AN AUTHOR'S GUIDE
TO PUBLISHING

Michael Legat was born in London and educated at Whitgift School, Croydon. He joined the Publicity and Production Department of The Bodley Head in 1941, and apart from three years' wartime service in the Navy, stayed there for nine years. In 1952 he was appointed Editorial Director of Corgi Books, following which he held the same position with Cassell & Company. Since 1978 he has been a full-time author, publisher's consultant and lecturer. He has served on the Management Committee of the Society of Authors, on the Literature Advisory Panel of South East Arts, and as a Director of the Authors' Licensing and Collecting Society and of the Copyright Licensing Agency. He is married and lives in Horsted Keynes.

AN AUTHOR'S GUIDE TO PUBLISHING

Third Completely Revised Edition

MICHAEL LEGAT

ROBERT HALE · LONDON

© *Michael Legat 1982*
First published in Great Britain 1982
Reprinted 1982
Reprinted 1984
First paperback edition (with revisions) 1987
Reprinted 1990
Reprinted 1991
Fully revised and expanded edition 1991
Reprinted 1992 twice
Reprinted 1993
Reprinted 1994
Third edition completely revised and reset 1998

ISBN 0 7090 6227 3

Robert Hale Limited
Clerkenwell House
Clerkenwell Green
London EC1R 0HT

2 4 6 8 10 9 7 5 3

Typeset in North Wales by
Derek Doyle & Associates, Mold, Flintshire.
Printed in Great Britain by
St Edmundsbury Press Limited, Bury St Edmunds.
Bound by
WBC Book Manufacturers Limited, Bridgend.

Contents

Foreword

This book is invaluable reading for all authors – and not simply beginners and those without agents. We can thoroughly recommend it as a balanced, helpful and informative guide to the profession of authorship.

Mark Le Fanu
The Society of Authors

Author's Note

I wish to make it clear that the ideas put forward in this book are not necessarily those of its publisher, nor of my other publishers, nor of my agent, nor of any publishing firm for which I have worked, nor of the Society of Authors nor of any other authors' organization. They are mine alone, so no blame will attach to the book's readers if they regard them with a certain suspicion. The views are, however, based on over fifty years experience of the book trade, and I hope therefore that the wariness will not be justified too often.

I am grateful to my publishers for allowing me the opportunity of revising and updating this book. It was first published in 1982, and a new edition, with a number of alterations and additions, appeared in 1991. Although the main principles of publishing, with which the book is largely concerned, remain the same, the present version has been rewritten and expanded to take account of the many changes of detail and daily operation which have come into use in the past six years, and also to look briefly at the new developments which will affect the trade in the years to come.

I should like to express my thanks to Mark Le Fanu, General Secretary of the Society of Authors, for his invaluable assistance and advice; to John McLaughlin, John Hale, Martin Kendall and Robert Hale for their helpful comments and suggestions; to Philippa MacLiesh (formerly of the Society of Authors) and to the late Ian Rowland Hill (formerly of the Writers' Guild of Great Britain) for additional help.

I also acknowledge with gratitude the permission granted by the following organizations to quote copyright material: the Hutchinson Publishing Group Ltd (a short extract from *Allen Lane: King Penguin* by Jack Morpurgo; Robert Hale Ltd (their formula for calculating the length of a typescript); the Society of Authors and the Writers' Guild of Great Britain (the Minimum Terms Agreement); the British Standards Institute (extracts from British Standard BS 5261; PART 2 1976 *Copy preparation and proof correction - Specification of typographic requirements, marks for copy preparation and proof correction, proofing procedure*); the Society of Authors (the Model Royalty Statement).

M.L.

To the memory of C.J. and of Peter
and to all my friends in the writing business,
whether they are authors or agents or
publishers or booksellers or critics or
whatever, and of course to Rosetta

1

The World of Publishing

In the years which immediately followed the Second World War, there were really only two kinds of publishers – hardcover and paperback – and in the main, although there were in some cases close relationships, they acted independently. The paperback houses published a general list, with a strong emphasis on fiction, while hardcover publishers included not only those which brought out books covering a wide range of subjects, but also the specialists – medical publishers, law publishers, educational publishers, etc. Since then, the world has changed. Independent hardcover publishers still exist, but almost all of them publish quite a high proportion of their books in paperback form, while the paperback houses all work in partnership and under common ownership with a hardcover company. Many old-established publishing houses have folded, or have been absorbed into conglomerates, most of which have their own paperback imprints.

And the world is still changing. More and more publishers are now bringing out books (if we may still call them that) in the form of CD-ROMs, and electronic publishing and the multimedia will undoubtedly grow and develop.

One thing which has not changed, and seems unlikely to do so, is the effect on publishers of copyright. It is the factor which decides what they do, and where and when and for how long they can do it.

Copyright
Books by authors who have been dead for over seventy years are, at least almost always, out of copyright and any publisher who brings out such a book is not restricted in any way. But authors who are writing today own the copyright in their work, and normally

13

retain it when signing a contract with a publisher (and indeed should always do so, unless there is very good reason for some other arrangement – see p.205). In return for various commitments on the publisher's part and agreed financial rewards (discussed in Chapter 6), the author gives the publisher a licence to publish. There are three main elements in that licence: the rights granted, the territories which the agreement covers, and the length of time for which the licence will be operative.

Volume Rights

The publisher who buys a book direct from an author will usually ask for control of all rights throughout the world. This is to say that the firm not only has the right to produce various editions of the book, or to license others to do so, but is also able to sell US and foreign rights, and serial, film, radio, television, electronic, and a number of other subsidiary rights (which will be discussed later in this chapter), in each case passing to the author an agreed share of the proceeds from such sales.

If, on the other hand, the book is bought from an agent, it is likely that the publisher will be restricted to Volume Rights (usually within the territories in which the publisher normally operates – see p.32), which is to say the right to produce, or license others to produce, hardcover or paperback editions of the book, to sell bookclub rights, and usually second serial (i.e. serial rights sold after the first publication in book form) and anthology rights, the sale of such rights often being subject to the agent's approval. All other rights are retained, given the author's agreement to such an arrangement, in the control of the agent, who will sell them, wherever possible, on the author's behalf. Of course it is open to the author who deals directly with the publisher to follow the example of agents and to retain various rights, provided that the publisher is still willing to publish the book on those terms, but there is little point in doing so unless the author is equipped to sell the rights in question. Few publishers make no effort at all to sell the rights they are granted, for the very good reason that their share of any moneys resulting from such sales increases their profit or at worst diminishes their loss on the book concerned.

It is very important, whatever arrangements have been made, to remember what rights you have granted to your publishers. Once you have given them control of any rights you are no longer free to sell those rights yourself. If you should by chance come in contact

14

with someone who wants to buy serial rights, for instance, or translation rights, you must pass the information to your publishers and allow them to follow it up. Apart from the legal obligation to do this, failure to tell the publishers what you are up to could cause great embarrassment if they happened to be in the midst of delicate negotiations over exactly the same rights with some other interested party. The same applies, of course, if it is your agent who has control of the rights.

Hardcover Publishers
There are several hundred hardcover book publishers in Britain, publishing an infinite variety of books, including the firms already mentioned which produce only books for a very specialized market. Some are huge companies, bringing out hundreds of new books every year in a general list embracing fiction and non-fiction of all kinds, but also sometimes including books for a specialist field. In fact, something like ninety per cent of the output of the British publishing trade is concentrated in the hands of fewer than a dozen giant groups of companies. At the other end of the scale are the tiny concerns, sometimes run by one mad enthusiast who undertakes everything from the work of the most junior assistant to that of the managing director, publishing perhaps only one or two books a year, and these include many of the so-called 'small presses', largely devoted to the publication of poetry.

Two major developments of recent years have been the growth of what, for want of a better term, we can call the 'integrated' publishing house, and the proliferation of conglomerates.

Integrated Publishers
A large number of hardcover publishers have taken to issuing paperback editions of many of their books, often producing both hardcover and paperback simultaneously, sometimes leaving a time gap between the two editions, or perhaps publishing the book only in soft cover form. Such paperbacks, usually known as 'trade paperbacks', are a somewhat different animal from the mass-market paperbacks published by such companies as Corgi, Pan, Arrow, etc., being printed in much smaller quantities, usually with a better quality of production, and selling for a substantially higher price. The 'integrated' publishing house may produce a few such books, but usually earns its title because it consists of both a hardcover business and a mass-market paperback division, and buys

many of its books with the object of producing both the hardcover and the mass-market paperback editions. This integration (sometimes referred to as 'vertical publishing') allows the acquiring editors in the two concerns to work together in the purchase of books, giving the publisher greater purchasing power; the joint deals of the two editors can often involve huge sums of money, which become economically viable at least in part because they can think of the two editions of a book as a single entity, using the same jacket/cover design, for instance, setting the book in print only once, co-ordinating the publicity, and generally working together to make sure of the book's success. This can include the sale of American and foreign rights, and of various subsidiary rights. The arrangement can be very attractive for authors.

Conglomerates
In common with many other industries, but often for different reasons, publishing has become, in the last few decades, progressively more difficult an enterprise to run economically. It has always been a gambling business, and its problems have been exacerbated because of the vast variety of books and the uncertainties of any trade based on selling goods which are not essential in the way that food and clothing are, and which are no more than marginally profitable unless they achieve the rare status of best-sellerdom. In addition, publishing demands substantial amounts of capital investment, and is therefore readily afflicted with cash-flow problems.

One result of these difficulties has been the development of various forms of conglomerate. Some publishing companies, including both large and small concerns, have been forced to seek the protection of giant, diversified groups which do not suffer from a shortage of cash, and which have been attracted to publishing partly because of its faintly glamorous and culturally commendable image, and partly because of a belief that the various businesses within the group will indulge, to the benefit of all, in the process known as cross-fertilization. Another kind of conglomerate results from the banding together of two or three publishing houses, or even more, sometimes by voluntary amalgamation but often by purchase, when the wealthier concern swallows those in greater financial difficulty. In many such cases the purchaser is an American publishing house (which may itself already be a conglomerate), and there has been some traffic in the opposite direction, with British firms buying into the American scene.

Conglomerates always say, when they gollop up yet another old-established publishing house, that the latter's editorial department will continue to function and maintain its individuality, while its service divisions (production, sales, warehousing) will be integrated with those of the group in the interests of economy and efficiency. It does not always work quite like that, and some victims of the giant groups have disappeared without trace, editorial department and all. One is also entitled, I fear, to greet with an ironic laugh the claims which have been made that, because of their greater resources, conglomerates can publish worthwhile books which might be uneconomic for small independent companies, and can afford to take on and nurture those talented authors who need time and experience to build up a reputation which will make them financially viable for the publisher.

However, conglomerates are not all bad, and the economic sense behind them is obvious, as is the advantage for the Americans who have bought British firms, or who have set up their own branches in this country, in having both major English language markets under the control of one international company.

When this book was last revised, there was some feeling that decentralization might be the order of the day during the 1990s, but this appears to have been wishful thinking. There are always alarums and excursions in the publishing trade, and the conglomerates have not escaped their ups and downs, but, generally speaking, they seem to be happy and successful with their complex corporate structures. They may not remain exactly as at present – it is quite likely that they will swallow up additional small concerns, and sell off those of their imprints which do not bring in sufficient profit – but their essential nature will still be that of the conglomerate.

It is encouraging that new, independent firms (including some which have been bought out from conglomerates) continue to set up in business, and many of them have managed, as a result of careful control, to thrive despite the difficulties of the economic climate.

CD-ROMs

The book as we know it today – printed pages bound together in some kind of cover – has been with us for some five hundred years. There are those who predict that books will soon be seen only in museums, and that they will be replaced by CD-ROMs and other electronic miracles either already extant or yet to be invented. The CD-ROM ('ROM' stands for 'Read Only Memory' – but there is no need to bother here with what that means) is a development from the music Compact Discs with which most of us are familiar. A CD-ROM can contain text, illustrations, animation and film (all in colour or black and white), and sound. One disc can accommodate twice as much material as is contained in the whole *Encyclopaedia Britannica*, and a more advanced form of disc is likely to have a capacity fourteen times as large as that. A special attachment to your computer is needed in order to 'play' the CD-ROM, but the machines are not over-expensive, and will undoubtedly become cheaper.

The medium is ideally suited to reference books, and more and more of them are appearing as CD-ROMs, which are highly portable, take up very little space indeed, and are immensely practical in use, making it simple to locate the subject you are interested in, and any related material, at the touch of a button.

You may feel, however, that real books can never be replaced when it comes to fiction or any kind of book which one normally reads from cover to cover, rather than just looking at one particular section for information. It is impossible to read the CD-ROM without a computer, and who wants to read for pleasure looking at a screen all the time? Well, children already do. The modern child is completely at home with computers, and it is possible that schoolbooks in their present form will disappear completely within a few years. It will seem entirely natural to those children when they grow up to read via the machine and the screen. And as for the problem of carrying a computer around with you, they will no doubt become even more portable than the present-day lap-tops, so there will be no difficulty there.

Publishers try to move with the times, and many, while still producing books, are also publishing in the new technology. In the world of entertainment reading, children's books will undoubtedly lead the way, because of the freedom the CD-ROM gives to add animation and sound to the text and illustrations, but some new novels have already appeared in this form, and I don't think it is going too far, given the pace of technological developments and their effect on our daily lives, to predict the death of the book as we know it before many decades have passed. This does not, however, mean any greater difficulty for authors in getting their work published – on the contrary, the expectation is for a larger demand than exists at present.

The Internet

As I write, Literature Online has been launched, making more than 200,000 literary works available on the Internet. (There are also bookshop facilities on the Internet, incidentally, allowing a purchaser to track down and buy a book without leaving home.) Undoubtedly this is just a beginning, and within a very short time there will have been all kinds of developments at which the mind today can only boggle. More threats to the old-fashioned book, perhaps, but if its imminent demise saddens you, then be at least a little comforted. It won't happen immediately – indeed, some people will tell you that it will never take place, pointing out that initial experiments with CD-ROMs of non-reference books have not 'taken off', and that the Internet will be of major use only to scholars and researchers. Anyway, most of us, by the time that the book really has disappeared, will be in Marvell's 'fine and private place'.

Niche Publishing

Declining sales and the increasing tendency to produce trade paperbacks, not to mention new technology, may mean the end of hardcover books, and 'hardcover publishing', as a description of the business may soon be a misnomer. 'Niche publishing' may become a more appropriate term. Niche publishing is the popular concept of the closing years of the twentieth century; it means publishing for specific, often limited, but measurable markets, rather than publishing on a much broader base for a market which may or may not exist in a size which will make the publication profitable. Niche publishing is not a new idea – many publishers have been working successfully on that basis for decades – but it will certainly become a more carefully observed watchword as the publishing industry tries to turn itself into less of a gambling business than it is at present.

Paperbacks

There are far fewer mass-market paperback publishers than hard-cover houses, with perhaps no more than a score of major imprints in this country. All of them have close links with hardcover houses – sometimes the hardcover house owns the paperback firm, sometimes it is the other way round, and sometimes they are simply partners (the ultimate ownership may be one of the big conglomerates in the USA, Germany or Australia). Whatever the connection, the paperback concern is usually separately managed, and although it tends to publish books which have appeared first in hardcover form from its associated company, it also takes some books, usually bestsellers, from those independent publishers who do not have their own mass paperback business.

Some years ago it could be said that, on the whole, and with the exception of Penguin Books, which has always brought out 'up-market' titles, paperback publishers concentrated on very popular books, with fiction predominating. Although it is still in that area that the major sales are achieved, virtually all paperback companies nowadays include an imprint devoted to literary works, and have other sections covering children's books, non-fiction, illustrated books of various kinds, etc., forming a very wide range indeed. There is also a considerable variety of format, and paperbacks appear in all sorts of shapes and sizes.

The scope of paperbacks available in the shops is increased by the fact that it is not only from the mass-market houses that paperbacks appear. Almost all publishers now produce some of their books in softcover form, although, as already explained, these are somewhat different from the mass-market product.

The cheapness of paperbacks in comparison with hardcover books does not depend, as many people believe, on the costs of the thin board cover and the binding process (the back edges of the signatures, or folded sheets, being guillotined off and the separate pages of the book then being glued together, whereas the hardcover book is likely to have its signatures sewn together before the binding case is drawn on) being much less expensive than the boards and cloth and more complex binding of hardcover books, but because the paperback business is predicated on large quantities. The minimum print quantity for a mass-market paperback book is usually in the range of fifteen to twenty thousand (although it may drop to ten thousand, or occasionally even lower), while bestsellers may be produced in quantities of a quarter of a million or more. Certainly the paper is of poorer quality, the print may be smaller, the binding is somewhat cheaper, and the author's royalties are usually lower than for hardcover books, but it is the mass production of large quantities which keeps the retail price down. The publisher's profit is possibly limited to a very small percentage of the retail price – perhaps a few pence per copy only – but since so many copies are sold, the sales income is sufficient to cover over- heads and produce a net profit and to provide for the large sums spent on the promotion of bestsellers.

Although there are examples of the hardcover and paperback editions of a given book being published simultaneously, it is more usual for there to be a gap between the appearance of the hard- cover book and that of the paperback of at least six months and more often a year or longer. This delay is imposed by hardcover publishers because, although it is true that members of the public who buy paperbacks are not in the main buyers of hardcover books, hardcover buyers can easily be seduced into the purchase of paperbacks, and if both editions are published more or less simul- taneously, sales of the hardcover can be seriously damaged. A delay is also sometimes necessary to ensure that the normal public library sale is not prejudiced by the immediate availability of a paperback edition. With major books, especially those of American origin, it is commonplace for the paperback edition to be published overseas in the Open market (see p.32) very much earlier than for the domestic market, in order to meet the competition of the American paperback edition of the same book, and the British and American houses are often engaged in warfare over these lucrative export markets, each trying to produce an edition first so as to capture the bulk of the sales.

Paperback publishers nowadays bring out an increasing number of 'originals' (books published for the first time in paperback), and frequently commission them. If you sell your book direct to a paperback house, you will receive a smaller royalty in most cases than you would from a hardcover publisher, but of course you will not have to split it as you would if the hardcover publisher had sold the book to the paperback house and then shared the proceeds with you.

It does not matter whether you submit your book to the hard- cover or paperback arm of an integrated publisher – editors on both sides of the business are aware of each other's needs and interests. In some cases a book may be published by an integrated firm only in hardcover or trade paperback format (because it does not have a large enough appeal for the mass market), or in mass market paperback only. Moreover, the hardcover arm may publish a book which is not paperbacked by its associate, but by a different house (perhaps because of long-standing arrangements with that

particular author), and the paperback arm continues to buy softcover rights in bestselling books published by those hardcover
concerns which have no mass market imprint of their own.

Bookclubs
Bookclubs sell by direct mail, offering books, both hardcover and
paperback, at less than the normal price, which they achieve by
purchasing copies from the publisher at high discounts, reducing
the author's royalty, and often binding their members to the
purchase of a given number of books per year. This commitment,
although the member's obligation is usually no more than the
purchase of one book every quarter, gives the club a captive
market. At regular intervals the club's 'choice' is sent and billed
automatically to members, unless they return a form saying that
they do not wish to receive it; undoubtedly many copies of the
choice are sold by this method to members who do not really want
the book, but are too lazy or forgetful to return the form rejecting
it.

The quantities of books that bookclubs take vary from one or
two hundred to tens of thousands. Publishers welcome a book club
order, since it is usually given before the book is printed, and can
thus increase the print order and spread the origination costs of the
book. Booksellers, on the other hand, abhor the clubs, especially
when their introductory offers allow new members to buy expensive books for a ridiculously low price, at the same time as the
bookseller is trying to sell the same title at full price. However, the
bookclubs have always claimed that they service an entirely different market – that their members are not normally bookbuyers –
and there is certainly some evidence to suggest that the various
forms in which a book can appear (hardcover, paperback, bookclub, condensed book, etc) are not totally competitive. The support
which the public gives to bookclubs seems to fluctuate; at the time
of writing, they seem to have passed through a fairly prosperous
period, and to be experiencing some difficulties, and certainly the
quantities of individual books taken by bookclubs have dropped
substantially from their heyday some years ago.

Sometimes bookclubs print their own editions of books. In such
cases the author will probably receive a slightly higher royalty than
when the publisher supplies copies from stock. The bookclub is
unlikely to print its own edition unless it is expecting to dispose of
very large quantities of the book, and will usually cut costs by using

the publisher's plant, so that it is in effect producing a reprint under its own name.

In addition to those which take a very wide range of books of general interest, there are many specialist bookclubs devoted to one particular subject, such as cookery, ancient history, religion, and so on. There are also bookclubs dealing only with paperbacks.

US Rights

If your book is sold to an American publisher, the contract will be basically similar to the agreement you sign with a British publisher, and will grant much the same rights. It will almost certainly be a much longer document and may also be very much tougher on the author than most British publishing contracts. You should never, of course, sign any document without reading it carefully and under- standing not only its benefits to you but your obligations under it and the restrictions it may place upon you, and care may be partic- ularly necessary with American contracts. Royalties tend to be a little lower in the States than in Britain, but the quantities of books sold are often higher.

If your book is lavishly illustrated, particularly if colour printing is involved, or if it is a somewhat elaborate production, it is quite likely that the British publisher will try to sell sheets to an American publisher who will buy them at a price only slightly above cost and inclusive of royalty. Your share will then be a percentage of the price received by the British publisher, and this is generally a ludicrously small amount in comparison with what you would receive if you were given a normal royalty on the American retail price of the book. It seems very unfair, but the economics of this kind of publishing rarely allow of a better deal for the author, and it is often a question of accepting this small reward or getting nothing at all.

Nowadays you might find yourself signing a contract with the British branch of an American publishing house. Since such branches operate in many ways independently of their parent companies, the contract may not differ greatly from that which you would sign with any British house, but if both the British branch and the American owners want to publish the book (lucky you!), you will be asked to grant world volume rights (or perhaps world English language volume rights). This should of course be reflected in the size of the advance, and you should also aim at receiving full royalties on the American edition, rather than sharing them with the British branch. Similar advice applies if the British publisher is the owner and has an American branch, or if the British and American houses are joint partners.

All moneys due from a US publisher (and the same applies to foreign language publishers) will be paid to your British publisher or to your agent, and of course their shares of the income will be deducted before it is passed on to you. If you sign a contract directly with an American publisher (or with a foreign language publisher) you will become liable for income tax in the United States (or in the foreign language country) unless you apply specially for exemption on the grounds that you pay taxes in your country of residence. Many countries have reciprocal double tax exemption arrangements with Britain. The Society of Authors, or the Writers' Guild, or your agent, bank manager or accountant would be able to advise you.

Foreign (Translation) Rights
Foreign rights can be very lucrative, despite the fact that foreign publishers usually pay a lower rate of royalties (allowing them to include the cost of the translation in their budgets without inflating the retail price). It is customary for the foreign publisher who takes on your book to agree to publish a faithful translation of the work, and it should not be altered in any material way without your consent. You may well find, however, that minor changes have been made. In theory, the author should be consulted about all alterations, but in practice it is probably better to accept them with a good grace after the event, provided of course that they have not damaged your work, and enjoy the financial rewards. The foreign publisher will usually be granted volume rights in the book in the language concerned, and may therefore achieve for you a sale of the foreign language edition to appropriate paperback houses, bookclubs, magazines, and so on.

(It should perhaps be pointed out at this juncture that when publishers buy the rights to a foreign language book, it is they who hire a translator to render it into their own language. Usually they will commission the translation on an outright basis, paying the translator an agreed flat sum per thousand words, but in some cases, as the Translators Association of the Society of Authors would recommend, it is possible for the translator to receive a royalty. English language publishers quite often receive requests from people who want to translate books from their lists into foreign languages; the reply is always is that no commission to translate a book is likely to be given until a foreign language publisher has bought the rights for that particular language, and that the foreign publisher will decide who shall have the job, probably selecting a translator who is already known to the firm concerned.)

Subsidiary Rights
Serial It is important to distinguish between first serial rights and second serial rights. First serial rights, which are not always granted to the publisher, but retained in the control of the author or agent, refer to the appearance of the book, or extracts from it, in newspapers or magazines *prior* to its publication in volume form. Second serial rights, which are often controlled by the publisher, refer to the appearance of the book, or extracts from it, in newspapers or magazines *after* publication in volume form. However many times the book may appear in this way after publication, the rights concerned are still 'second' serial (not third, or fifth, or umpteenth), and to make it even more clear as mud, you might like to note that 'serial' in this context is really another name for 'magazine' or 'newspaper', and does not mean a serial or instalment form of your book.

Anthology and Quotation These rights cover the use of your work in anthologies of poetry or prose, and the granting of permission to others to use extracts from your work in their own publications. For poets and short story writers in particular Anthology Rights can often provide a substantial income.

Digest Book Condensation Condensed books, mostly fiction, are sold by direct mail to subscribers. The shortening of the book may be a salutary experience for the author, demonstrating just how much of the original version was unnecessary verbiage; it may also cause considerable pain at the disappearance of splendid pieces of writing and possibly the total elimination of scenes and characters. The condensations are, however, done with considerable skill and as much sympathy as possible by the experienced editors employed by the condensed book publisher, and authors who are upset by what they do should console themselves with the cheques that they will receive for these rights.

Digest This differs from 'Digest Book Condensation Rights' in that it refers to the right to publish a shortened version of a book in a newspaper or magazine, rather than in book form.

Strip Cartoon To many people in this country, alas, a 'book' is a magazine. To others, again and even more alas, it may be a collection of strip cartoons, the contents of the original book having been abridged, the dialogue made brief and punchy, and excitement added with words like 'POW' and 'ZAP' and a proliferation of asterisks, exclamation marks and other typographical devices. It has happened to Shakespeare. It could happen to you. If it does, cry your way to the bank.

TV, Radio and Recorded Readings, TV and Radio Dramatization, Film and Dramatic, Sound and Video Recording These rights are, I think, self-explanatory. Recorded books, mostly read by well-known actors, have become very popular in recent years. It is perhaps worth noting that, if you are lucky enough and your book sells to a film producer or company, the moneys involved are sometimes supplemented by a share of profits on the film, which is fine if the term used is 'gross profits', but rather less exciting if the share is of 'net profits', since in the film industry net profits sometimes disappear altogether, even on the most successful films. Better deals are for a share of net or gross receipts. What happens most often with film rights is that an option is purchased for a comparatively small sum, and such options have a habit of lapsing without the film being made. There is nothing to be done about this except to be grateful that you received a sum of money for nothing.

Merchandising For most authors these rights remain unexploited, but if you should happen to be a Beatrix Potter or an Edwardian Lady just imagine how much you will rake in from the posters, notepads, money-boxes, coffee mugs and all the other products which will sell because of the use of your material.

One-shot Periodical This term usually means the (very unusual) publication of the complete text of a book in one issue only of a newspaper or magazine.

Hardcover Reprint and Large Print Hardcover reprints are sometimes licensed to a firm which produces books in a special format, perhaps as a series ('Classic True Accounts of World War II', for example) or for promotional purposes. Large-print books, which are increasingly popular, are usually straightforward reprints of the original text, but set in a large size of type so that they can be read by the partially sighted. The specialist publishers of these books pay an advance and royalties in the normal way. If the US rights have not been sold, the large-print publishers sometimes ask for the right to distribute their edition in the United States. In contrast to large-print arrangements, it is customary when a request is received to translate a book into Braille to grant permission without fee for either author or publisher.

Electronic Modern technology advances with extreme rapidity. As already mentioned, many books are now appearing in CD-ROM format. Other forms of electronic communication include Virtual Reality, in which sound and vision take the 'reader' into the heart of the material, so that it becomes personally experienced, and the World Wide Web and the Information Superhighway, all of which can be used for the publication of an author's work. By the time that this revised edition appears in print, new 'platforms' (i.e. methods of communication) will undoubtedly have been discovered, and this is likely to continue as technology develops. All these rights tend currently to be included under the simple heading 'Electronic', or possibly 'Multimedia'. They are already of very considerable importance, and as the multimedia grow and are used more widely, it may be necessary to split them into the various platforms. The Authors' Licensing and Collecting Society has published a useful booklet, *Guidelines for Writers in Electronic Publishing and Multimedia*, which was prepared by the Association of Authors' Agents, the Authors' Licensing and Collecting Society, the Personal Managers' Association, the Society of Authors and the Writers' Guild of Great Britain.

Reprographic Reprography (a term first used in the 1960s) is a portmanteau word, made up from 'reproduction' and 'photography', and its most common application is to the familiar photocopier. Reprographic rights, which can be very lucrative, are, in most cases, handled for the author by ALCS (the Authors' Licensing and Collecting Society) and on the publisher's behalf by PLS (the Publishers Licensing Society), these two societies controlling CLA (the Copyright Licensing Agency) which collects moneys due under the licences it issues (see p.222).

Public Lending PLR (Public Lending Right), the payment made to authors when their books are borrowed from public libraries, is, by law, the author's money and no one else's. You should not therefore sign a contract in which a clause gives your publisher a share in your PLR. Even your agent, if you have one, takes no cut of it. (See p.220)

Other There seems to be no end to the things that can happen to a book, and some contracts, after covering all the subsidiary rights that both parties to the agreement can think of, add a further clause which refers to other rights, and thus covers any rights that have been overlooked or any which do not exist at the time of the contract but which may emerge as a result of modern technology.

Packagers
Packagers are people who conceive, commission, edit and produce books for regular publishers to sell. Thus they do all the work of the ordinary publisher up to the marketing, publicizing, selling and distribution of the work. The books are usually fully illustrated, with a considerable amount of colour work, and the packager's aim is to sell the book not just to a British publisher, but simultaneously to an American house and to foreign language publishers as well; if foreign language editions are sold, the black plate which includes the text will have to be printed separately, but the colour for all the editions can be printed at one time, which will be much more economical than printing them separately for each publisher involved, and since several publishers' print quantities can be put together, the total print run will be high enough to reduce all the origination costs to a very reasonable sum per copy. Some pack-agers have turned into publishers, themselves bringing out the packaged books which they have conceived, but only if they have succeeded in selling editions around the world.

Having had an idea for a book, a packager commissions an author to write it, paying a lump sum according to the number of copies printed, or in some cases making a handsome outright payment, or paying a substantial advance on account of a modest royalty on net receipts. The author might stand to gain more by receiving normal royalties from all the publishers concerned, but any shortfall in this direction is made up for by the fact that all the money is paid in advance, before the books have been sold into the shops, let alone to the public, since each publisher will have paid the packager a sum inclusive of the royalties to cover all the copies ordered. As a matter of principle any author who is asked by a packager to write a book should aim to get some kind of royalty rather than just an outright payment. After all, packaged books are often very successful. At the least, a further sum should be payable if the book is reprinted.

Sponsored Books
Sponsored books used to consist almost entirely of histories of large businesses, produced to celebrate some anniversary, paid for out of the firm's advertising budget, and distributed to staff and customers. Such books were not usually on sale to the general public. Nowadays, however, many large organizations see the sponsoring of books, whether or not the subject is directly connected with the interest of the organization, as a useful kind of publicity. The books are published by a hardcover house in the normal way, the only real difference being that all or a proportion of the costs are paid by the sponsor, who often takes a share of the profits on the books. Some sponsors have retailing facilities available, or are prepared to spend considerable sums in publicizing the book, and this may result in an abnormally large print quantity being ordered. This is very pleasant for the author, although there are some cases where the sponsor will try to buy the copyright for an outright sum, and even if the amount is generous, the author will probably suffer under this arrangement in the long run. Or they may propose a low royalty, explaining that the author will still be well paid since the sums due on the high sales envisaged will compensate for earning less than the norm on each copy. Yet another ploy is for the sponsor to propose that the author should become an employee of the company while writing the book, which would automatically give ownership of the copyright to the firm, and although the salary offered may sound very tempting, again the author should resist.

Vanity Publishing
Some authors who cannot secure commercial publication for their books pay to have them published by vanity publishers. Vanity publishing is a technical term with a specific meaning. If you pay a printer to put your little volume of poems into print, and you then sell the copies to your friends and anyone else who will buy them, it may be vain of you, but it is not vanity publishing; if the publisher Lord Whatsit writes his memoirs and has them published by the house which he owns, that may be vain of him, but it is not vanity publishing; if a regular publisher is persuaded to take your book on because you are prepared to subsidize it in some way, perhaps by

contributing to the costs or by promising to buy a large number of copies at trade prices, that is still not vanity publishing. In the first case, you will be paying only for the costs of production of your volume of poems, and the printer's profit, and will be able to retain all the moneys gained from selling copies; Lord Whatsit's book will not be taken on, even though he owns the firm, unless it is of publishable standard, and there will be a normal contract such as any other author would receive, allowing for the payment of an advance and royalties; similarly there will be a contract for the publication by a regular publisher of a book which the author has subsidized, and it will probably provide that the financial subsidy will be returned once the book has proved to be profitable, and will certainly allow for the payment of royalties.

Vanity publishers, on the other hand, are the sharks who express great enthusiasm for your work, however poor its quality, but explain that publishing conditions are so difficult nowadays that they cannot go ahead unless you make a contribution to the costs. You will get your money back, they say, because the royalties they will pay on sales (apart from the copies that you yourself purchase, which will be royalty free) will be exceptionally generous. In fact, however, you will be making far more than a 'contribution' – you will be paying for the entire costs of production and the publisher's profit too – and, strangely enough, the huge royalties never materialize. If you want to sign up with a vanity publisher, go ahead. It's your money, and you're entitled to do what you like with it. But whatever the vanity publisher may say about having a large and extremely capable sales force, don't expect to see copies of your book in the bookshops – booksellers know the vanity publishers' imprints and refuse to stock their books. And don't expect to see any of your money back. You will get nicely produced copies of your book, but that's all, and you will have paid through the nose for them. Vanity publishers take your money and give your ego a boost that you could probably find much more cheaply in a bottle of liquor or a new dress or whatever turns you on.

How do you recognize vanity publishers? By their contracts (always absolutely watertight legally, so don't think you will get anywhere by suing when the results fail to meet your expectations), which will not bear any resemblance to the kind of contract discussed in Chapter 6 of this book, differing in such giveaway instances as not mentioning any advance payable by the publisher, specifying royalties in the region of thirty-three and a third per cent (often not payable on the first four hundred copies printed – which is quite likely to be the entire print run – and certainly not on any copies purchased by the author), and of course the clause specifying the amount of subsidy that the author will pay. Before you have got to the stage of a contract, however, you can recognize vanity publishers by their advertisements, asking authors to submit their work – 'Books wanted,' they say, or 'Authors wanted'. Regular publishers have no need to advertise in that way – their problem is more likely to be how to cope with the vast number of typescripts submitted to them unsolicited and without any encouragement on their part.

Self Publishing
If you want to see your work in print and cannot find a regular publisher to take you on, then, rather than go to a vanity publisher, you might consider self publishing. Contact a reputable printer, who will produce the book for you. Yellow Pages will help. You may have to shop around, but it is usually not too difficult to find a printer who is not only capable of doing a good job for you, but who can advise you on such matters as print sizes, paper quality, bindings, etc. Alternatively, there are several small firms, listed in the *Writers' and Artists' Yearbook* under 'Editorial, Literary and Production Services', which will do the whole job for you for quite modest charges. Whichever way the book is produced, your biggest problem is likely to be distribution: how will you sell copies of your book without a sales force to persuade booksellers throughout the country – indeed, throughout the world – to put copies on sale? But even if all you can do is to sell copies to your friends and perhaps persuade your local bookseller to display copies of the book (you will almost certainly have to supply them 'on sale or return', so that you will be paid only for copies which are actually sold, and of course the bookseller will expect a share amounting to at the very least twenty-five per cent, and more likely forty per cent), you are still likely to do considerably better than if you go to a vanity house. Two books which give helpful advice on self publishing are *Publishing Your Own Book* by John Wynne-Tyson (Centaur Press) and *How to Publish Yourself* by Peter Finch (Allison & Busby). There is also an organization, called Author–Publisher Enterprise, for self publishing authors, which offers encouragement, advice and practical help (see p.228).

Desktop Publishing

The development of sophisticated personal computers has made it possible for many authors to produce work in a finished state which can be described as 'camera-ready'. This term is usually used of a text which is heavily illustrated and for which the text has been set up in type and the pictures reduced or enlarged to the size in which they are to appear, the whole then being pasted up into pages ready for the photographic process which will produce film from which the book can be printed. Authors who can produce work in this state are clearly in a favourable position for self publishing, but the term 'desktop publishing' is also used when they are supplying this material to a regular publisher. The PCs which produce work of this quality and variety are priced beyond the means of many authors, but the costs are not in fact astronomic, and they tend to drop regularly. It can be confidently predicted that more and more authors, whose work is suitable, will become desktop publishers, and that self publishing will also increase.

Territories

The rights which a publisher controls are restricted in the licence which the copyright holder grants by two factors: the territories and the licence period, determining where the publisher's rights may be exercised, and for how long.

For most of this century, for English language books which had an appeal on both sides of the Atlantic, the world as a market was neatly divided into three parts: the exclusive British market, where only the British publisher's edition of the book could be sold; the exclusive United States market, where only the American edition could be sold; and the Open market, in which the British and American editions could compete with each other.

These divisions were easily defined: the British market consisted of the United Kingdom and the British Empire, including all its dominions (with the possible exception of Canada), colonies and protectorates and a number of countries, such as Egypt and Iraq, where British influence had been traditionally strong; the American market consisted of the United States of America and its colonies and protectorates; Canada was normally exclusive to the British publisher if the book were of British or British Empire origin, and exclusive to the American publisher if it were of United States origin; and the non-exclusive Open market was everywhere else. Even after the British Empire became the Commonwealth and certain countries such as South Africa and Malta became independent republics, the British publisher's traditional market remained a recognized entity and covered the same territories.

In the 1970s, however, at the instigation of the United States, it was agreed that the split of territories between British and American publishers should be re-defined in the case of each book, and the fact that a given country had been traditionally part of the exclusive market of one of the publishers should no longer mean that it was necessarily so for every book. This was of considerable advantage to American publishers, who had long cast envious eyes on some of the Commonwealth markets, despite having a self-sufficient home market, and who could now sometimes insist that territories such as Australia or India should become part of the Open market, thus allowing their books entry; it gave no pleasure at all to British publishers, who were, and still are, quite heavily dependent on export sales, and who found themselves always on the losing end when the territories were divided up. The situation has been additionally complicated by the fact that some territories which had always been regarded as belonging to the Open market could become part of the British or American publisher's exclusive area, and the growth of publishing industries in countries like Australia or South Africa, which previously relied almost entirely on Britain for its books, has resulted in further fragmentation of the old divisions. Australian rights are quite commonly sold separately, particularly when the book is of US origin. Canada, too, has a thriving publishing industry, and increasingly often, especially with agented books, the exclusive Canadian rights may be separately sold. Similar arrangements may be made for other territories which are populous enough to make publishing viable within the area.

The divisions of the market may not be as neat as they were, and are sometimes additionally blurred by the fact that nowadays a number of firms are owned jointly by American and British publishers, but contracts for English language books are still likely to specify various territories as exclusive to one or other publisher, and the remaining parts of the world as the Open market.

A further problem has arisen as a result of Britain's membership of the EU. Since trade barriers are prohibited within the Common Market, it is possible for a European wholesaler to purchase copies of a given book from the American publisher and then export them to Britain, thus infringing the British publisher's exclusivity in the home market, but relying on the provisions of the various EU treaties to be stronger than the agreement regarding territories between the British and American publishers. The enterprise can be profitable to the wholesaler because of the fact that British and American retail prices may differ considerably, and whereas in the past the British price was usually below that of the American edition, the reverse is often now the case. Fluctuations in exchange rates make it a volatile situation. It should be pointed out that the issue is one of potential market violation and not necessarily of infringement of the author's copyright. However, the author may be drawn into any dispute as the original grantor of the various exclusive and non-exclusive territories.

Because of the dangers which EU regulations pose to their sales in Britain, which should really be the most inviolate of markets for them, some British publishers attempt to add Europe, or at least the EU, to their exclusive market, thus preventing the American publisher from selling the book in question in those territories, and obviating the threat of an invasion of the home territory. This move is clearly not popular with American publishers, some of whom will not sign up any books by British authors which do not allow them at least right of entry into the European territories. In some cases, in order to persuade agents and authors to grant these additional rights despite American disapproval, British publishers have offered a full home royalty on sales within the EU instead of the normal, considerably lower, export terms.

Of course, there is less likely to be any problem if your book is bought by one of the Anglo-American conglomerates. Although the branches on either side of the Atlantic may operate independently, they frequently buy the English language rights for the whole world, which they can then control as they wish. There is no difficulty either for a British book which is not of sufficient interest in the United States to be published there, or for an American book which does not find a British publisher, since the publisher in either of these cases would obviously have exclusivity in the Open market, and probably all over the world.

Foreign language publishers do not have the same problem of sharing out the world as English language publishers do. A German publisher, for instance, will usually have the whole world available for the German language edition of a book, and most foreign language publishers similarly have exclusive rights in their language throughout the world.

(Incidentally, it should be made clear that sales of copies of a British or American, or indeed any other English language publication in a foreign country have nothing to do with the foreign rights which are referred to in the contract for a book written in English. These rights are concerned with the translation of the work from English into a foreign language and its publication by a foreign publisher, and indeed are often less confusingly called translation rights. If copies of the book in the original English language editions are sold in France, Germany, Japan, or any other foreign language country, they come under the clause in the publisher's contract referring to export sales, not under foreign rights.)

If you write in English and sell your book directly to a publisher, then that publisher will probably buy world rights, and will attempt to sub-lease English language rights to firms in those countries which are outside the original publisher's normal sphere of operations (for instance, a British publisher would try to sell US rights to an American house, while an Australian concern might hope to sell both British and US rights). The details of which territories will be exclusive and non-exclusive to each publisher will be decided at the time of the sale. If an English language publisher fails to sell rights in a territory where the firm does not usually operate, then in rare cases it may be possible for copies of the publisher's edition of the book to be put on sale in the country concerned, but the quantities concerned are usually small; such sales are of course export sales.

Licence Periods

In most publishing contracts, the author gives the publisher the various rights defined in the agreement 'for the period of copyright'. This last phrase may be further defined by some such wording as 'and all renewals and extensions thereof in each country'. The effect, in most cases, is to give the publisher the ability to exploit the rights in the book from the time of publication until up to seventy years after the author's death. If the book goes on selling, the publisher will of course continue to pay the specified royalties to the author, or eventually, to the author's heirs. If the book is not kept in print, or under certain other circumstances which are usually clearly defined in the contract, the rights will revert to the author, although the publisher may be able to retain them if the book is still in a print in an edition which has been sub-licensed to another firm or organization.

A granting by the author to the publisher of a licence for the entire period of copyright, as explained above, has been the tradition virtually ever since formal licensing agreements between authors and publishers (as opposed to the outright purchase of copyright) were first made. It seemed immutable, but at the beginning of the 1980s the Society of Authors and the Writers' Guild began a campaign to improve the terms offered to authors, and asked why publishers should not work on a limited licence of, say, twenty years, or even ten years, with the right thereafter to negotiate a new contract for a further period if they so wished and if the author were willing for that publisher to continue to have the rights. Authors would feel both that they had more control over their work, and that the arrangement should make publishers more efficient, because failure to do a good job might mean losing the author to a rival at the end of the licence period. Publishers, the Society and the Guild argued, knew very well that many books have a far shorter life than ten, let alone twenty, years, so that a licence covering that period would be adequate, while if a book continued to be active up to the time when the contract was due for renewal, the publisher could feel fairly certain of having done a good job, which would make the author think twice before taking the book away. Moreover, since publishers normally limit the sublicences they grant to a period of between five and ten years, they should hardly complain at an application of the same principle to their own licence, especially as it would be a more generous one.

Although a few contracts with a limited licence period have been signed, on the whole publishers have been very reluctant to accept the concept, and it seems unlikely that they will have a major change of heart in this matter in the immediate future, although the Society and the Guild continue to champion the idea.

2

The Publisher's Market

Booksellers

The main outlet for publishers' books is, not surprisingly, book-shops. Booksellers come in a considerable variety of size and approach. Largest of all are the chains, and most members of the general public, if asked to name a bookshop, would say, 'W.H. Smith' in England and Wales, or, 'John Menzies' in Scotland. As we all know, these chains are not only bookshops – they sell CDs, audio tapes, videos, toys, stationery, magazines, and a great many other products. Then there are the chains like Waterstones, Dillons, Ottakars, Books Etc which are devoted exclusively to books – or almost so. As in the branches of the more diversified chains, you will find discounted books in these shops – books which are sold at less than the publisher's recommended retail price. The chains depend almost entirely on central buying – that is to say, the head office decides what books the branches will stock, and buys them in bulk from the publishers – although some of the bigger branches may have at least a degree of autonomy. Because of the large quantities purchased, the chains have always been able to demand and obtain high discounts, and after the Net Book Agreement became ineffective in 1995 (see p.45), the discounts on certain bestsellers rocketed. The chains can and will obtain books to order which are not on their shelves, but there is often a delay, and in some cases you may be told that the chain does not deal with this or that publisher.

The staff in most of the chain bookshops is likely to be far less ignorant about books and publishers and authors than was the case some years ago, and this is especially true in the shops which are solely dedicated to books, which have made a considerable effort to become 'user-friendly' – welcoming and less off-putting to the customer who finds bookshops intimidating – and their assistants are usually intelligent and helpful. On the other hand, it would seem that the more a chain diversifies, so that books form a decreasing part of the stock, the less informed the staff in the shops are likely to be. If you want to find a bookseller who is really knowledgeable and who is in the business not just to make money, but also for love of books, then you should go to one of the small independent bookshops. The owners of these shops survive on a comparatively small turnover (the bookbuying public is not a large one), despite the fact that they cannot benefit from the high discounts available to the chains, and indeed most of them have suffered to a greater or lesser extent by the abandonment of the Net Book Agreement, which has lost them sales of some of the top bestsellers, since they cannot compete with the price-cutting of the major chains. Some have closed as a result, but the majority remain in business, and contrive to do so mainly because they are able to offer an excellent service and to build up a personal relationship with their regular customers. Knowing their clientèle can often take some of the gamble out of the bookshop's ordering, because they have a good idea of what those people will buy and in what quantities, and the excellent service builds up a loyalty factor in the customer which can be of great importance. Tremendous advances in information technology and distribution allow the independent bookshop to provide the customer with accurate and informative details of available books, and to supply them within, if not twenty-four hours, a matter of two or three days.

Although the small owner-run bookshop is constantly under threat, the real problem is not competition from the big chains so much as the fact that they are selling what the vast majority of the population regard as a luxury item, especially if compared to essentials such as food and clothing. Even those who buy books from time to time mostly consider paperbacks to be over-priced and hardcover books to be quite ludicrously expensive, forgetting to compare them with such transitory pleasures as a meal out or a theatre ticket, and ignoring the fact that books can last a lifetime. However, threatened or not, it seems likely that the independent bookshop will survive, although its stock of hardcover books may eventually be almost entirely replaced by mass-market and trade paperbacks, and multimedia products.

Wholesalers
Wholesalers are, of course, important to the publisher too, and

have become increasingly so in recent years as more and more of the independent booksellers have come to rely heavily on wholesalers to supply books to order. Indeed, without the co-operation of the modern breed of highly efficient wholesalers, the independent booksellers would find it even more difficult to make a living. It has been predicted that at some time in the future publishers will sell their books to the major chains and to wholesalers only, and will not deal directly with independent booksellers, but at the time of writing many publishers are in fact moving back to the earlier practice of supplying bookshops direct.

Although British wholesalers also supply books to foreign countries, most overseas sales are achieved through local wholesalers in the countries concerned. However, where a substantial market for books in English exists, notably in Australia, the larger publishers mostly have their own companies, which distribute their titles as well as publishing some indigenous books. Incidentally, because of the frequent American invasion of territories which used to be exclusive to the British publisher, and because of the rise of local publishing in many such areas, the overseas markets have not proved an area of expansion for British books in recent years.

In addition to their sales to bookshops, publishers look increasingly nowadays to non-traditional outlets, such as garden centres, sports shops, and, since the Net Book Agreement became ineffective, certain supermarkets. The last named have been particularly tempted to carry books as part of their stock because, like the big chain bookshops, they can offer them at discounted prices, but they have had varying degrees of success.

Paperbacks are of course very widely sold in regular bookshops, but are also available in newsagents and sweetshops, and more and more often in supermarkets, tobacconists, hairdressers, gardening centres, and other non-traditional outlets. Libraries too take paperbacks in substantial numbers. Although paperback publishers do sell directly to the chains and to some other retailers, a very large part of their sales is made to wholesalers, who supply and service the thousands of small retail outlets for the books.

Public Libraries

Public libraries are an important market for publishers, but demand has diminished substantially in recent years, largely because of cuts in local council spending. Local authorities see the library service as one of the least important items in their budget, (education, roads, policing, refuse collection and various other services must obviously take priority) and this attitude is fuelled by reports which show that the total annual borrowings from public libraries are slowly but regularly declining – although, happily, this does not appear to be true in the case of children's books. Nevertheless, British libraries have always been, and look like remaining the best in the world. No other country has so extensive and well-stocked a system making books available at no cost (except indirectly to the ratepayer) to everyone. We may justly be proud of our public libraries as one of our greater national glories, but they are also a considerable millstone around the necks of our publishers and authors, for they have turned us into a nation of book borrowers rather than book buyers. We have one of the smallest annual *per capita* hardcover book-purchase figures among the affluent nations. How many authors have despaired at hearing their friends promise to get their books out of the library, as though this would be of great benefit to them? Admittedly, authors like to be read, but even though Public Lending Right (see pp.220–2) has brought many of them a welcome, but mostly modest, addition to their income, what authors really want to hear is that their friends are going to buy copies of their books. This is not simply because the author gets a royalty on sales of the book, which will be much larger than the PLR figure per borrowing, but because the more copies that are sold the more likely the publisher will be to accept the author's next book, the more likely the bookseller will be to stock it, the more likely the author will move towards bestsellerdom, or at least to a greater success than at present. On the other hand, it must be said that public libraries do an excellent job of publicizing books and authors, and one of the reasons for the recent increased borrowing of books for children must surely be the events that so many libraries organize for youngsters, including story-time readings and visits by authors.

By far the biggest figures for library borrowings are those relating to fiction for adults. Nevertheless, one of the results of further reductions in the amounts that councils are willing to allot to libraries is likely to be cuts in the amount spent on fiction. It will not disappear completely from the shelves, but there will be a change of emphasis, and indeed libraries already see their primary role in modern society as repositories of knowledge, offering borrowers the fullest possible range of non-fiction books, rather than as providers of entertainment. Indeed, some observers believe that the sole reason for a decline in borrowing figures is the fact that libraries have already cut back on the purchase of novels, and so offer the fiction-reading public a poorer choice.

Most publishers sell their books to public and other libraries through specialist wholesalers known as library suppliers.

Print Quantities and Prices

In fixing the print quantity of the books on their lists, publishers look at their available markets, and try to make the right guess at how many copies will be needed. Print quantities of hardcover books vary enormously, and so do their retail prices, ranging from a few score copies of an extremely expensive limited edition to fifty thousand or more copies of a major bestseller priced more modestly. Bestsellers are rare, and the majority of books on a general publisher's list are likely to have initial print runs of between one thousand and ten thousand copies, with prices in a limited and familiar range, and this includes trade paperbacks which generally retail for some pounds less than a hardcover book. It is worth noting, by the way, that fiction, following a long-established tradition, is almost always priced more cheaply than non-fiction – a biography, for instance, is likely to cost a minimum of £4 or £5 more than a novel of comparable length, and if it is heavily illustrated may easily be priced at £10 or £15 more.

As already noted in Chapter 1, the high print quantities for paperbacks can start below ten thousand copies, but can rise to a quarter of a million or more. Prices tend to be standardized.

The Cult of the Bestseller

Bestsellers may be rare, but they are essential to a publisher's prosperity. Publishing is a business which exists on small margins, with the majority of titles on a list teetering between making a small loss or a small profit. There are also always the disasters – the books which, quite unpredictably and often for no good reason that anyone can discover, end up making a large loss for the publisher. Bestsellers are needed to cancel out the losses and to provide a substantial proportion of the firm's profit. This is particularly true of mass-market paperbacks, but it is not simply the economics of publishing which have made it so, but the retail book trade's insistence on fast turnover. It is difficult to interest the most powerful bookbuyers in the country – the big chains and the wholesalers who service newsagents – in the paperback of a book by an unknown or even moderately successful author; what they want are bestsellers which will rapidly move off the shelves and keep the tills ringing. Happily for them, bestsellers not only usually have quite a long life, but are likely to drag the author's previous books to best-sellerdom on their coat tails, so that the publishers reprint and reprint again, and more and more spaces on the racks are filled by that author's books.

If you listen to hardcover publishers talking together you will undoubtedly hear them saying that everything is increasingly difficult and that they don't know how any of them will manage to survive more than a year or two more. I have heard that kind of talk for the past fifty years. But the cult of the bestseller really does have one very serious outcome, which particularly affects new fiction. Hardcover publishers used to be able to afford to take on new and unknown novelists and publish two or three of their books knowing that they would almost certainly make a loss, in the belief that by the fourth or fifth book the writer would have established a reputation and learnt enough about the craft to produce something which would sell well enough to make a profit. (The belief was not always justified, by the way, but a few successes would make up for quite a number of failures.) Because the hardcover market for fiction has shrunk over the past fifty years or so, allied to a number of economic changes and pressures, an expected loss can no longer be contemplated – virtually every book which a publisher takes on must promise a profitable bottom line. In practice this means that it is essential nowadays for any publisher who signs up a new novel to be able to sell the paperback rights – the publisher's share of the royalties makes the difference between profit and loss on the publication. But the paperback houses (of which, remember, there are comparatively few) tend to be best-seller orientated, which means not only that they put almost all their efforts behind one or two 'lead' titles every month, but also that if they have on their list any bestselling authors who are also prolific, they are likely to keep a large number of their titles in print, and this inevitably diminishes their appetite for less well-known authors. So they will probably take on new authors only if they seem already to be nudging at bestsellerdom, and it has there-fore become extremely difficult for hardcover publishers to nurture a new talent which has not yet developed fully, in the way in which they did in days gone by. The publishing trade, including the mass-market paperback business, is very much aware of this problem, and does its best to take on and promote new writers, and of course new first novels continue to appear – but they do need to have a high level of skill and maturity.

Even Penguin, the trendsetter, the company which, starting in the 1930s, brought about the 'paperback revolution' and changed the face of publishing in the second half of the twentieth century, has been affected by the cult of the bestseller. Having established itself in a position from which it was able to publish successfully books not aimed at the most popular end of the market, it was eventually forced to take a number of steps to secure its continued existence, including the introduction of pictorial covers, and the addition to the list of popular bestsellers. The company also established Penguin shops within bookshops, where the whole range of Penguin titles would be permanently available. In the last twenty years or so, Penguin's competitors have expanded their range by the introduction of 'up-market' imprints, which are very successful. Such lists, which often include 'originals' (books published for the first time in paperback) have given hope to new novelists, provided that their work has at least some pretensions to being regarded as literary.

The villains of the piece would seem to be the profit-driven booksellers (from which I would exclude the small independent booksellers, who have always been willing to give a chance to an untried talent if they could). They must be aware of the need to foster new writers, and indeed they periodically produce plans for doing so, but they are usually still interested only in those who are outstandingly successful. Perhaps they cannot be blamed, and the real problem lies with our materialistic, money-mad, modern world. Or it might be argued that they are right to demand that books should be of a high enough standard to please the public, and if your early efforts don't make the grade, then you've simply got to go away and work at your craft until your work can meet the challenge. There's something to be said for that point of view. Talent, like murder, will out, but it's now the author who has to nurture it until it is ready for outing.

The Life of Newly Published Books

The bulk of sales on a general hardcover publisher's list, and this applies particularly to fiction, will be sold on publication and in the first six months thereafter. Bestsellers may have a longer life (although even they can fade quite rapidly), and some books are fortunate enough to become backlist titles or standard works, and will go on selling steadily for a period of years. They are the exceptions, as are those very few books which suddenly come to vigorous life long after the initial impetus has disappeared (frequently because of a television serial based on the book, or because it has become a 'cult' book, or for some equally unpredictable reason). Interest in an author's earlier books can sometimes be revived if he or she writes a bestseller, or preferably a whole string of bestsellers. Sometimes the enormous improvement in sales comes about because the author's story-telling ability has blossomed over the years, and the re-publication of earlier, less well-written books may be somewhat embarrassing (although not so embarrassing as to prevent either publisher or author, or their bank managers, from enjoying the proceeds). In most cases, however, the author of almost any book will find that a very high proportion of the total sales will be shown on the first royalty statement received after publication, and indeed if the book came out at the beginning of a royalty period, the proportion may be as high as eighty or ninety per cent.

Much the same is true of paperbacks, but, as already noted, a book which becomes a major bestseller will almost certainly turn the same author's previous and subsequent books into bestsellers, and they can often go on selling for many years.

Remainders
Remainders are those copies of a book which are left when sales have come down to an extremely low level or have ceased altogether. At that point the publisher's sales department will probably decide that the book should be 'remaindered', which means selling it to a remainder merchant, who is a kind of specialist wholesaler. The remainder merchant purchases unwanted books from publishers at a very low figure indeed (usually less than the cost of manufacture) and then sells them to the public, mostly through specialized outlets, at knock-down prices.

Publishers sometimes remainder only a part of their stock of a given book, keeping some copies available to sell, mostly to special order, through normal trade outlets at the full price. A partial remainder, as it is called, clears space in the warehouse, and brings in a few pennies from what would otherwise be totally dead stock. It works quite well for the publisher, except when ructions develop after a member of the public buys a copy at full price and ten minutes later sees it in a remainder outlet for a quarter of the cost. Almost all agents object strongly to the practice, but unless the contract specifically forbids it, have to content themselves with a sharply-worded grumble to the publisher.

Book Fairs

International book fairs are an important part of the publishing scene. They take place in almost all countries of the world. The best-known and largest book fair is held every autumn in Frankfurt-am-Main, Germany, and others include those held annually in London, Jerusalem, and Moscow, and BookExpo America (formerly run by the American Booksellers Association) which is located in a different US city every year. For publishers of children's books there is the annual Children's Books Fair in Bologna, Italy. Book fairs provide opportunities for the sale and purchase of rights and also for booksellers to order books, and the majority of publishers feel that it is essential to attend them, often spending a considerable amount of money on a stand to display their books and on hospitality for their customers. However, many other publishers stay away, save their money, and feel that they do not lose anything by not attending. Attendance by an author at any of the book fairs is far from obligatory, but probably worthwhile at least once. If you are a major 'name', your publishers may want you to be there so that you can be shown off – or indeed you may want to take the opportunity of meeting all your publishers all over the world in one go, as it were. If you are not in that class but are the sort of author who likes to try to sell your work by personal approach, you will have the opportunity of speaking directly to dozens of editors, and may persuade some of them to consider your book (but do make sure that any publishers that you may already have know what you are up to). If you are a quiet, retiring type who has, perhaps, just had a first book accepted, you will probably be suitably humbled by the sight of the hundreds of thousands of books which, like yours, are going to be out there in the marketplace looking for people to buy them. The atmosphere at a book fair is always slightly unreal – it is hot, noisy, almost feverish, and the person you are talking to will probably be looking past you for most of the time, watching in case any of the passer-by is someone even more worth talking to than you.

The Net Book Agreement

The publishing and bookselling trade finally abandoned the Net Book Agreement in the autumn of 1995. Since it is still talked about, and may continue as a matter of controversy for some time to come, it is perhaps worth rehearsing the history of the Agreement. It came into being originally in 1900, at the behest of booksellers, who saw it as protective device, but with the support of publishers. It prevented booksellers from selling books at less than the price fixed by the publisher (except in the special cases of National Book Sales, and remainder sales), and for nearly a hundred years the NBA gave stability to both sides of the trade. After the introduction of the Restrictive Practices Act of 1965, the Agreement was twice investigated by the Monopolies Commission, which on both occasions decided that the Publishers Association was right in its argument that it worked to the benefit of the public at large.

However, certain booksellers began to press for the abolition of the NBA, and in 1995 their campaign grew in strength, aided by the certainty of yet another investigation by the Monopolies Commission, and by murmurings from the EU about the possible illegality of the Agreement. In September of that year a few major publishers surprised the trade with a decision that in future their books would be non-net, and once that had happened, in the space of a few days the Net Book Agreement was to all intents and purposes dead.

Those whose actions made the NBA no longer operative argued that once booksellers had the ability to sell books at less than the publishers' recommended retail prices, the public would greatly increase its purchases. Even if the price-cutting were to extend only to bestsellers, people coming into a shop to buy a 'bargain', would be tempted while they were there to buy other books. It didn't quite work out that way. First of all, prices could not generally be cut across the board, but only on books the sales of which were large enough to allow of bulk orders and consequent high discounts. Moreover, not all publishers were willing to give those very high discounts even on their top selling titles. This was confusing to the public, who often expected every book to be cheaper, whereas in fact the great majority of books were sold at the price recommended by the publisher, just as though the Net Book Agreement were still in force. Nevertheless, sales of the major discounted bestsellers did indeed increase, almost entirely through the big bookselling chains, which, in addition to getting their high discounts, could afford to cut their own profit margins. Independent booksellers lost sales of those top selling titles, which made their businesses even more precarious. And the public has not in general terms increased its book-buying at all.

So who has gained? Some small booksellers have gone to the wall, but most have managed to carry on. It would seem that just as much damage has been done to a number of publishers, who have substantially trimmed their profit margins because of the very high discounts they have had to give on the books on which they would normally expect to make most money. Some pessimists believe that this will result in making it more difficult than ever to get published, but at present there is no proof of any such negative development. As for the authors of discounted bestsellers, some may have benefited, but for others the increased sales have been offset by decreased royalties. The leaders of the revolution against the NBA still claim to have been right. But a very substantial number of publishers, booksellers, librarians and, indeed, authors feel that its abolition was a mistake, and live in hopes that one day the Agreement may be restored, and since the only real discernible result of the NBA's disappearance has been an increase above the rate of inflation in the price of books, the general public would probably benefit from its return.

In the meantime, some booksellers are also calling for the abolition of the Recommended Retail Price (RRP). This is the price which publishers put on their books, which they have continued to do despite the disappearance of the NBA. Those who want to get rid of RRP say that booksellers would then be able to price books according to what the traffic would bear – some books would be sold more cheaply and others at a higher price than the publisher would have suggested, and prices would vary from bookshop to bookshop. It sounds like a nightmare scenario to me, but if it comes about, no doubt we shall get used to it, in time.

VAT

Another major concern within the book trade has been the possibility of the imposition of VAT on books. Purchase Tax, the forerunner of VAT, was first introduced in 1940 by the then Chancellor of the Exchequer, Kingsley Wood. He had every intention of imposing the new tax on books, but a strong campaign was mounted by authors and publishers, spearheaded by Stanley Unwin, who, in a celebrated letter to The Times, argued that a tax on books was a tax on knowledge. His letter continued: 'It would be humiliating if, in a war for freedom of thought,' (the Second World

War was raging at the time) 'the sale of books in which man's highest thoughts are enshrined should be hampered by taxation.' The Chancellor eventually gave in. Once Britain had joined the EU, it seemed likely that harmonization of taxes would mean that VAT would be levied on books, and although, up to the time of writing, succeeding Chancellors have shied away from imposing it, the threat remains and the whole trade gets itself into a tizzy as each Budget Day approaches. Is the alarm justified? It would certainly mean an increase in the price of books, and that will affect sales adversely, especially since the public at large already thinks of books as expensive. In addition, new authors will find it more difficult to get into print, many independent booksellers will go out of business, and so will small publishers. Perhaps. I certainly do not want to see a tax on books, and the next time the threat appears to be imminent, I shall join the campaign against it with enthusiastic vigour. Nevertheless, I have to say that I sometimes wonder whether the effect would be quite as disastrous as the prophets of doom predict.

3

Submitting Your Work to a Publisher

Preparation of the Typescript
Handwriting was all very well for Jane Austen, but nowadays few
publishers would be willing to consider a manuscript (using that
term in its true meaning of material written by hand). On the other
hand, we have not yet reached the stage, which will unquestionably
come at some future date – probably far off – when they will all
require submission to be in disc form, emanating from a personal
computer (commonly referred to as a 'word processor'). Until we
get to that point, a typescript is required (even if it is often loosely
and perversely still referred to as a 'manuscript'), whether it is
produced on a typewriter or is 'hard copy' from the word processor. It should be in double spacing on one side of the paper only,
with ample margins (say, a minimum of 2.5 cm) at top, bottom,
right- and left-hand sides of the page. Why is this important? First
of all, because your material will be easier to read. Double spacing
will also allow room for corrections which do not warrant retyping.
Margins at the side will permit the compositor (the person who
puts the book into type) to put each page into a kind of stand which
has grips on either side to hold it in place while he copies it.

There are different rules for the layout of poetry and plays.
Poems should be typed exactly as they are intended to appear in
print, in single spacing with any indentations or other singularities
just as you want them. Plays demand special and complex layouts,
advice on which can be obtained from David Campton's excellent
book, *Becoming a Playwright* (published by Hale).

The paper used should be A4 (297 x 210 mm), or what is known
as American A4 (280 x 217 mm), which is the size of the 'continu-

ous' paper commonly supplied for some word processor printers. I believe that most publishers would prefer you not to use the facility on your electronic typewriter or word processor which will 'justify' the type on both sides, spacing the words out so that both left- and right-hand margins are straight ones. Do your best to keep to the same number of lines per page, and the same margins, and if you use more than one typewriter it is preferable that they should all have the same size of type – these considerations make it much easier to work out the length of the book, quite apart from the fact that the typescript will look neater.

Many authors tend to economize on typewriter ribbons. It doesn't help. Why put an obstacle in the way of your book by making it physically difficult for the publisher to read? Equally, masses of messy corrections are to be avoided. That doesn't mean that you can't make the occasional alteration, but the cleaner the typescript looks, the better. If you do make a correction, make sure that the change is totally clear, and if it is of any length or complexity, retype the page. Editors do take notice of a typescript's appearance. Sloppy, badly-presented typescripts are not only unprofessional, but make it look as though the authors do not care sufficiently about their work.

If you are using a typewriter, you should make at least two carbon copies of your typescript. When submitting a book, always send the top copy to a publisher rather than a carbon. If the book is accepted for publication, a second copy will be required by the publisher, and your first carbon copy will be acceptable. The second carbon copy is for yourself, and you should retain it with the utmost care. You may want to refer to it in working with your editor, and you will certainly need it if the other copies are lost or damaged. Typescripts sometimes go astray in the post or are mislaid in the most scrupulously monitored of publishers' offices (and not all are that!), or can be damaged by fire or flood, and if any such disaster should take place, it is much easier to have the book retyped or photocopied from your own carbon than to have to start writing it again from scratch. Photocopying a typescript is just as acceptable, if not more so, than carbon copying, if you can afford it. If you are using carbons, again don't indulge in false economy, but replace the carbons as soon as the copies begin to look grey.

Increasingly nowadays authors use word processors. A word processor is, in fact, simply a computer controlled by a program which allows the users to record whatever words they may wish to compose, the words then being stored on discs, from which they may be retrieved so that they may be read and, if necessary, altered, and from which copies may be produced on the attached printers. Word processors vary from the cheap and simple Amstrad PCW8256 (which at the time of writing is the cheapest machine on the market, and which many authors find entirely adequate for their purposes, although the quality of printing is less than perfect) to the expensive, luxury machines which allow of the production of graphics and other illustrations as well as words, and which have a wide range of printing facilities, including the choice of many different type styles and sizes, colour work, and so on. If you are embarking on desktop publishing (see p.32) you will certainly need a fairly sophisticated PC, even if not one at the very top of the range.

Among the many attractions of word processors are the ease with which corrections can be made, the speed with which the work can be printed, and the ability to produce as many copies as you like, without having to mess about with carbons or go to the expense of photocopying.

However, the remarks above concerning typewriter ribbons apply equally to the ribbons used on some printers. Don't economize on them – make sure that your work is always easy to read. If you have the facility to produce work in either 'draft' or 'high quality' mode, use the former for your own copy of the typescript, but the latter, always, for work which you are going to submit to a publisher.

Although it is still customary to submit a book initially in typescript form, if the book is accepted and the publishers require a second copy, if you use a word processor, they may well prefer to have the copy on disc. It is, of course, a simple matter to make a copy disc, and you should in any case always have a back-up copy for your own use. If the publishers want a copy disc, they will probably tell you whether it should be supplied in the programme which you normally use (such as *Windows*), or whether they would prefer it, for instance, in ASCII (American Standard Code for Information Interchange – a code which enables different computer systems to communicate with each other).

The pages of your typescript should be numbered consecutively from the first page to the last, not starting from '1' again at the beginning of each new chapter. If you have ever dropped a typescript of separate pages and tried to put it in order again, you will appreciate how much more difficult a task it is if the chapters are each numbered separately, besides which it is often helpful to know how many pages there are in a typescript without having to add up the total chapter by chapter. Put 'The End' at the end, even if you don't want it to appear in the final printed version; endings are sometimes inconclusive, but if 'The End' is there the publisher will know that that is where you intended to stop.

Publishers vary in their likes and dislikes about how a typescript should be fastened together. The universally unpopular method is that in which the pages are bound solidly together, which makes the book impossibly heavy and awkward to read. Looseleaf binders are often used; the ring variety is not too bad, but pages frequently slip out of the kind which relies on a spring to keep them in place. Paperclips should be avoided, if only because other pieces of paper so easily get caught up in them. My own preference in my days as a publisher was for entirely loose leafs; now that paper no longer comes in handy boxes, the typescript can be contained in one or more wallet-type folder. However stapling is acceptable, either in chapters or in a regular number of pages, but only one staple, at the top left-hand corner, is needed.

How long should a book be? A glib, but nevertheless true answer is that it should be as long as it needs to be. If you set out to write, say, eighty thousand words, you may find that you have to pad your material or conversely to condense it. Let the book find its own length. There are no rules – very short and very long books do get published – but there are guidelines. In most cases, publishers do not want anything much under thirty-five to forty thousand words (except for children's books) and tend to look apprehensively at work which runs to more than a hundred thousand words, although family sagas often exceed that length. If you can keep to somewhere between fifty and eighty thousand words you will probably stand more chance. But, as I have already said, there are no hard and fast rules, unless you are writing for a series, when you may have to stick closely to a length decided in advance by the publisher. The best thing is to do your market research – find out the length of already published books which are similar in scope to yours, or write to a publisher and ask what length would be considered reasonable for a book of the type you have in mind. But do make sure that a desired length does not become more important than the content – don't try to cram too much into a short space, when it will all seem under-written, or stretch out your material to fill up the pages, when it will appear thin and the padding will show.

How many chapters should your book have? Again, there are no rules. Some books have no chapters, and others are broken into hundreds of short sections. In non-fiction the different aspects of the subject usually fall almost automatically into separate chapters. In writing fiction it is sometimes more difficult to decide, but if you come to a 'natural break' in your narrative, then you have probably come to the end of a chapter. But I doubt if any books of the right kind of total length have ever been turned down for having either too few or too many chapters.

It is not absolutely necessary to indicate on the front page of your typescript how many words it contains, since most publishers are practised at gauging the length of the books they receive, but it does no harm to show the extent, and indeed it may be a help. The publishers of this book, Robert Hale Limited, issue an excellent guide to the calculation of the length of a typescript and, with their permission, I now quote it:

> The purpose of calculating the wordage of any typescript is to determine the number of printed pages it will occupy. The precise word count is of no use, since it tells nothing about the matter of short lines resulting from paragraphing or dialogue (particularly important with fiction).
>
> Calculation is therefore based on the assumption that all printed pages have no paragraph beginnings or endings and the type area is completely filled with words.
>
> To assess the wordage proceed as follows:
>
> 1. Ensure the typewriting is the same throughout in terms of size, length of line, etc. If not the procedure given below should be followed for each individual style of typing and the results added together.
>
> 2. Count 50 full lines and find the average number of words, e.g. 50 lines of 560 words gives an average of 11.2 words.
>
> 3. Average the number of lines over 10 characteristic pages, e.g. 245 lines on ten pages gives an average of 24.5 lines.
>
> 4. Multiply the averages of 2. and 3. to get the average per page, e.g. $11.2 \times 24.5 = 274$.
>
> 5. Ensure the page numbering is consecutive, then multiply the word average per page by the number of pages (count short pages at beginnings and ends of chapters as full pages).
>
> 6. Draw attention to, but do not count foreword, preface, introduction, bibliography, appendices, index, maps or other line figures.

Some authors are in the habit of putting 'First British Serial Rights' on the front page of their typescripts, in the mistaken belief that this is what they are offering to the publisher. They should be offering Volume Rights, or at least British Volume Rights, or possibly All Rights. First British Serial Rights (or in these days of unrestricted trading within the EU, First European Serial Rights) are what you offer to a magazine or newspaper when you submit a short story or an article, or if you submit your book to them before or instead of showing it to a book publisher.

Do put your name and address on the title-page and last page of the typescript.

Words are the main tool of the author's trade, and they should be correctly used and spelt and punctuated. I have always considered that failure in these respects is the sign of an unprofessional approach, but I do recognize that some writers have an impenetrable blindspot in certain of these matters, particularly often with spelling, and that even the most careful scrutiny of dictionaries and grammars cannot entirely solve their problems. The spell-checking facilities available on many PCs are useful, but again may not be the complete answer for the near-dyslexic author. I would suggest that before finally typing or printing out their books, such writers should prevail upon a friend with the right capabilities to go through the books and make the necessary alterations. Such glamour attaches to authorship that it should not be difficult to find someone who will undertake this chore. Teachers are very suitable, although it is as well to choose one who has retired or is at least elderly – the younger ones may be as hopeless as you yourself. You may also find it worthwhile to get hold of a copy of my own book *The Nuts and Bolts of Writing* (published by Hale), which was written with the specific aim of helping writers to improve the quality of their work in respect of spelling, punctuation and grammar, and was, in fact, suggested to me by my publisher in a moment of anger and despair at the poor standard in such matters of so many of the typescripts submitted to him.

Sending the Book Out

Having got your typescript ready, in the best possible condition that you can manage, where do you send it? In the *Writers' and Artists' Yearbook* you will find a list of publishers and their addresses. Some indications of the kinds of books that each firm publishes is given, but the information is often too brief and general to be more than the roughest of guides. *The Writer's Handbook* gives rather more detail about publishers and their requirements, but even the additional help which it provides may not be entirely adequate. Rather than using a pin with either book to decide which publisher you will try, it is a good idea to visit your local bookshop and library to see which companies regularly bring out books of the kind which you have written. It may be stating the obvious, but it is of little use to send, say, a romantic novel to a publisher who produces nothing but school text books, or an art book to a publisher who never ventures into that field. On the other hand, you should beware of working too closely on what you discover in the bookshop; if you have written, say, a new biography of Mary, Queen of Scots, it is almost certainly a waste of time to send it to a publisher who has recently brought out a book on the very same subject, or who has a standard work on it on the back-list; try another house which has a list of biographies.

To some extent the question of which publisher to choose may become a little easier if certain of the people who work in publishers' marketing departments, who are growing in power and influence (see p.72), are correct in predicting that one of the future aims of publishers will be to establish themselves as brand names. By this they mean that publishing houses will attempt to become known for publishing certain genres of books. Some brand names already exist – Mills & Boon, the premier brand name for romances, is the perfect example, and there are numerous other firms which are noted for particular categories of books. This concept, incidentally, also ties into the idea of 'niche publishing' (see p.19).

Should you choose a large publisher or a small one? You may prefer to be with a small publisher, on the grounds that it is better to be a big fish in a small pond than a small fish in a large pond. Of course, no matter what the size of the pond, if you're a bestseller you'll be a big fish, and if you're at the other end of the scale you may not be more than a minnow. Assuming, however, that you're just of medium size, you may feel that you will get more individual attention in the small firm, while you may benefit in the large one from its more effective selling organization, but neither of these possibilities is necessarily so. It cannot even be said with any certainty that your work stands more chance of being accepted by a big publisher, despite the fact the firm brings out a great many books every year – its standards are likely to be just as high as those of a small house. The best thing is to forget the size of the publisher and choose simply those which your market research tells you are the most likely to be interested in your book.

When you have selected your publisher you can simply send your typescript to the company. In these days of very high postal costs for parcels it is, however, wiser to write first asking if you may submit the book. Tell the publisher, briefly, what it is about. If it is a novel, specify what genre it is (straight, romantic, family saga, thriller, detective, etc), and perhaps add some details about any particular point of interest, such as the setting, the period, or the fact that the main characters are gay. If it is non-fiction, give a few details about your qualifications for writing it, the market for which it is intended, and what makes it different from books on the subject which are already available (to write non-fiction success-fully, you really do need considerable expertise and, if possible, a new angle); if it is aimed at a specialist audience, it will be worth-while to give some estimate of how many people you think will be interested and likely to purchase such a book (if you have written an innovative book on training parrots to talk, let us say, you may be able to tell the publisher that there are x thousand parrot-owners in the country).

Do not boast that all your friends have enjoyed the book. Publishers are never impressed by such information, partly because they don't know your friends and so have no idea whether or not their judgement is to be respected, and partly because they will suspect that your friends will have told you how much they liked the book even if in fact they loathed every word. On the other hand, if you happen to have secured an endorsement from some eminent person, especially one who is an authority in the field in which you are writing, by all means say so. Equally, if you are writ-ing, for instance, a book on safety in the home and have shown it to an organization such as RoSPA, who have given it their approval, say so. If you have had some success as a writer – that is to say, previous books commercially published, or regular articles or stories accepted for publication in newspapers and magazines – it is certainly worth mentioning the fact.

Over the years I spent in publishing I received thousands of letters about books which the authors wished me to consider. Some were grovelling ('I would consider it a great honour to be published by so renowned a firm as yours'), some were overbearing ('I have decided that you shall publish this book. Kindly send me your terms by return'), some were jokey ('My Mum thinks it's smashing, but I do recognize that she may be a teeny bit prejudiced in my favour'), some were apologetic, and tended to misquote ('A poor thing but my own'), some were so long that I felt I didn't need to read the book itself, and some were so illiterate that I knew I didn't have to. Caroline Sheldon, the literary agent, lists three other letters that turn her off: those that begin 'Don't miss this opportunity', those that admit 'the first three chapters aren't very good', and those that boast 'this story won a prize in our village competition'. The letters that she would like best, as I did, were those which are brief and to the point, businesslike, professional.

Send a stamped addressed envelope with your letter of enquiry. It is discourteous not to do so, and since publishers are buyers in a buyers' market, and are inundated with such letters, they may not reply at all if you don't.

It may be worth your while to find out the editor's name, so that you can address your letter to him or her personally (although, if it is a large editorial department, it may be read and answered by someone else). If you do so, however, make sure that you get the name right. Some people are very sensitive about misspellings of their names (personally, I am inured to it after long experience) or about being addressed as 'Ms' when in fact they are 'Mr' or 'Mrs' or even old-fashioned 'Miss'.

If the publisher is willing to consider the book, then post it or deliver it yourself, if you are near enough to do so. Enclose postage for its return. Don't, if you deliver it, expect to see anyone in the office other than the person in reception – at that stage no one is interested in you, however fascinating you may be. Your book's the thing, and it is your ambassador. And if you feel that you have to see someone to explain something about the book – some information which you can't put briefly in a letter – you are probably unwittingly condemning the book as a failure. It should be able to speak for itself in every respect. After all, you aren't going to be able to stand in bookshops explaining it to potential customers, are you?

When you send your book to a publisher you should receive an acknowledgement of its arrival. If you do not, it may mean that the parcel has been lost in the mail (which is comparatively rare), or it may be simply that the publisher has decided to economize by not sending out these expensive pieces of paper (cost of stationery, secretary's time, postage). Some authors enclose a stamped addressed postcard which the publisher can mail back to you when the parcel arrives.

Synopses and Specimen Chapters
Instead of sending the complete book, you can send a synopsis and two or three specimen chapters. The practice of doing so has become commonplace – indeed, such submissions considerably outnumber nowadays those of complete typescripts, publishers having become much more willing than in the past to look at material in this form – and it not only saves the author postage and usually means that a verdict comes much more quickly, but, if the synopsis and chapters are sent before the book is completed, may result in a commission to finish it. There is also the advantage that an interested publisher has the opportunity of making suggestions for changes at an early stage.

For the majority of non-fiction books, the synopsis-and-specimen-chapters approach is probably the best way of trying to interest a publisher, but do, as already mentioned, include details of your qualifications and of the market at which you are aiming. You can also write to a publisher at an even earlier stage, simply putting forward an idea for a book; if the publisher likes the idea, a synopsis and specimen chapters and editorial discussion can follow, and perhaps lead to the commissioning of the book. If you happen to be a recognized expert in your field, the first approach may come from the publisher, inviting you to write a given book, but it is quite likely that a synopsis and specimen chapters will still be called for, just to show that you are capable of writing to an acceptable standard and that you and the publisher have the same concept of what the book is meant to be like.

For fiction, however, the situation is a little different, the problem being that in an imaginative work, which often depends on the author's ability to create colour and excitement and to handle the crises in the story with a sense of drama, even the best of synopses and specimen chapters cannot give an entirely reliable picture of the book as a whole. Publishers frequently commission novelists whose work they know, especially if they have themselves published that author before, on the basis of a synopsis (often without the specimen chapters), but comparatively few first novels are signed up at so early a stage. If you are just starting out, then, and send off a synopsis and specimen chapters of a novel, you are likely to get either a firm rejection, or a letter asking to see the book when it is completed; the latter request is encouraging, but it is not a commitment to publish, so you should not raise your hopes too high.

(Incidentally, I must say that I have little sympathy with those would-be novelists who are unwilling to settle down to produce a book without first having a publisher's commitment to make it worth their while. New authors have to prove themselves. Few are so gifted that they can write an acceptable book without first learning their craft – and there is no better way to learn the craft than by actually doing it.)

It is important to distinguish between a synopsis and a blurb. The latter, usually printed on the front flap on the jacket of a hard-cover book, does not tell the whole story, whether the book is fiction or non-fiction. It aims to tantalize, to raise questions, and to suggest that all kinds of excitement are in store, without revealing what they are, so that the reader is made to want to read the book to find out what the excitements are, and the answers to the questions which the blurb poses. But the publisher wants a synopsis, which should reveal all, not a teasing blurb, so that it is possible to judge, among other things, whether you can resolve your story satisfactorily, or whether your non-fiction book is going to fulfil the hopes of those who buy it.

If you are commissioned to write a book on the basis of a synopsis, you do not have to stick to it absolutely rigidly. Obviously, you must do your best to deliver the book that the publisher expects, but minor differences from the original synopsis will probably be quite acceptable. Your publisher is used to the fact that authors change their ideas sometimes in the course of writing, or find that something which sounds perfectly fine in brief will not work properly when it is expanded. If the changes are at all major, you should of course let your publisher know about them in advance, especially if they alter the scope of the book in some way.

Many established writers produce all their books 'on spec' – that is to say, without a contract until the book has been finished and accepted for publication. Others are fortunate enough to be commissioned for each of their books, but in those cases, even though the author is very experienced and trustworthy, the publisher will probably ask for a detailed synopsis, which the editor will use to convince others in the publishing house of the excellence of the proposed book, and which the rights department will be able to send out to buyers of subsidiary rights and foreign publishers in the hope of making sales in advance of publication.

An approach which is not to be recommended is the submission which takes the form of two or three pages, extracted apparently at random from a completed novel. They are of course selected by the author because they are the most exciting in the book. Intended to whet the publisher's appetite, such submissions are merely irritating and a complete waste of time and postage. It is in fact an unwritten law, known to all editors, that the authors who use this method of submission are generally entirely lacking in talent; one can always tell this, because if the pages sent represent the best of the writing in the book, then the rest must be abysmal indeed.

Multiple Submissions

Most tutors of Creative Writing and authors of books on the subject will tell you not to give up easily. They advise you not to be depressed if your typescript is regularly turned down and they remind you of the number of rejections that John Braine received for *Room at the Top* before it was accepted and published with enormous success. But if each time you send out your work you have to wait for months before it comes back with a rejection slip, it may take you years before you too achieve your desired acceptance. Can you do anything about that?

Some years ago the majority of publishers would have held up their hands in horror at the thought of an author having the temerity to submit work simultaneously to more than one publisher. If they had discovered that such a crime had been committed, the book would have been returned to the wicked author forthwith. However, manners and codes of behaviour change. A long time ago now publishers began to accept the idea that agents would often conduct an auction for a new book which was considered commercially important, sending copies to all the publishers who seemed to be contenders for it, and demanding that their best offers should be made by a due date. Having been forced to accept the principle of multiple submissions in this way, the majority of publishers found it rather easier than they had imagined to respond to increasing calls from non-agented authors to allow them to minimize the delays in awaiting verdicts by no longer objecting to looking at a typescript at the same time as other publishers were also considering it.

Multiple submissions are now commonplace, but there may be a few dinosaur publishers around who have not yet caught up with contemporary trends, and it is therefore probably sensible, when writing a letter of enquiry to a publisher about your work, to ask whether that house has any antipathy towards multiple submissions. If you prefer not to make that enquiry, but simply to assume that no one will object to not having an exclusive offer, then at least I would suggest that you should inform the publishers, as a matter of courtesy, that you are submitting the work elsewhere at the same time.

Agents
You may decide instead of submitting your work directly to a publisher to send it first to an agent, and in many ways this can be a very wise move. The advantages of using an agent are many: agents know the state of the market much better than you are likely to, for they are in regular touch with all the principal publishers and are aware of the kinds of books they are looking for at any given juncture; they send books out at their own expense; they will negotiate the contract with the publisher, getting the best possible deal for the author, ensuring that the latter's rights are always preserved, and can often help to keep the publisher up to scratch, so that the book is handled well in every respect; they collect any moneys due, and check that they are correct; they will undertake the sale of many of the subsidiary rights; and, one of an agent's most important functions, they will stand between the author and the publisher in the case of any dispute, enabling the author to remain on friendly terms with the publisher despite the fact that, through the agent, they may be at loggerheads; they may also be able to save you from having the dispute in the first place, for although they are the representatives of their authors, and therefore on their side, they do also have a wide experience of publishers and their problems (indeed, many agents have spent part of their careers as publishers) and may be able to explain things that you don't understand, and tell you whether your complaint is justified or not; they will also probably be able to give you some advice about tax on your earnings as an author (although you may need the services of a fully qualified accountant); and they will often give useful editorial advice on a typescript.

For all these services, agents normally charge their authors 10% or 15% of their earnings from writing, plus VAT, but a higher percentage may be taken on foreign earnings, because British agents usually make foreign sales through the agents who represent them in the foreign countries concerned; the foreign agent takes a commission on the moneys earned in whichever country it may be, and transmits the balance to the British agent, whose own percentage is sliced off before it is passed to the author. Some authors resent having to pay a double commission in this way, and in certain circumstances their feelings may be justified. It is obviously a matter to be discussed directly with the agent.

The majority of agents do not charge for reading typescripts submitted to them by potential new clients, although the practice of asking for a fee has become more widespread recently, and will probably continue to grow. It is advisable to write to an agent first asking if you may send your material for consideration (give a fair amount of information about the book and about yourself, including any qualifications you have for writing it, details about its potential market, and something about your future writing plans).

Apart from the possible reading fee, no good agents, having added you to their list of clients, will take their percentage until they have sold your book and the money comes in. The agent's cut is usually well earned. But it is not easy to find an agent who is willing to take on a new client, and in fact it is often easier for an unknown author to get a publisher than to be accepted by an agent. Agents tend to be unwilling to act for an author unless they are convinced that within a reasonable period their percentage of the author's earnings will be making a worthwhile contribution to their costs, their overheads and their profits, and that means, in effect, that they are looking for clients who will be making upwards of £5,000 a year from their writing, and therefore putting at least £500 a year towards the agents' expenses. You may doubt your ability to bring in that sort of money to an agency, especially when you learn that most agents are unwilling to act for their authors over the sale to newspapers and magazines of articles and short stories (because the amount of money involved is rarely large enough to make their percentage worth the work which is involved for them). However, the kind of new client whom an agent would consider ideal in terms of earning capacity is not always easy to come by, and you may still get taken on, even if you seem unlikely to achieve the desired income.

If you experience difficulty in finding an agent to accept you as a client, your best bet may be to try one of the newer, smaller agencies (look in the *Writers' and Artists' Yearbook* for the dates when they were founded). You may not be getting quite the same expertise and experience, but the new agent's enthusiasm and need to establish the success of the agency may work to your benefit.

Do not despair if you cannot get an agent. There is a widespread belief that the only way to get published is through an agent, but it is not true, and a huge number of highly successful authors have begun by submitting their work directly to publishers. Some publishers certainly discourage or even refuse direct submissions from authors, dealing only with agents, and the number of such houses is increasing, but others go almost to the opposite extreme, regarding agents as enemies and refusing, as far as they dare, to work with them. But both these groups are minorities. Most publishers are quite happy to deal directly with authors and to have a 'slushpile'. This term, used for the pile on an editor's desk of unsolicited typescripts submitted direct from authors, sounds very derogatory, and the implicit contempt in it derives from the fact that well over ninety per cent of any publisher's slushpile consists of poor-quality material or books of a kind which the firm does not publish. Nevertheless, the majority of publishers devote considerable care and attention to the slushpile, searching for the very few publishable books that it may contain. Who knows? Nestling there may be a new Catherine Cookson, or the next Booker winner, or an even more successful diet book than those already on the market.

If a publishable book is found in the slushpile, it has some advantages for the publisher in not being agented, and these lie not so much in the fact that the terms in a direct contract may be slightly less favourable to the author than those in an agented contract – such differences are not likely to be substantial – but in the opportunity a direct contract gives the publisher to control all rights. The advantage is not simply in taking a percentage from any income which the rights generate, but in being able to offer the book to rights buyers, which may result in a reciprocal offer. Taking the example of US rights, it works like this: periodically British publishers go on business trips to the States with the hope of buying British rights in books controlled by American publishers, and of selling American rights in books which they, the British publishers, control to American publishers, and American publishers come to Britain on similar buying/selling visits; it is obviously of advantage, when the publishers are setting out to buy, to have something to sell, and what the publishers have to sell, in these cases, are not the agented books (which they may recommend, but cannot sell because they do not control the rights), but something which has come from that apparently contemptuously described slushpile.

On the other hand, it must be remembered that a book submitted by an agent is always going to get serious consideration in the publishing house. The publisher knows before reading a single word that it must have some merit, or the agent would not have agreed to handle it, and that it is likely to be of interest, because the agent knows what sort of books that publisher wants. And the more enthusiastic the agent is, the more seriously the publisher will consider it. In the end, however, it is the book itself which matters, and a book which arouses real excitement in a publishing house is going to get into print whether it comes from an agent or directly from its author.

In the past, the idea that there should be formal agreements between literary agents and their clients would have seemed very strange, and even the letters that may have been exchanged would often be very vague in many respects. The world changes, however, and nowadays it is usual for an agent taking on a new client to present a formal agreement setting out the terms of the relationship. Such a contract is likely to be fairly simply, and especially if the agent belongs to the Association of Authors' Agents (members are marked with an asterisk in the *Writers' and Artists' Yearbook*) is probably not the kind of thing that you need to worry about unduly before signing. Nevertheless, as with all contracts, you need to study such a document carefully before you do sign, and it will certainly be worth your while to seek advice on the matter if you have any doubts. The Society of Authors or the Writers' Guild, if you are a member of either, would be able to advise you.

Naturally, agents vary in their competence. You may find after a while that you are dissatisfied with yours. There is nothing to stop you changing to another agent if you can find one to take you on, or to give up having an agent altogether. However, you should give the first agent notice of your intention to change, and that agent is entitled to continue to act for you and to take the agreed commission on earnings in respect of any books which the agency has handled for you, provided that the original contract which it negotiated has not been terminated. If you have a written agreement with your agent it will undoubtedly specify what is to happen regarding existing contracts with publishers in the event that you and the agent part company. If you do not have such an agreement, it is worth thrashing the matter out in some detail so that neither party is in doubt about the situation.

Agents cannot of course perform miracles. If you get an agency to act for you, it does not necessarily mean that it will be able to sell all your ideas or completed books. Nor are agents in the business of teaching incompetent authors how to write. And since they are not bankers, subsidizing impecunious authors is not part of their remit either – indeed, neither agents nor publishers should be expected to advance money to an author other than under the terms of a contract.

Further information about agents is to be found in my book *An Author's Guide to Literary Agents* (published by Hale).

Waiting for the Result of a Submission
Having submitted your book to a publisher, how long can you expect to wait before receiving a verdict? Anything between two and eight weeks, and often – indeed, usually – longer. Some publishers are remarkably dilatory in this respect, and stories are common of books kept for a year or more before a decision is made. If the publisher has kept in touch with the author during that time to explain why it is taking so long to make a decision, there may be less cause for complaint, but in most cases the author hears nothing. This seems to me to be quite outrageous.

Don't think, by the way, that this treatment is given only to new authors – well-established writers who have already had a number of books brought out successfully by the publisher in question can suffer long delays too.

As will be explained later in this book, a decision as to whether or not to publish cannot always be arrived at swiftly. But some publishers contrive to make up their minds a lot faster than others, so why can't they all be quick? And if they positively cannot speed up their processes, why can't they have the courtesy to let you know that they are tentatively interested in the book, but need more time while they prepare estimates or perhaps obtain further specialist readings?

Is there anything you can do about a publisher's slowness? It is easy enough to say that you should withdraw your typescript in the face of unreasonably delayed decisions, but we all know that authors are reluctant to do anything which will possibly antagonize the very people they are hoping to impress and with whom they want to establish an amicable relationship. There are not many options open to you. Of course, if you are an author of very high standing, even the most awful of publishers will be bowing and scraping and rushing round madly to convince you that you are dealing with a firm whose efficiency extends in every possible direction, including speed of decision-making. But for others the only answer is to suffer the delays. Do you suffer in silence? Yes (unless you have been published previously by the firm in question, when you should be able to chivvy a little), for perhaps three months, after which it would be reasonable to write to the publishers and enquire what is happening. If you still get no satisfaction, then you have chosen an inefficient publisher (and there are several around). There is not a great deal that you can effectively do. At the end of six months without a decision, it is time to get stroppy, and demand the return of your typescript. That may mean the end of your chances with that particular publisher, but if the firm has proved itself to be lackadaisical, you will be better off elsewhere. Nothing can compensate you for the lost time, and since the law books are silent about how long a publisher takes to make a decision, there is nothing to be gained from consulting your solicitor, unless the material you sent to the publisher has a special value (as with irreplaceable photographs, for instance), when a legal approach may be helpful in getting it back.

Reasons for Delay

So far we have been concerned largely with unreasonable delays in publishers' decision-making, but not all publishers are reprehensible in this respect. Nevertheless, there may be considerable variations in the time that an efficient publisher may take with different submissions.

Sometimes the work may be returned almost immediately upon receipt. This does not necessarily mean that your book or idea has not been seriously considered, although it may be simply that you chose a publisher who was not interested at that juncture in the kind of book you had written. Often, however, a speedy return indicates no more than that you were lucky enough to send your material in when there was not a great pile of typescripts on the editor's desk waiting to be read, so that you were able to get prompt attention. Not all of the book may have been read – perhaps only a few sentences. Don't feel hard done by. Publishing may seem at times to be a particularly haphazard business, run largely by incompetent amateurs, but in fact the people who work in it are professionals, and that includes those who assess the typescripts, such as your own, which are submitted to the firm. The easiest aspect of an editor's professionalism to learn is the ability to identify those books which the firm will *not* want to publish. Mistakes can be made – most publishers, if pressed, can tell you of the great best-seller which they let slip through their fingers – but for the most part an editor really does know what the firm isn't looking for, and can recognize such work very quickly. And if your masterpiece is stupidly turned down after the merest glance, and the next publisher it goes to pounces upon it with excited little cries and pays you an enormous advance for it, the first editor will shrug, knowing that, even if a chance has been missed, another interesting book will undoubtedly make its way to the firm before long.

If your book does not come back immediately, it may have spent most of its time in the publisher's office working its way from the bottom of the pile to the top. It isn't always a steady progression. Sometimes a book will usurp your position in the queue because it is by one of the publisher's established authors, or because an agent has sent it in suggesting that it is a potential bestseller and asking for a prompt decision. Most publishers receive a very large number of typescripts for their consideration, and delays are inevitable.

After a preliminary reading, perhaps by an outside reader, perhaps by a junior editor, if the reader thinks the book interesting, a further reading will probably be arranged. Comparatively few books by unknown authors are taken by publishers on the basis of one reading only, unless perhaps the book lands first of all on the desk of a director or a senior editor whose decision can be taken without question. Even then, publishers will prepare estimates in some detail before accepting a book, and this may take a considerable time, especially if the book is complicated (for instance, with many diagrams to be inserted into the text, or numerous headings and subheadings and material to be set in different sizes of type, and so on).

Many books are rejected at the estimate stage. However enthusiastic the editor may have been, the publisher wants to see a profit on the book, and if the potential market for it does not appear to be large enough, then it will be impossible to spread the costs of origination (that is to say, the setting of the book in type, the preparation of the jacket, and all the other costs which have to be borne before a single copy can be produced) so as to come to a retail price for the book which will not inhibit sales by being too high and which will still allow a profit to be made. A very few publishers are still willing now and then to publish a book on which it is expected that they will make a loss – it might be a novel of exceptional literary merit, or perhaps poetry – but such instances are very rare, and indeed may be regarded as eccentricities.

Perhaps this is an appropriate place to point out that when publishers decide to publish a book, they are, on average, committing themselves to an expenditure in the region of £7,500, that being what it will cost to pay the author an advance and to produce an edition of a few thousand copies. The figure does not allow anything for overheads, which will come out of the gross revenue if sufficient copies are sold to pass the break-even point. It is not surprising then that publishers check their figures with great care, and tend to take on only those books whose profitability they feel is certain.

Sometimes additional delay is caused, before a decision is made, because a hardcover publisher wishes to discover whether the book is likely to be taken for publication by a paperback publisher, bringing in a share of the advance and royalties paid. This can be done quite quickly and easily if the company is integrated, owning both hardcover and softcover arms, but an independent hardback publisher may need to send the material to several of the paperback houses to see if they will bite. Some authors may query whether this course of action is morally justified, arguing that the book was submitted in confidence, as it were, and should not be shown to other parties without the author's permission, but it is a fairly common practice, and in many cases is an essential part of the process whereby a publisher decides whether or not to take on a particular book. The addition of some kind of income from paperback or other subsidiary rights is often the only factor which makes it possible for the publisher to sign up a book the hardcover edition of which is not expected to sell in large enough quantities to be self-supporting.

An unfortunate cause of the delay in communicating with you could be that the publisher has lost your typescript, and does not want to confess to having done so. It does happen, even in the best-run offices. Most acknowledgement forms which publishers send out contain a statement to the effect that they accept no responsibility for the loss or damage of a typescript while it is in their possession, and you will not automatically get compensation for the loss, unless you have taken out your own insurance, which is a wise thing to do if you can afford it. That, however, really applies only if you have produced your work on a typewriter, so that the only way you can replace the lost material is by photocopying the carbon copy, assuming that it is of good enough quality, or by typing the whole thing again, or paying for it to be done. Word processors have turned the loss of a typescript from the disaster that it used to be into a comparatively minor irritation, since you will be able in a few hours to make a copy from your disc at a minimal cost. And then you simply start the process of submission all over again.

The Rejected Typescript

If your book is rejected it will probably come back to you with nothing more than a formal statement that the publisher does not want to make an offer for the book. A few publishers take the trouble to explain why they are turning a book down, but the majority do not, and I am not sure that you can expect it of them. It would of course be of immense value to you if the publisher said exactly what was wrong with your material, but just think how many books are rejected every week – probably nine out of every ten submitted – and then consider how much of that week would have to be spent in writing in detail about books which the firm is not going to publish. If you do get a letter explaining the rejection, you should take it as a hopeful sign – not that the decision is likely to be changed, but that at least the editor found enough in your typescript to justify taking the time to write about it.

If, having received a formal rejection, you persist and write to ask why your book has been turned down, you may not even get a reply. This is not really as discourteous as it may sound. Many editors would like to correspond with the authors whose work they reject, in an effort to help them, but they simply do not have the time. Looking after the books and the authors that they are going to publish leaves them very few spare moments. Besides, they are paid to concern themselves with the interests of their employers, which do not include correspondence with rejected authors. Don't write, even if you get a helpful rejection letter, apart perhaps from saying 'thank you', unless the editor has plainly invited you to do so. Simply send your book off to another publisher.

Occasionally a rejection letter will include words of encouragement and praise, even though the book is being turned down, and perhaps expressions of regret that the publisher cannot make an offer for it, and in terms which go beyond the merely polite. You can almost certainly take such letters at face value – editors don't generally hand out compliments unless they really mean them. Editors also sometimes recommend, although they are rejecting the book, that you might try sending it to other publishers, whom they may name. Again, be encouraged by such advice – editors have no perverse wish to waste other editors' time, even if the others are competitors.

How often should you submit a book before giving up? The answer depends on your patience and how much you are prepared to spend on postage, and possibly on retyping the book, which is bound to get slightly tatty after several readings and which may require some updating (although of course if you use a word processor this will not prove a major difficulty). If you receive any kind of encouragement, despite the rejections, it is certainly worth continuing to try. On the other hand, if you have received nothing but formal rejections, you should perhaps ask yourself, after the typescript has come back, say, six times, whether there is indeed something wrong with it. Of course you may find it impossible to see its failings, and friends are usually not much use in this respect, since they will rarely tell you the truth about the book if they don't think it's very good, for fear of hurting your feelings. If you put it away for a fairly long period – three months or more – you may find at the end of that time that you can judge it more impartially. On the other hand, you can just keep on sending it out, hoping that one day it will find a home, and taking heart from the many stories of very successful authors who collected large numbers of rejection slips for their first book before placing it happily.

Your problem is to find someone in a publishing house somewhere who loves your book. Liking is not enough. You need an editor who is really enthusiastic, and who will if necessary fight the company to persuade them to take the book on. In some publishing houses this attitude is recognized to the extent of being known as 'the love factor', and a book will not be taken on if it is missing.

Many would-be authors believe that you've got to 'know someone' to stand any chance of acceptance. It isn't true. Of course there's no denying that it helps, but – cross my heart! – only to a very, very minor extent. Knowing someone in publishing will probably guarantee that your book will be read by someone fairly senior in the firm in question. But it will be a professional reading, and it will still be perfunctory if your book has no merit or is unsuitable for the list of that firm, despite the fact that you 'know someone'. What if the book is a bit better than that? Well, it will get a more careful reading, just as any other book of some merit would. But that doesn't mean that it's going to get published. Do you really suppose that publishers choose which books to publish on the basis of whether or not they know the author? I'm afraid that publishing is too tough a business to work on that sort of approach. The thing that gets you a contract is not who you know, but the quality of your work and its ability to bring out the love factor in an editor.

There is of course one sense in which 'knowing someone' does work to an author's advantage. I know the publisher of this book, and he knows me, and he takes very seriously any suggestion that I make to him of a book I could write for him (although he doesn't always commission it), and he also sometimes suggests ideas for books to me (a development which, naturally, I welcome).But it's not really the fact that we know each other, or indeed that we can call ourselves friends, which makes this happen – it's because he knows *my work* (and, I hope, loves it).

If you don't succeed at first in finding an editor who loves your book, keep on trying (subject to what I have said above about a whole string of formal rejections). You can even try the same publisher more than once, after a decent interval, because publishing personnel change, and your book may land on the desk of a different editor from the one who saw it last time, and he or she may be the lover you're looking for. However, if you are going to send it to a publisher who has already rejected it once, you should not do so unless there was some kind of encouragement in the first rejection, and unless you have improved it in accordance with any suggestions that the editor made or any ideas of your own. And you should certainly not send it again without indicating that it is a second submission.

4

What Are Publishers Looking For?

The Commercial Approach
Primarily, these days, publishers are looking for books that will make money. In times gone by, when publishing was an occupation for gentlemen (nowadays, even if you feel that it is an occupation for incompetents, it is more accurately described as an occupation for business men), publishers were able, as has already been mentioned, to take an overall view, and if they had a bestseller on their list would be able to use some of the money that it made for them in publishing other books which were worthy but which would almost certainly make a loss. Provided that the year's results ended up in the black, it did not matter too much if you published, for instance, small volumes of poetry which might have been printed in red ink for all the contribution to the firm's profit that they would make.

In recent years, accountants have increasingly dominated publishing. Some of them do understand what publishing is all about, including such concepts as undertaking the publication of unprofitable first novels in the belief that the author will ultimately become successful, but in many firms there is now an insistence that every single book must reach a fairly high level of profitability, and the editor's role has become subjugated to that of the money-man. It is a very unfortunate development – except, of course, if you think of Stanley Unwin's dictum, 'The publisher's first duty to his authors is to remain solvent.' The accountants would argue that without their control many more publishing firms would go out of business than those which have already collapsed.

Some observers of the publishing scene feel that the days of the accountant's supremacy are over, and that the new controller of what is and is not published is the marketing department, which will demand that the potential market for a given book should be identifiable, that its size should be capable of accurate assessment, that it should be large enough to make publication economically viable, and that the publisher's ability to reach it should be assured, all before the book is taken on. It is the marketing department's ascendancy which has led to the presently popular concept of niche publishing, which has already been defined (see p.19), and which is essentially concerned with bringing out books aimed at a specific and quantifiable market.

Whether the accountants or the marketing people are now dominant, the editor no longer exercises nearly as much power as in bygone days, and this is almost certainly why it is far more difficult nowadays for new novelists to find a publisher unless their books are immediately and obviously commercial.

For the book which deserves to be published but does not necessarily command a mass-market appeal and for authors who need time and encouragement while trying to perfect the skills of writing before their talent comes to full flower, some kind of sponsorship might seem to be the solution, whether it comes from the Arts Council or from commercial concerns in the public sector. But Big Business doesn't seem interested, and the Arts Council has no money to spare. Of course, the Arts Council and the Regional Arts Boards do award bursaries to assist writers, and there are various other bodies which have funds available (see p.217), but in almost all cases such moneys are used to subsidize writers while they are working on their books, or because they have fallen on hard times, rather than to persuade a publisher to take on a book which seems worthy but unlikely to be profitable.

However, all is not woe. Some new and comparatively small (or, indeed, very small) publishing houses are successfully pursuing an enlightened policy, and there are a few survivors from an earlier era who have never allowed the powers of the editorial department to get out of balance with those of the marketing and accounts departments.

It is not just books which will make money that publishers want, but authors who will do so. Every publisher who takes a new book on to the list hopes that it will be followed by others from the same author, and a publisher's belief that the author is a one-book writer may contribute to a decision to reject a submitted title. A perfect example, taken from the past, is *The Egg and I*, a humorous book by Betty Macdonald. Despite having had a considerable success in the States, it was rejected by many British publishers at least partly on those grounds, and was finally taken on by the late Peter Guttmann of Hammond, Hammond (a publishing company which is no longer active), who himself doubted whether Betty Macdonald would write another book. In fact, she wrote several more, and very successful they were, which was a bonus for Hammond, Hammond.

The Skills of Authorship

It is easy enough to say that publishers want books and authors which will make money for them – not necessarily a great deal of money, but sufficient to make a contribution towards overheads and a small profit in addition – and that the more commercial your book the easier it will be to find a publisher for it, but such comments, apart from stating the obvious, are not particularly helpful to the aspiring author.

Specific advice on what publishers want is hard to give. Jill Black, a former Director of The Bodley Head, said, 'The truth is that we don't know what we're looking for; but when we see it, it shines from the page.' Nevertheless there are some general points to be made.

First of all, I think, publishers look for evidence that the author understands and can use the tools of the writing trade, by which I mean not only spelling, punctuation and grammar, but more importantly a mastery over words, so that the desired shades of meaning are unerringly and clearly conveyed. Also needed is a sense of style, which is largely to do with the varied rhythms of the phrases and sentences, but which also involves a feeling for prose which is suited to its subject, and is neither over the top in lushness nor so plain as to be colourless. The writing should be to the point, without waffle, and the author needs to remember neither to patronize the reader with unnecessary explanations nor to assume a knowledge which that reader does not have. All this amounts to authority in the writing – it is something which every editor can recognize within a few sentences at the beginning of a book.

Another kind of authority is needed in respect of the contents of the book, and it comes from knowing your subject thoroughly if you are writing non-fiction and from knowing your characters and your setting in depth for a novel. The book also needs to have a satisfactory shape, to be well-organized, broken into appropriate chapters or sections, and for a novel there may be a requirement to use flashbacks, cliffhangers and other such devices with skill. In fiction the editor will also be looking for a strong narrative drive, so that the story progresses inexorably, but with good variation of pace, and for characters with whom the reader can empathize.

It is obvious (or should be) that the book should have something to say, which does not necessarily mean that it has to have some significant message, but that the author had an objective in writing it – something to tell the reader, whether it is how to decorate the bathroom, or what James I was really like, or simply a good story.

What about originality? A publisher will always be drawn to the typescript which is original in some aspect – the humour or wit, perhaps, the twist in the plot which gives a new angle to a familiar theme, or the unconventional view of something, whether it be the decoration of your bathroom or the life of James I, which has never before been subjected to that approach. But it is difficult to be genuinely original, and authors trying to be different from every-one else are often driven into the wildly experimental, which is rarely likely to command a large enough market to interest the average general publisher.

Perhaps it is better to aim to excite, so that because of your style, your mastery of words and all the other qualities I have mentioned, the editor is gripped by your work from the first page to the last, whether the book is a novel, a biography or a 'how-to' manual. That's when what you write will shine from the page. (This, inci-dentally, is why the first page of a book is so important; you've got to grab the reader – especially an editor – right at the start, and then never let go.)

Naturally, there are exceptions to all these rules and guidelines – publishing is so individual and bizarre and multifaceted that every statement one makes about it needs qualification – and books which do not meet any of the requirements listed above, or which do so only partially, are frequently and often successfully published. It can be very confusing for would-be authors, especially when they compare their own rejected work with books which have been published, perhaps by the very firm which rejected them, and decide, with as much dispassion as they can contrive, that the published books are inferior to their own work. The first thing to remember in that situation is that you cannot compare like with unlike. If you are what is known as a serious novelist and you look at published romantic novels and think how feeble and contrived and generally despicable they are in comparison with your own work, or if you are an academic who can see no justification for the success of certain pseudo-scientific books based on imagination rather than solid evidence, do remember that these books are not written for you, that they have their own market, their own techniques, and that the people who write them are mostly extremely capable craftsmen who know exactly what they are doing and do it with considerable flair. Popular taste may be debased, but it's not nearly as easy as you might think to produce work which catches it.

'All right,' you may say, 'I will compare my work only with those who write in the same vein as I do. How is that X and Y get published, when they don't write as well as I do and their subjects are more limited in interest than mine?' The answer may simply involve a matter of taste – the publishers may disagree with your assessment of X and Y's work in comparison with your own, and has published them believing that they are better books than yours. Books are accepted for publication not by some impartial and infinitely wise committee of assessors, but by individuals with their own likes and dislikes. Or it could be that X and Y are on that publishers' list because they submitted their books when the firm was looking for just such work and theirs were the best that came along; now that they are on the list, there is no room for yours, although you might be a better writer. Or maybe X and Y are established to some degree, and even though the publishers may not feel that their latest books are up to the highest standard, their quality cannot be considered poor enough to make the publishers hesitate over whether or not to publish them, and they believe in X and Y as worthwhile authors and want to go on publishing them, hoping that their next books will be better. As I have already suggested, publishers are interested in authors rather than books, and are looking for a writers who, with a number of books, will build up a reputation so that the books sell in increasing numbers as each new one comes out, or who, if the first book is an immediate success, will repeat that success with many more books.

Of course, the bigger name you are as an author, the more you have publishers at your mercy, not only in securing better terms, but sometimes in persuading them to publish a book at which they might otherwise have looked askance. If they refuse to take the book on, they know that with your reputation another house will be only too glad to publish it, however bad it may be, in order to get you on their list. I would suggest, however, that if you are just such a world-famous author and your publishers express doubts about your latest offering, you should listen carefully before rushing into the arms of one of their competitors. Bad books can damage even the most brilliant of reputations.

The most important point to remember when, as a frustrated author once said to me, 'you look at all the rubbish that does get published,' is that the publication of a book still depends, despite the influence of the accountants and marketing gurus, on the personal tastes of an editor. Editors, believe it or not, are human, and the variety of their individual quirks and foibles is infinite. I could cite dozens of cases in which colleagues of mine in various editorial departments have been tremendously enthusiastic about books in which I could see no merit at all. Sometimes they proved me wrong, sometimes my doubts were justified. All editors make mistakes, all editors have successes which astonish their colleagues. It is said that thirty-eight different publishers turned down John Braine's *Room at the Top* before it was finally accepted. On the other hand, *Jonathan Livingstone Seagull* landed on the desk of an editor called Eleanor Friede, who was enthusiastic enough to more or less force through its publication against the advice of her colleagues; for some years the book seemed to justify the reservations of the Jeremiahs and was counted as a failure, but then it suddenly became a 'cult' book and a world bestseller.

Hyped Books

Some authors feel very aggrieved that certain books, often with little to distinguish them from the herd, and in some cases even of below average quality, get 'hyped' into bestsellerdom. How does it happen? It usually begins with the enthusiasm of an agent, who begins to talk the book up and persuades a publisher to believe that the book is a potential bestseller, worth a lot of money. One sale for a staggeringly high amount allows the bandwaggon to roll, and the book sells for extravagant sums all over the world. There is often an element of the Emperor's New Clothes about it. It certainly isn't fair, when much better books earn their authors little or no money, but then life isn't fair, and success in any field nearly always depends on a certain amount of luck as well as ability. You have to be in the right place at the right time to have your book hyped; you, or your agent, must recognize that right time and place and seize the opportunity when it comes; all that involves a great element of luck.

Do hyped books work? Well, quite often, but sometimes they

fall flat. When they do succeed it is usually because the book has the quality of being in tune with the reading public's mood, but also because the publisher has mounted a highly successful publicity campaign, including considerable advertising to bring the book to the public's notice. You may have heard that publishers are generally agreed that advertising, other than to the trade, does not sell books, but it can do if the advertising is really intensive. The expectation of high sales for the hyped book allows for a substantial publicity budget, and as well as large advertisements, often inserted several times, in newspapers and magazines throughout the country, the publisher will have to produce point-of-sale material such as posters, showcards, special cardboard display stands known as 'dump bins', and so on. Other options may include advertisements on buses, hoardings, and in the London Underground, and launch parties and a tour for the author. And then there is television, which is probably the most effective advertising medium available – provided that you produce a really professional advertisement and screen it often enough for it to have an impact. In total, we are talking of costs of many tens of thousands of pounds. And even then it may not work.

Why, given two books of similar merits and accord with public taste, both available at the same time, does one attract the hype approach while the other is neglected? Because of the irrationality of the human element, and because of the way the wheel of fortune turned. The hyped book just happened to appeal to a small handful of people who believed that it could be promoted into bestsellerdom and were prepared to spend money to push it in that direction; and it had the right kind of luck.

What Publishers Don't Want
Since it is so difficult to be specific about what publishers want, it may be helpful to take the easier course of saying what they don't want.

Topical books The normal publishing process takes about nine months from the acceptance of a finished typescript to publication – longer if the book is complicated in some way (e.g. any illustrated book with a complex layout). Books can be produced in a much shorter time, and sometimes are – almost instant publication can take place for a book recording some major event which has caught public imagination, such as a royal wedding or a short and effective war. But these are exceptions, mostly appearing as paperbacks, and the event has to be of such wide interest that a really massive sale can be envisaged, thus justifying the enormous extra effort and expense that are necessary to whittle the normal nine months down to a few days. But a topical book without a huge market will have little appeal to any publisher, especially as so often its topicality, which will have disappeared by the time the book comes out, is its only merit.

Categories of books not normally on the publisher's list Publishers sell to booksellers, and booksellers tend to think of publishers as specialists in certain areas. It is really the concept of brand names, and as niche publishing grows in importance, more and more publishers are likely to be trying to establish themselves as the experts in certain fields of publishing. Some houses, for instance, are known as publishers of art books. Now, if Rows & Crowne, a publisher who has not previously entered that market, brings out an art book, the bookseller's reaction may often be, 'If it were any good, it would be published by one of the regular art book publishers. They probably all turned it down. Therefore it can't be much good. No, I won't order any copies.' That is of course an over-simplification, and booksellers would deny that they can be so conservative and shortsighted as to turn down a saleable book simply because it bears an unexpected imprint, but it is certainly true that publishers often find it quite difficult to broaden the scope of their lists because of trade resistance. The moral from the author's point of view is that market research must be thoroughly done, and if the book is a specialist one, it should not be sent to a publisher who is unlikely to want to experiment with it in an unfamiliar field. There is an additional reason for choosing a publisher who has some reputation for bringing out books in a particular category, which is that the publisher who regularly publishes books aimed at specialists will know how to reach the markets concerned, and may also have a mailing list which will bring the book to the attention of those people who are most likely to buy it.

The jack of all trades Publishers, booksellers and the public like to know where they are with an author. They like authors to write the same sort of book each time, and it is certainly much easier to build a reputation if you stick to one field. But another reason why publishers tend to look a little doubtfully at an author who offers them a series of widely differing books is that the jack of all trades is so frequently master of none. If you can write a book on any subject under the sun, you may be quite brilliant, and therefore an exception – or possibly you deserve the rather uncomplimentary description of 'a hack writer', with its implication that your work is of a low standard. The one thing that shrinking markets have done for books is to improve their overall quality. There is far less room for the hack than there used to be.

Autobiographies Everyone, they say, has a book in him or her. True, but in most cases it should stay there, principally because so few people have the ability to get it out of themselves in a form that anyone else will want to read. But one of the other problems is that the book which most people have in them and want to write is their own life story. 'I have had such an interesting life. I'm sure I could write a book about it,' or 'After all your experiences, you should write a book – you really should.' Unfortunately, thousands upon thousands of men and women lead lives which they and their friends find of riveting interest, but unless they are famous, or infamous, or can write superbly and perhaps evocatively of a bygone age, few readers outside their immediate circle will find them equally absorbing. And if you cannot claim fame or the pen of a Laurie Lee, who is going to buy your book? Your friends and relations will expect to be given copies, and no one else will bother. It won't even get into the libraries, because its interest is so limited. Write the book, by all means, for your children and grandchildren to read, but don't expect to get it published commercially. This advice also applies to most humorous accounts of your experiences – especially about moving house, a favourite subject for amateur authors, since almost everyone's experience of moving house is traumatic and, if you have that sort of sense of humour, funny; in order to write an autobiographical funny book successfully, your experience or your humour (and preferably both) should be exceptional, so that the book is lifted beyond the commonplace.

Biographies of obscure historical personages or subjects of minor local interest You may have discovered the truth about Sir Humphrey Drivell, the dull, stay-at-home eighteenth-century squire of the village of Upton Downbottom, but unless your account of his life, like *The History of Myddle*, for instance, also gives an unusual and detailed account of a bygone village community, few people are going to want to buy or borrow the book. No one has ever heard of Sir Humphrey Drivell, and that means that very few people will want to read about him. The same applies to a history of St Ethelwulf's Church, Upton Downbottom; you may be able to find a local printer who will produce a few copies for the benefit of the Upton Downbottom villagers and you and your relatives and friends, but the market for the book will be so small that no commercial publisher is likely to be interested. Again, I would not wish to discourage anyone from writing such a book, which might be fascinating and of immense value to its very limited audience, and it could be something for which self publishing would be the answer. Just don't expect to get it commercially published.

Short Stories A few years ago it was almost impossible to get a volume of short stories published unless you were a bestselling novelist, or unless you were writing science fiction or horror stories. And even if you were a household name, your collection of short stories would get a much smaller print quantity than your new novel. Recently, however, there has been a modest increase in the number of published books of short stories, but you probably still need to have established something of a literary reputation to stand much chance of your collection being accepted. A few anthologies of short stories are published every year, which provide an outlet for individual stories, but the average short story writer stands much more of a chance of publication in magazines.

Poetry Despite the fact that public interest in poetry has grown very considerably in recent years, it is comparatively rare for a poet's work to be sold in quantities which make publication a profitable business, and such expectations are almost always the result of the author having established a reputation as a poet over a long period of years, or perhaps being well-known in some other field. Your poetry is therefore likely to be turned down very quickly. Nevertheless, there are still a few houses with general lists who are prepared to publish volumes of poetry even though it may lose them money to do so, and if your work is of real merit, you will probably find recognition from one of these firms. There is, however, some hope, even if you are not in the genius category, because there are hundreds of small concerns specializing in the publication of poetry in the so-called 'little magazines' or in booklet form. Sometimes the material is duplicated rather than printed. The financial rewards, if they materialize at all, are likely to be minuscule – in some instances you will get no payment other than a few free copies of the publication – but the appearance of your work may help to establish your reputation (especially if you are diligent at selling copies at readings in pubs) and lead you eventually to a slightly more lucrative offer from a regular publisher.

'Bandwaggon books' As soon as a certain style of book becomes a bestseller – usually something which is sufficiently different from the normal range of publications to become almost a new genre – half the authors in the world seem ready to leap on to the bandwaggon, rushing to their word processors to produce imitations. Years after the James Bond books first appeared, would-be Ian Flemings are still slaving away at pseudo 007s, and heaven knows how many world statesmen have come near to fictional assassination since *The Day of the Jackal* first appeared, while I have no doubt that there are many Hitchhiker clones roaming around the galaxy, Guide in hand. There are two reasons why books of this kind are not often successful: the first is that few of these imitators are talented enough to write books which are anywhere near as good as the originals; the second is that such fashions in writing can often change remarkably rapidly, and allowing for the normal delay in getting a publisher to accept your book and then publish it, the fashion may have disappeared.

Genres which are out of fashion It is not easy for any author to discover which genres are currently unpopular with publishers, except by finding out when a book is rejected with all sorts of complimentary remarks about it but with the depressing comment that there is currently no demand in the market for work of that nature. At the time of writing, the historical novel is in the doldrums – no publisher wants to take on a new historical novelist – and yet this genre has been very successful ever since the days of Sir Walter Scott. It seems possible that eventually the wheel will turn and the historical novel will come back into its own – by which time something else may be relegated to the doghouse.

Obscene, scurrilous, politically extreme or otherwise controversial books A highly controversial book is almost always of interest, but, although almost anything goes nowadays, not if it steps beyond the bounds of the public's taste, which means that most publishers, who themselves are in tune to that taste, are likely to shy away. However, markets for books which most people would find offensive do exist – there are publishers, for example, for pornography, for extreme fascist or anarchist views, for all kinds of outrageous material, and even politically incorrect books get into print – so it is a question of doing your market research carefully. As for the scurrilous book, beware of the laws of libel.

Children's books The editors of children's books are usually people of enormous patience. Scores of mothers and grandmothers make up stories for their little ones, decide when they are well received by their young audience that they could be published, and submit them, often accompanied by illustrations done by a friend whose lack of talent is equalled only by that of the story-teller. Writing for children is extremely difficult, and has not been made easier by the fact that nowadays it is necessary to be politically correct, while the length, complexity and especially the vocabulary of the book must be acceptable in the view of editors, librarians and booksellers (everyone, in fact, except the children themselves) for the age range for which the book will be published. It is really a most difficult market to break into, and it becomes very little easier as you move up the age scale, coming eventually to teen-age novels. All writing for young people is difficult. If you can get it right, you will be welcomed, but be prepared for disappointment. And if you send in illustrations, do make sure that they are of professional standard.

Novels about failures The plain fact is that failures are usually rather boring or depressing or both, simply because they are failures. You need exceptional skills to make them interesting.

Novels which have contrived plots Try to avoid stories which are based on, for instance, identical twins, or amnesia, or in which all problems are solved by the generosity of a previously-unheard-of wealthy relative who arrives from Australia in the last chapter.

Expensive books In general, publishers don't want books that are very expensive to produce because they are intended to be in odd shapes and sizes or because they involve the pasting in of pull-outs and pop-ups and other gimmicks, or demand to be printed in seven colours throughout. Such books are published, of course – indeed, pop-ups and odd-shaped books have both become very popular – but unless you have something really outstanding to offer, as a beginner you almost certainly stand a better chance by sticking to ordinary, common-or-garden books which can be produced in one of the standard formats such as Metric Demy 8vo, Metric Crown 4to or Metric Large Crown 8vo.

Libellous books The threat of a libel action is enough to make the strongest publisher go deathly pale. Quite apart from the fact that it may mean an extremely expensive court case, ending with an award against the firm of very heavy damages, and even more crippling costs, all copies of the book will probably have to be withdrawn and destroyed. And although in theory the publisher can reclaim all expenses from the author under the indemnity clause in the contract (see p.120), in practice the author rarely has the resources with which to reimburse the publisher. See also pp.207–9.

Publishers Do Want New Authors
There are always exceptions to prove the rule that publishers don't want the kinds of books listed above. Perhaps the chances for them are less, but you can never be quite certain because there are still a great many publishers about who are eccentric, unpredictable, erratic in their tastes as well as in the way they conduct their businesses. It is, after all, a fairly crazy business, in which every product is different, and each of them is, to a greater or lesser degree, a gamble. It is also a fascinating way of life (and 'way of life' is the right phrase, for few people in publishing are involved in their work only during office hours), with constantly changing interests and problems, and those who work in the industry (even the maligned accountants) do so on the whole not just because of the rewards – there are comparatively few really rich publishers about, precisely because it is a gambling business and it is only too easy to lose on one book all the money you have made on another – but because they like books and, surprisingly enough, authors.

It was Sir Frederick Macmillan, I believe, who first said, 'Publishing would be fun if it weren't for authors.' Undoubtedly he had his tongue in his cheek. Authors can be infuriating, childish, disloyal, temperamental, greedy, vain and any other pejorative adjectives that you can think of – just like other human beings. Publishers can be all those things too – just like other human beings. On the whole publishers are eager to love and cherish their authors. They begin by loving a book, and with any luck, they will then transfer that love to its author.

That then is the message: publishers are not ogres, implacably hostile to writers; on the contrary, they are always eager to find new books and authors on which they can lavish their affection. And one of the reasons why they want new authors is that old authors give up writing, or lose their touch, or go out of fashion, or die, and replacements must be found. So if you are a first-timer, be of good cheer and send your book out in an optimistic frame of mind. But please remember that although the annual total of new books produced in Britain is frighteningly high – well over 100,000, and the figure rises every year – standards are rising too. Be as certain as you can that your book is equipped to fight its way into a crowded market. You need to be professional, just as you would if you were entering any other field, and that includes being sure that what you write will appeal to a wide enough public.

Despite all the difficulties, I have never believed and still do not believe that there are any mute, inglorious Miltons around, unless they wish to remain mute and inglorious. If you have what it takes, you will get published. Just keep on trying.

5

The Publishing Process

What happens between the time that you submit a book to a publisher and its publication? Why does it take so long? Processes vary from publisher to publisher, but in general it will go something like this:

Editorial
Your synopsis or typescript will arrive on the desk of an editor, or possibly on that of a secretary whose job it is to log all incoming submissions in a ledger, in which what happens to the material will also be recorded.

In the case of a synopsis and specimen chapters, when the material reaches an editor, it will probably be looked at fairly quickly. If it is non-fiction, it may be rejected almost immediately on the grounds that the author can't write, or that the subject is of far too limited appeal, or that the publisher already has a similar book on the list, or for some other fairly obvious reason. If it does seem of interest, the editor will probably discuss it with other people in other departments, and may also do some market research to see what else on the subject is available. The result of these consultations may lead to a negative decision, or to estimates, discussions with the author, and a commission. In many ways it is easier for a publisher to make a decision about a non-fiction book than about a novel, and a synopsis and specimen chapters of a work of fiction will be more likely to be treated somewhat similarly to the process for a completed typescript in that genre, and as has already been suggested, even if the editorial department is impressed by the synopsis and specimen chapters it is comparatively rare for a newcomer to be commissioned to write the novel, unless it really seems to have blockbuster qualities, and the more likely outcome is a request to see the book when it has been finished.

An initial submission in the form of a completed typescript will be glanced at briefly by the editor to whom it comes. In some cases an immediate decision can be made as to whether it should be read by that editor, or passed to an outside reader, or given to another editor in the house who specializes in that kind of book, or rejected without further ado. However, in some publishing houses, such decisions will be taken at a weekly editorial meeting.

If the book is non-fiction, and especially if its subject is specific rather than general, it will almost certainly be sent to an outside reader who is an expert in that field, and very often to more than one such authority. Apart from these specialists, many publishers also employ general outside readers, and in some firms almost all books, including fiction, are given an outside reading, either before or after the book has been considered within the house. Who are these general readers, and what are their qualifications? They are often ex-publishers, sometimes themselves authors, sometimes merely friends or acquaintances of the publisher; they are expected to know a little in general terms about the market for non-specialist books, and to be able to distinguish between good and bad writing, but their main qualification is quite simply that their tastes are known to the publisher, which allows for their comments to be evaluated. In any case, their function is not entirely that of giving a verdict on the books they read; they also usually provide a detailed summary of the book's contents.

If you feel anxiety that your typescript may be delivered up to the mercies of a comparatively unqualified person, then be assured that most publishers use their general outside readers primarily as 'weeders' or to confirm a judgement already made in the publisher's office. When outside readers recommend rejection, they are usually right, provided that they are reasonably experienced (and if the publisher has any doubt about their expertise, the book will almost certainly receive another reading before the final decision is made). Moreover, an outside reader's report on a book, and especially that part of it which gives reasons for recommending rejection, will be studied by a senior member of the editorial department, and if those reasons seem at all inadequate, again another reading will be called for. On the other hand, if the reader recommends publication or thinks that the book is at least worth considering, then it will undoubtedly be read by other people too, to confirm that the reader's enthusiasm or interest is justified. Very few books, other than those by established writers, are ever accepted on the basis of one reading only, and indeed many books are given several readings before it is finally decided to take the book on or to reject it.

Although the reports on a book may be generally favourable, the editor may not yet be ready to move to the next stage, the preparation of an estimate. The readers may indicate that the book is potentially publishable, but that additional work is needed on it before it can be accepted, and in this case the editor will perhaps invite the author to come to the company's offices to discuss the matter. Some authors approach such meetings in an aggressively defensive mood, unwilling to concede that their work is less than perfect as it stands; it is their right to do so, but it is also the publisher's right in such circumstances to decline to go ahead. Most sensible authors will listen to what is said, and accept the criticisms or at least discuss any proposed alterations in a reasonable way. Good editors can contribute materially to the improvement of a book, and indeed that is their object, or should be. The other side of the coin is that a bad editor can completely ruin a book and turn it into something very different from what the author intended; in such cases the author is fully entitled to resist, but must be prepared to accept the fact that this may result in the publisher deciding not to publish the book.

Authors whose books are rejected speedily often believe that the books have not been read at all, and some even resort to various devices to prove this (such as putting one of the pages upside down, or carefully inserting a hair between two pages of the typescript). Apart from the possibility that the editor may spot these traps and leave them unaltered, just to annoy you, you may as well face the fact that publishers do not read every word of every typescript submitted to them; on the other hand, none is rejected without even a glance (unless the publisher happens to be one of those who will deal only with agents). Some are rejected without being read as soon as the publisher can see that they deal with subjects which the firm does not publish, or that they are not of book length (authors often submit short stories to book publishers in the apparent belief that they also publish magazines, while others seem to think than ten thousand words or less will make a full-length book). For the rest, a few pages will be read – sufficient for the editor who usually has a considerable amount of experience and who knows what kind of book the company is looking for, to decide perhaps that the book is not of interest. Or perhaps the editor will get some way into the book before deciding that it is too dull, too unauthoritative, or too controversial, or simply too badly written for it to be worth bothering with. Even if initially interested, the editor may skip a great deal, or use a technique which I call 'skim-reading', whereby one turns the pages very rapidly, letting the eye travel swiftly over the page to get a general idea of the book without reading very much of it word for word; it sounds a very cavalier way to treat a submission, but editors do become expert at coping with the vast numbers of typescripts that flow into their offices day by day, and rarely fail to recognize a book which needs more serious consideration. In many houses, even these rapid rejections will be discussed at an editorial meeting, and a book may get another reading from a different editor as a result.

Publishers do make mistakes and reject books which they should have taken, but you can be assured that any typescript with a certain amount of quality, if it is one which will fit the publisher's list, will be considered carefully and read in its entirety. It is for this reason that I dislike the term 'slushpile', because it suggests the publishers consider such material inevitably to be rubbish. As I have already said earlier in this book, this is just not true. There may be a pearl there, and the last thing the publisher wants is to miss something worthwhile. Adequate, unexciting, publishable books are readily available, but the number of outstanding titles that come along is very limited, and no publisher likes to let one of those get away.

Estimating

Assuming that the editorial reports are favourable and that any rewriting required is, or can be, satisfactorily carried out, the book will probably be discussed again at an editorial meeting, and the go-ahead given for the preparation of an estimate. This involves consultation by the editor with the production department in order to assess the cost of manufacture, and with the sales and marketing departments to gain their support for the project and to fix a tentative first print quantity and estimate of sales, so that the potential income can be calculated. Often the subsidiary rights department will also be consulted and asked to predict what subsidiary rights income may come in, and indeed in some cases the book will be shown to, for instance, paperback houses, in the hope of obtaining a firm offer for paperback rights, the publisher's share of which will help to subsidize the hardcover edition. In the case of the integrated publisher, when a book is being considered by the same organization in both hardcover and paperback, there may be a single estimate covering both editions.

Sometimes the estimate prepared will not show a satisfactory profit margin, and in that case, the editor, or someone in one of the other departments, may suggest altering the specifications in some way – perhaps a more economical type face could be used, thus reducing the extent (i.e. the page length) of the book, which will mean a saving on paper, printing and binding costs, perhaps a reduction in the number of illustrations could be considered, or perhaps the sales department could be persuaded to increase the print quantity or the retail price of the book, or both. Sometimes several estimates have to be prepared before the formula is right, after which it is necessary in many companies to get approval from a number of department heads before the editor can finally write to the author to say that the firm wishes to publish the book. Often, after preparing a number of estimates, no satisfactory figures can be reached, and the editor then has reluctantly to reject the book.

The processes described are obviously time-consuming, which explains at least in part why authors so often have to wait so long for a decision. During the waiting period it is often true that no news is good news, but equally a long delay, while it probably means that serious consideration is being given to the book, is no guarantee of ultimate acceptance.

Contract
If all has gone well, the publisher makes the author an offer to publish the book, usually specifying the advance that will be paid and the basic royalties, but rarely going into other details, which await the preparation of a contract.

This will probably entail further discussions within the publishing house, so that whoever prepares the contract will get all the details right (although if the book is agented, the agent usually draws up the agreement on the standard form used by that agency). Authors should read each contract that they are sent with care, remembering that danger can lurk in the small print. It is not a good idea, when you get your new contract from Messrs Rows & Crowne, to think that since you have already signed a number of agreements with them for previous books you can sign this one without reading it. They may have changed their basic contract form, or there may be a number of differences in the wording or in the splits of moneys from subsidiary rights, or the points at which royalties increase, and so on. If there is anything in the contract that you wish to query or change, write to the publisher about it – do not simply make alterations on the contract and return it, but settle any disputed matters first. The Society of Authors and the Writers' Guild both offer their members detailed advice on contracts, so it will be worth your while to join, if you are not already a member. See also Chapter 6 for comments on what you should look for in an agreement.

Some publishers send the author two copies of the contract – one to be signed and returned, the other already signed by the publisher to keep. If there are any changes, mark them and initial them on both copies. Other publishers send only one copy of the contract, giving the author a copy to keep only after the first one has been signed and returned. In such cases it may be a sensible precaution to take a photostat of the copy sent to you to sign before you return it; otherwise you may not be absolutely certain that the counterpart you actually receive is exactly the same – not that your publisher is likely to cheat in this respect, but it is a cheap and easy way of checking that no chance mistake has been made, and of protecting yourself against the few unscrupulous publishers that do unfortunately exist.

When you return your signed agreement, it will be filed by the publisher, and probably consulted thereafter quite frequently – whenever subsidiary rights are sold, when it is time for royalty statements to be prepared, and so on. In some firms an extract of the contract is made, with all the details on it which are likely to be needed, so that the whole document does not have to be consulted every time.

In most cases, an advance, or part thereof, is payable on signature of the contract by both parties, and a note will be passed to the accounts department, so that an appropriate cheque can be drawn.

Copy Editing
Once you have accepted the initial offer, the book may be passed to a copy editor, although nowadays, in an effort to cut costs, some publishers are dispensing with this stage, relying on the author to have done a large part of the copy editor's work, and leaving the rest of it to the production department and/or the designer, or even to the printer. The increasing use of PCs is hastening the disap-

pearance of the copy editor, because typescripts produced on a word processor tend to contain fewer typing mistakes – it is so much easier to correct your errors than it is on a typewriter, especially if your word processor has a spell-check facility, which picks up literal errors as well as spelling mistakes. This is a pity – copy editors can contribute very considerably to good, efficient publishing, and if they do disappear it will mean far more errors in published books, because not all authors can be relied upon to be punctilious in their writing, and even the best of word processors cannot make up for the sloppiness of so many of the typescripts which arrive, supposedly ready for press, on their publishers' desks.

If there are no copy editors in your publisher's office, this does not necessarily mean that the firm has abandoned copy editing – fortunately a large number of concerns still believe that the cost of copy-editing is money well spent – but many publishers nowadays use freelances for this and other work which can be done outside the office.

So what exactly do copy editors do? Their responsibilities go far beyond merely correcting the author's spelling and punctuation; they check the author's facts, they remove (or at least query with the author) inconsistencies, they may rewrite phrases, sentences or even large parts of the book (there are many published books which should really bear the copy editor's name on the title-page as co-author), and they mark the typescript for the printer, so that the latter has clear indications of, for example, italicization, indentation of paragraphs or of certain sections of the text, etc. Some authors resent the work of the copy editor, and with cause if they are unlucky enough to find one who interferes unwarrantably with the author's style or makes other totally unnecessary changes; but a first-class copy editor, who respects the author's intentions and knows what should and should not be done, can make invaluable improvements. The good copy editor will in any case always consult the author concerning any proposed changes, and a sensible author will listen co-operatively to the suggestions which are made.

Production

By this time, the author will probably have been asked to supply a second copy of the typescript and/or a copy disc, in which all alterations will be incorporated, and this will have been sent to the production department, whose designer will decide the type in which the book is to be printed, the type area on the page, the way that chapters are to begin, and other such details (much of this work may have been done at the estimating stage). If the book is extensively illustrated, the designer has a much more exacting job, and will have to work out the size and shape of illustrations and their position, and the exact amount of text which is to appear on each page. Given the designer's instructions, and now knowing the final print quantity, the production department will be able to work out the cost of manufacture, using the scale of standard charges for various sizes of books supplied by the typesetters, printers and binders which they usually use. Assuming that these figures are acceptable, the production department will in due course order, or allocate from stock, a suitable quantity of the appropriate kinds of papers for the text and for the jacket or the cover of a paperback edition, in accordance with the agreed print quantity, and if the book is a hardback, cloth (usually imitation nowadays) for the binding and 'brasses' with which the title, the author's name and the publisher's name or colophon will be stamped on the binding.

When the final copy-edited typescript is ready, the production department will send it to a typesetter for composition, together with any line illustrations which are to be integrated with the text. With more and more authors using PCs it will increasingly often be a disc, rather than a typescript, which goes to the typesetter; from a disc, with the addition of certain commands, the type for the book can be set without the text having to be re-keyed (that is to say, a compositor does not have to 'type' the book). If the book is to have tone illustrations printed on art paper in separate sections, these will often be printed by a different printer from the one who prints the text. This also applies to the jacket design, which, together with the material which is to appear on the back and the flaps, will also be sent for preparation and proofing. Incidentally, although an artist may have prepared the illustration for the jacket, the lettering is often done by a designer, who may be a freelance but is often the publisher's own designer in the production department.

In due course, proofs of the book will arrive from the typesetters. Two sets are usually sent to the author – one to be corrected and returned, the other to keep. When correcting proofs it is advisable to use the proper markings and signs, and some of the most common of these are shown in Appendix I. Corrections are extremely expensive – out of all proportion, it would seem, to the initial setting charge for the whole book – and should therefore be kept to a minimum. Mistakes made by the typesetters are their responsibility and are not charged for, and should be corrected in a different colour ink from that used for any alterations the author wants to make. The latter, if they exceed a certain percentage of the original total setting costs, will almost certainly be charged by the publisher to the author, so the rule must be to get your typescript or disc as perfect as possible before it is sent to the printer, and at proof stage to make only those changes which are absolutely essential. Also be sure to note all corrections in the set of proofs that you keep.

Proofs sometimes come in galley form, that is to say on long sheets of paper, and not divided up into the pages which will finally appear in the book. This method of proofing is used if large numbers of alterations are expected (and have been allowed for in the costing of the book!) or if the layout of the book is particularly complex. Sometimes proofs come on what looks like a computer print-out. More often page proofs are supplied, which look very much as the final book will appear, except that they have a paper cover and are probably not printed on the same kind of paper as will be used for the final version.

Normally the publisher allows the author two to three weeks for the correction and return of proofs. During this period, they may also be read by someone in the publishing house – usually the copy editor, but sometimes someone in the production department. The author's corrections and those of the publisher's proof reader will be incorporated in the marked set which will be returned to the typesetter. When all the necessary alterations have been made, the typesetter will provide camera-ready copy, film or a disk from which the printer will be able to produce the printed sheets of the book.

Although proofs still normally appear, they are, like copy editors, an endangered species. Since word processors make it easy to produce perfect copy, and the material does not have to be re-keyed but can be fed directly into the computer from which the typesetter works, proofs will in certain cases be unnecessary, although they are still likely to be needed for the preparation of an index and often for publicity purposes and for the sale of subsidiary rights.

The production department will, of course, pass the relevant orders to the printers and binders (sometimes, but not always, the same firm) for the manufacture of the book, and will monitor its progress through all stages up to delivery to the warehouse.

Jackets or Covers

The jacket design for a hardcover book and the cover design for a paperback are usually fairly widely discussed within the publishing house. Many publishers employ an art director whose sole responsibility is jackets or covers, and who will probably discuss the design for each book on the list with the editor concerned and with the sales and marketing departments. If it is decided to produce a jacket which is purely typographical (rare in the case of paperbacks) or is based on a photograph or perhaps an existing painting, such as a contemporary portrait of the subject of a biography, the art work may be designed and produced within the house. In such cases the art director may not see a copy of the book itself, and it is not necessary that he/she should do so. If, on the other hand, the jacket or cover is to carry a specially commissioned illustration, the art director will brief an outside artist, who will probably also be given a copy of the typescript. The artist will then usually submit a 'rough' – a sketch of what is proposed as the final artwork. This will be considered and approved or rejected by the editorial, sales and marketing departments. Increasingly the author is consulted about jackets or covers, and many publishers welcome comments, provided that the author does not make unreasonable demands. An author's complaint about the factual accuracy of the design is entirely valid, but adverse comments on the overall effect or the basic design, while there should be no inhibition to prevent any criticisms being made and the publisher should take note of them, are less likely to be matters on which to try to put your foot down. In general, publishers take a great deal of care with jackets and covers, knowing that they are a vital sales tool, and if the sales department in particular is satisfied with the general design, the author may have to bow to their belief that it is acceptable. Not unnaturally, publishers tend to put credence in their own expertise, and may simply tell you bluntly that your skill is in writing the book, and theirs in knowing best how to sell it.

The jacket of the hardcover will also carry the blurb, which is a description of the book, normally to be found on the front flap of the jacket, and very often on the first page of the book too. Your publisher will probably ask you to supply a blurb for your book, although your effort will usually be discarded or substantially rewritten, because most authors do not excel at describing their own work succinctly and appealingly, and however big their egos often shrink from using the adulatory adjectives beloved of profes-

sional blurb-writers. The back flap of the jacket may carry a continuation of the blurb (the best ones are short enough not to need this
extra space) or sometimes a brief biography and a photograph of
the author, while the back of the jacket, unless the illustration goes
all the way round, will probably be used as an advertisement space
for books by the same author, or other books on the publisher's list,
or, if the book is reprinted, for favourable quotes about it from the
reviews. A paperback will probably have a one-line blurb on the
front cover, and something more about the contents, or quotes on
the back.

The use that is made of the space available and the actual wording of the material will probably be discussed and decided upon
jointly by the editorial, sales and marketing departments. Again, it
has become usual for the author to be consulted about the blurb
and other material which appears on the jacket or cover, but even
the best publishing agreements, while giving the author the right of
consultation, make it clear that the final decision on such matters
rests with the publisher.

Subsidiary Rights

The work of the subsidiary rights department often begins at an
early stage. Extra copies of the typescript may be made, but in
other cases proofs will be supplied, so that the book can be submitted, if appropriate, to paperback publishers, bookclubs, magazines
and newspapers, and to foreign publishers. Some of these submissions may be delayed until finished copies of the book are available, but it is usually important to sell subsidiary rights, wherever
possible, in advance of publication, because such sales build up
interest in the book, and of course a bookclub order will almost
certainly affect the publisher's print order by increasing it.

The efforts of the subsidiary rights department are ongoing.
Sometimes simultaneous submissions will be made (to all the leading paperback publishers, for example), but often it is a matter of
trying one possible purchaser after another. Subsidiary rights
managers are usually tenacious, and will often continue to try to
sell their rights long after publication, and sometimes with considerable success. Of course, if your book is of a highly specialized
nature, there may be a very limited number of potential outlets for
it, and once they have all been tried, the subsidiary rights manager
will understandably abandon the effort, to reactivate it only if some
new buyer comes on the scene.

The subsidiary rights department conducts the initial negotiations for the sale of rights, and in some firms is responsible for all details of the agreement, while in others the final arrangements will be made by the contracts department.

Some of those publishers who will consider only those books which come to them from agents seem to be deciding that, since the agent retains many of the rights, it is hardly worth maintaining an expensive subsidiary rights department. This strikes me as foolish, but so do many other economies introduced by business concerns all over the world.

Sales

The sales department (in which for the sake of simplicity I include the marketing department) often plays a crucial part in the shaping of a publisher's list, not only in the decisions whether to accept this or that book, but also in reporting trends, sometimes suggesting specific titles or areas of publishing to the editors, and of course in the forecasting and budgeting processes which most businesses find essential. The marketing men are also increasingly influencing the make-up of the publisher's list, as already noted, by suggesting that the firm should specialize in certain areas, and thus become a 'brand name' for that sort of book.

In many publishing houses there is great rapport between the editorial and sales departments, each respecting the other. Unfortunately, all too often, in less well-run concerns, there is instead antagonism. 'The sales department makes no effort with all the fine books I give them,' says the editor; and the sales people reply, 'If only the editors would find us some good books, we could improve our figures out of all recognition.' Authors may feel that there is more justice in the editor's complaint than that of the sales force; nevertheless, it is very, very rarely true that the sales department makes no effort. In most cases, the sales representatives, although they may have basic salaries, are also paid a commission on the sales they achieve, so they have a personal incentive in addition to the need to keep the firm in business and so retain their jobs.

Each of the larger publishing houses has its own sales force, a team which works exclusively for that firm, but smaller publishers may group together to share a sales force, or use freelance representatives. Another possibility for small publishers is to arrange representation (and often warehousing, invoicing and despatch, too) by one of the larger houses; for the very small new publishing house this is sometimes the only way that its books can be presented to the trade, but it is rarely satisfactory, because naturally the big publisher's representatives will begin their spiel to booksellers with the books on the main list and will come to the small publisher's titles only when the buyer may not want to buy any more books and is thinking of the next appointment anyway. It's pretty tough for new small publishers.

As soon as a new book is given a tentative publication date, or sometimes even when it is first signed up, the sales department informs the sales force, giving as many details as possible at that stage, and selling then begins. However, the main vehicle of communication between the publishing house and its sales force about the firm's new books is usually the Sales Conference, at which someone, often the editor concerned, will tell the sales persons about the books, endeavouring to enthuse them and trying to give them all the information which will help them to achieve good sales. Although many editors have never themselves been 'on the road', especially nowadays when it is no longer the habit for new entrants to the publishing business to spend some time in every department, they all need to be sales persons too, for they have to 'sell' their new books in the first place to the sales and marketing directors before it is even signed up, and then to the representatives at the sales conference. If they fail to convince the sales force of the value of the books, then, although they will still try hard, the reps will obviously not approach booksellers and other purchasers with the same confidence.

Sometimes certain booksellers and wholesalers are invited to attend the sales conference. Occasionally authors are commanded to attend. If this should happen to you, remember that you have two things to do: you have to convince the sales force of the quality and sales potential of your book, emphasizing any special markets which would be particularly interested in it; and you have to persuade them, if you can, that you are a likeable person, since it is after all a part of human nature to try a little harder for a friendly, pleasant author than for one who is perhaps too conceited or stand-offish or who talks down to the reps. A touch of humour helps, and so does a subtle combination of self-confidence and self-deprecation. If you are invited to speak at a sales conference and the whole idea terrifies you because, like many authors, you are extremely shy or because you know that you are an abysmal public speaker, then it is probably best to decline and leave the editor with the job of presenting your book. Don't be surprised if you are not asked to attend a sales conference – it is a rare honour.

Of course it is not only to booksellers that the publisher sells the books. Wholesalers, library suppliers, supermarkets, specialist outlets and, of particular importance to the British trade which depends so much on its ability to export, the overseas customers, all have to be canvassed. The publisher's bigger customers are called on at regular and fairly frequent intervals, but for some of the smaller shops the period between calls may be a long one, so the representatives must have all the necessary information about new books well in advance, so that they can be sure that everyone on whom they call will have heard of the book and had the opportunity to order – or rather, to be prevailed upon to do so. It is important for authors to realize that booksellers have no obligation to order any given book. They have to be persuaded that they should do so.

How the publisher's representatives do this is with personal enthusiasm, by using their knowledge of the customer (in some cases they may indeed 'make no effort', knowing that the bookseller concerned has no market for that particular book), by trading on their own reputations (if they have guided the bookseller wisely in the past, their advice will be more readily taken) and that of their firm (which includes not only the quality of its list, but also its record in such matters as prompt delivery and accuracy of its invoices, and its vigour in publicity and promotion). Of course, they use jackets, catalogues and advance information sheets, which will include the publisher's plans for advertising and point of sale material, all of which are the most common sales aids. Sometimes the bookseller will be given a proof copy of some special book.

Very few of the sales that the reps make nowadays are 'firm' – almost all are 'on sale or return', meaning that the bookseller has the facility, after a reasonable period, of returning any unsold books to the publisher for credit. Very often it is only by such methods that the reps can persuade the bookseller to order the book, and when you consider how many books are published every year, it is hardly surprising that they often fail.

Many of the chains of bookshops have central buying arrangements, and often it is the sales director who deals personally with these and other large accounts, calling on them and selling the list. The power of the central buyers is alarming, especially in respect of the paperback market. Predictably, they will support the proven bestselling authors, but for first-time writers it is a case of make or break: a buyer's enthusiasm for a book by a new unknown author can turn it overnight into a bestseller, while a negative reaction, despite all the sales director's attempts to get the buyer to share in the conviction that the book can be a success, will give it the kiss of death. The first-time author therefore not only faces the difficulty of finding a publisher who can be persuaded by the strength of the material to invest time and money and effort into the book, but must then go through what amounts to a second editorial selection process, and a far more arbitrary one, often based largely on the jacket design.

The sales department will also be responsible for selling appropriate titles into non-traditional outlets, such as sports shops, garden centres, National Trust shops, and so on, and will arrange special deals, which might include sponsored books (although the editors may take a major part in this), and the kind of offer which involves saving the tops of cereal packets and sending them off in order to buy a book at a reduced price. Additionally the department deals with the increasing number of time-consuming but profitable direct sales to members of the public who have not been able to find a particular book in the shops.

It is also primarily the job of the sales department to call for reprints, which is always a matter for great care, for although all copies of the publisher's edition may have left the warehouse, the sales people have to be sure that they are also leaving the bookseller's shelves and that sufficient re-orders are likely to come in to justify the reprint.

Finally, it is in the sales department that proposals to remainder slow-moving books will originate, and negotiations with a remainder merchant will follow.

Publicity and Promotion
Publicity and promotion are vital tools of the sales and marketing departments, and in many firms this part of the business is under the direct control of the sales director.

Since this is the area in which many authors feel that their publishers fail most dismally, I shall examine it in some detail.

When your book is accepted for publication you will probably be asked to fill in a form asking for such information as any bookshops where you are personally known, any papers or journals where your book has an especially good chance of being reviewed, and organizations which might be circulated with details of your book. Authors should fill the forms in with care, despite the fact that some publishers seem thereafter to file the information away and take no action on the author's suggestions. Good publishers do follow through, although sometimes they may neglect certain aspects, usually because of lack of sufficient money in the publicity budget.

When hard times come (and they never appear to be totally absent as far as publishers are concerned), the publicity and promotion budget is almost always the first place where the publisher looks for economies, and the people who work in that department are used to doing so on a shoestring. The amount of money that they are allocated in any given year has to be spread among all the books that the firm is publishing in that period, and not surprisingly the books on which most money is spent are likely to be those which the publisher considers to be the major ones on the list; once they have been allocated their large share of the budget, the lesser books split the remainder between them, and end up with very little each. Hence, perhaps, your publisher's inability to produce the leaflet you envisaged, and hence almost certainly a reluctance to advertise your book in the national press.

In fact, publishers believe, almost without exception, that national press advertising is a waste of money. It is cosmetic, serving only to appease and boost the author's ego. 'But if the book is not advertised,' you may say, 'how will the public know about it?' Well, there are other ways, which we will come to in a moment, but be honest – do you really buy books because you have seen them advertised in the national press? All right, you do – but you are an exception. The vast majority of people buy books (or more often borrow them) because they have read a review, or because of recommendation from a friend or from a bookseller, or simply because they happen to see them in a shop (paperbacks in particular are known to be often 'impulse buys'). Publishers are slightly less grudging towards local newspapers, which charge much less for the insertion of advertisements and are possibly of some value if the author is known in the area where they circulate, but even then feel that their money can be better spent elsewhere.

One of the truths of the advertising business is that a small amount of money is not nearly as cost-effective as a large amount, and alongside that principle it can also be said that something which is not already in demand can only be stimulated effectively by a blanket coverage. Indeed, two or three hundred pounds-worth of advertisements in the national press is likely to achieve nothing, whereas several thousand spent on various forms of advertising, including the press, may begin to bring results. If you don't believe me, ask any advertising agent. The one exception to this applies if your book is non-fiction and is aimed at a specialist market, when advertisements in magazines devoted to the subject concerned are likely to be both worthwhile, precisely because they are going directly to the people who are most likely to buy the book, and comparatively inexpensive.

However, in the main, publishers prefer to concentrate on advertising to the trade, for it is to the trade that they sell their wares, not to the general public, and the battle for the success of a book is a long way towards being won if they can persuade the bookshops and the wholesalers to order good quantities.

First they produce a catalogue of their new titles. Your book will appear in it, sometimes accompanied by an illustration – perhaps your photograph, or a reproduction of the jacket, or an illustration from the book – but almost invariably with a blurb. The catalogue information will also include a tentative publication date and price and various other details about the book, many of which pieces of information will turn out to be inaccurate, because catalogues are prepared a long time in advance of the publication of most of the books in them, and changes in plan frequently occur. Your placing within the catalogue may give you pause for thought. How exciting to find your book occupying the leading position! How humiliating to find that your masterpiece is tucked away at the back, and has been given no more than a quarter of a page! In the latter case, you may feel hard done by, but you just have to accept the fact that although most publishers believe all their geese to be swans until publication proves otherwise, they do recognize that some are swannier and some geesier than others. If your publisher thinks your book belongs in the geesier section of his catalogue, it's hard luck.

The catalogue is sent out to the trade (booksellers, wholesalers, purchasers of subsidiary and foreign rights, etc.) and some copies go to members of the public who have asked to be placed on the firm's mailing list. A summary of the catalogue is often used as an insert in the Spring or Autumn Buyer's Guide editions of *The Bookseller*, which is the major trade paper (well worth subscribing to) and which twice a year produces these huge editions in which almost all publishers present their lists of new books for the coming months. The Spring and Autumn Buyer's Guides are a kind of gigantic multi-publisher catalogue. They also contain informative editorial coverage of forthcoming books, supplied by the publisher.

The publisher may also insert other advertisements for your book in ordinary numbers of *The Bookseller* and other trade papers. These will appear in advance of publication, but not usually as early as the Spring and Autumn Buyer's Guides.

Leaflets are sometimes prepared and sent out, but usually only for specialist books in which the recipients of the leaflet are likely to be keenly interested. The publisher needs to be sure of a good return from such publicity, for the cost of printing leaflets, plus envelopes and the labour of addressing them, and above all postage, is often prohibitive.

Sometimes a publisher will send proof copies of a book to well-known people, in the hope of getting pre-publication 'puffs' from them, which might be quoted on the leaflet, if there is one, or on the jacket, or in advertisements. A proof copy may also go to those journalists who write about forthcoming books in the trade press. Of course, they cannot mention every new book, so there is no guarantee that yours will be covered.

The publisher may also prepare showcards and other material for use in bookshops, including 'dump bins', which are those cardboard stands which contain several copies of a book, with promotional material printed on a sort of built-in showcard on the top and on the sides of the bin. Paperback publishers also provide most of the solid racks and 'gondolas' (the free-standing racks which you are likely to see in the middle of a shop rather than against the walls) which hold their books. All this is known as 'point of sale' material. Usually it is reserved for major titles, but if your local bookshop is willing to put on a display of your new book, your publishers may agree to supply a special showcard proclaiming the fact that you are a local author.

One of the most important weapons in the publicity department's armoury is the review copy. Most publishers send out large numbers of review copies of each book that they publish – sometimes as many as two hundred – to the literary editors of all major national and provincial newspapers and magazines, to specialist publications, to radio and television programmes, and indeed to any person or organization which might review the book. Many authors are bitterly disappointed by the lack of reviews of their books, and often blame the publishers. But it is not really their fault, and they are often as disappointed as you are. Reviews are important – even a bad one, unless it is totally destructive, is said to be better than none – and if you have any influence with a reviewer it is worth making sure that the publisher knows about it so that a review copy can be sent. The publicity people will, of course, use any favourable quotes from reviews in advertisements, on the jacket or cover of the book if it is reprinted, on the jacket or cover of your next book, and in any other appropriate way. We have all heard stories of the misuse of quotes from reviews – for instance, the words 'a magnificent . . . novel' being extracted from a review which actually said 'a magnificent example of how not to write a novel', but publishers, as we all know, are much too ethical to do anything like that.

A regular feature of publishing life used to be the parties which publishers threw to launch certain of their books. Launch parties are still held, but far less frequently than in the past, publishers preferring to spend their money on other forms of publicity, or even simply to save it. Some authors find it disheartening when their publishers tell them that they have no intention of celebrating publication in that way, and even decline an offer from the author to share the expense. Why should they refuse? Well, again it's a matter of cost-effectiveness. The guests at a party are made up generally of the author and a few family members and close friends, a fair sprinkling of the publisher's staff, a few journalists and literary editors, and a bookseller or two. Large amounts of liquor are consumed, and lots of canapés, and the room where the party is held and the staff to serve the drinks and food have to be paid for too, so it is an expensive business. The object of the exercise is to get publicity for the book and to persuade the booksellers to order it, but the amount of space that the press gives on these occasions is usually very limited, and the booksellers present have already ordered the book if they are going to do so. So little is achieved. If your publisher does throw a party for you, you can consider yourself honoured indeed.

The publicity and promotion department also spends quite a lot of its time trying, on behalf of the firm's authors, to arrange radio and television interviews, speaking engagements at literary luncheons, and the like. In the United States, where every city of any size has its own TV station, with round-the-clock broadcasting, a great deal of air time is taken up with 'chat shows', which makes it comparatively easy to get authors the chance to talk about their books on TV. In this country, with our limited number of channels, it is far more difficult, and the average author's chances of getting on a book programme or nationally-screened interview shows are very small. There are better prospects with radio, and while it may not be easy to land an interview on one of the main channels, you may have the chance of a broadcast on a local programme, whether they are run by the BBC or are commercial stations – slots for phone-ins, for instance, are often available.

Luncheons and other speaking engagements require some ability to speak well. If you can work up a good talk it may prove worthwhile publicity for you and your book, and you may be asked to give it to writers' circles and local literary societies, and Women's Institutes and Townswomen's Guilds, and so on. You will also in most cases receive fees for your talks, or at least expenses, which are sometimes offered in an amount which will exceed your actual expenditure and therefore amount to expenses plus a small fee. It is impossible to give guidance on the fees that one might expect, which depend on the size both of the organization concerned and of the audience, not to mention your own fame. There is also the question of what is expected of you – a forty-minute talk, followed by questions, perhaps, or something more than that. All that can be said is that if your talk is sponsored by one of the Regional Arts Associations, you can expect at least £75, whereas the fees that Women's Institutes are prepared to pay are more likely to be in the £10–£25 range. You may find occasionally that your 'fee' is the lunch or dinner after which you are to speak, but if you get on to the main after-lunch or after-dinner speakers' circuits (for instance, there are many Ladies' Luncheon Clubs), you not only get your meal and travelling expenses but fees which can be quite generous, and if you have achieved some sort of celebrity as an author these engagements can be very lucrative indeed.

Whatever your standing and whatever kind of group you speak to, always get as big a fee as you can, and if it is not very much, console yourself with the thought that the publicity is worth having. It is important to get as much as you can, incidentally, not merely because it keeps the wolf away from your own door, but because it sets and maintains standards for other authors.

If you are paid for a talk by a local authority or by a university, the officials will often try to treat you as one of the authority's or university's employees and will deduct tax and National Insurance from your fee; the best way of avoiding this is to get the authority to agree in advance that you are a free-lance, providing a one-off service which does not constitute employment and that they are therefore not entitled to make any such deductions from your fee. You may need to obtain a statement from your accountant or from your tax office to back up your claim.

The publicity and promotion department will also be involved, along with the sales and marketing departments, in film tie-ins and other similar marketing opportunities. It also is responsible for arranging tours for some authors, although again these are usually reserved for the more famous. Tours are exhausting – a series of frantic plane, train and car journeys, interspersed with drinks parties and a great deal of hand-shaking with local booksellers, journalists and other worthies. They also usually involve signing sessions. Most publishers, and most booksellers hate signing sessions, which work well only when the author is a really major bestseller or a nationally-known 'personality'. Far more often the session is a depressing occasion, with the publicity manager, the publisher's local representative and possibly the book's editor making embarrassed conversation with the bookshop manager, while the author sits miserably behind a pile of books, waiting for the customers who don't come. And if one does come, it is quite likely to be the representative's wife or partner, summoned by a desperate phone-call to come and pretend to be a member of the book-buying public; she will purchase a copy of the book, be grateful for the author's signature on it, and later will hand it back to her husband or partner, who will either put in back in the bookshop, getting a refund from the bookseller, or, more likely will tell her to keep it, and will put the cost on his expenses, disguised as 'entertainment'. Do everyone a favour, including yourself, and don't ask your publisher to arrange a signing session for you.

In some ways you yourself can do as much for the book as anyone else, and you should not be shy about blowing your own trumpet. Unless your book is too technical for them, your relations and friends will read it. Don't hesitate to ask them to recommend it in turn to their friends and to give copies of it for Christmas and birthday presents. Most non-writers find authors curiously glamorous, and you should not hesitate to capitalize on this. Tell a stranger that you are an author and immediate interest will almost always be shown, and you will be asked what sort of books you write. Don't be modest, but do your best to make this new acquaintance resolve to go and buy a copy. If your book is going to be paperbacked, keep quiet about it as long as you can, so that people buy the hardcover edition instead of waiting for the cheaper version. Use every trick you can think of to increase your sales. By the way, that includes not being too generous with your complimentary copies. You will probably want to give free copies to your nearest and dearest (and they will expect it, anyway), but make the others buy their own. You can promise that when they've done so you will sign the copy for them.

Final Print Quantity, Price and Publication Date

After the proofs have been returned, the publisher will take a final decision about the print quantity. This may vary from the figure originally discussed for the purposes of the estimate when the book was first under consideration. Very often, alas, the print quantity is lowered. Why? Because publishers, who are among the world's optimists, become less so as the time approaches for them to commit themselves to spending large sums of money on the gamble of manufacturing a book. Additionally, it is often difficult to maintain the initial enthusiasm – new books have come along to engage the attention of the editor, who may be far more interested in the book which is about to be signed up than in the one on which, although it is not yet published, all editorial work was completed months ago. That does not mean that the firm's enthusiasm has been totally lost – it is a matter of degree. Sales departments like to be cautious, and the editor may not fight them as vigorously now to keep the print quantity up or even increase it. Other circumstances may affect the decision too. For instance, the failure to sell subsidiary rights may have lessened confidence in the book, or the market may have changed in some respect, or the book may have been pre-empted by another publisher's book on the same subject, or (and this is often the most important factor) advance orders may, for these reasons or for no discernible cause, have been disappointing. Equally of course there may have been reasons why the print quantity should be increased – bolstered by success in the subsidiary rights market and good initial reactions from booksellers, excitement about the book may have mounted. Or it may be that the publisher is going to stick with the number first thought of. Whatever print quantity is decided upon, new sets of figures will probably be prepared, now that the costs of the book are more accurately known, and again approval for the estimate will have to be obtained from various departments within the publishing house.

The book's price will also be fixed. This is not an easy matter. As I have already said, the public at large believes that books are expensive, and the publisher has to take that into account when deciding on the retail price. The return must cover the manufacturing costs, the author's royalties, the publisher's overheads, and a profit – the firm is in business, after all, to make money. If the book is priced too cheaply, the publisher will lose on it; if it is too expensive, it may prove unsaleable. The more copies that can be printed, the easier the decision is, for the fixed costs on the book (i.e. the composition or setting of the book in type, the preparation of the illustrations, the setting up of the printing and binding machines, the costs of originating the jacket or cover, including the artist's fee, and other similar items) are spread over the entire printing, which means that the total costs per copy diminish the more copies are printed.

The cost of a book in relation to its retail price varies from publisher to publisher and from book to book, but very roughly it could be said that the average discount to wholesalers and retailers is about 45% (this allows for the higher discounts given to bulk buyers, such as the large bookshop chains, and overseas customers), manufacturing costs work out at about 20% and the author's royalty at 10%, leaving 25% to cover the publisher's overheads (including wages, telephone and mailing costs, rent, rates, interest on capital, advertising and promotion, warehousing, distribution, heating and lighting, depreciation, and the cost of the books that are not sold, either because they are given away for promotional purposes or because too many were printed) and profit, not to mention tax. The formula works out slightly differently for paperbacks, the average discount being 50%, manufacture 17½% and the author's royalty 7½%, again leaving 25% for the publisher's other expenses, and for profit, the net amount of which may not exceed 3%. It is not a formula for instant wealth for publishers, any more than it is for authors, and indeed it is worth remembering that publishing is in fact a small and not over-lucrative, high-risk business. The turnover of the entire British publishing industry does not approach that of a single firm such as ICI, and even at the highest levels those who work in the business rarely earn fat-cat salaries and certainly do not have the same sort of regular inflow of wealth that some of their bestselling authors enjoy. Bear in mind also that the publisher's profit is more often than not ploughed back into the firm for use on future projects, many of which will not come to fruition for many years, and the next time your affluent publisher takes you out to an expensive lunch (you should be so lucky!), just think how many books have to be sold to pay for it.

At the same time as the print quantity and price are decided, the publication date, which has usually been tentatively in mind since the book was signed up, will probably be firmly fixed. Publishers tend to bring their books out on dates which are regular to the firm concerned – the last Thursday in the month, for instance, or the first and third Tuesdays – and usually publish more than one book on those days, so that the titles can be invoiced and despatched at the same time. The decision about which month in which to bring out a particular book depends on a number of issues. First of all, there is the question of when the manufacturing process will have been completed and stocks delivered to the publisher's warehouse, and this in turn depends on everything going through as planned, without an unexpected delay at proof stage, for instance, or a sudden essential change of jacket design, and with the manufacturers keeping to the scheduled dates and producing work of acceptable quality; secondly, it will depend on the balance of the publisher's list – it will not be a good idea to publish all the major titles in the same month, nor, if the firm is a general publishing house, to have nothing but fiction one month and only non-fiction the next; thirdly, the publisher will be concerned about the time of the year and sometimes with specific dates – it is no use hoping to catch the important Christmas market by publishing in November or December, by which time the booksellers will have ordered all they want for the gift season, nor is there much to be gained by publishing a book about Wimbledon, as an example, in August when the Tennis Championships are over. Incidentally, it is worth pointing out that the Christmas market is important for a limited number of books only. Some books for children, including annuals, certain practical books, stocking-filler humorous books, annuals for adults, and those books which would in any case be bestsellers may have substantial Christmas sales, but the vast majority of books sell no better then than at any other time, and often less well.

Sometimes authors feel that their books have been hampered by being published at the wrong time of year. There is little that can be done about this, since it is entirely the publisher's province to decide when a book will appear, within the limits set by the contract. Nevertheless, most publishers, being business men, try as often as circumstances will allow to publish at the most suitable time for each book, because it is in their own interest, as well as the author's to do so. At the same time, you have to understand that not every book can be published in September or October (which many consider to be the best possible months), since the list has to be spread throughout the year. If you ask your publishers, they will probably be able to tell you good reasons in favour of every month of the year – e.g. 'January is a splendid time to be published – far fewer books come out then, so you stand a better chance, to say nothing of all those people wanting to spend their book tokens – besides which, the shops have been cleared of Christmas cards and all the other space-consuming seasonal material.' Equally, when they decide to delay the book until February, they will be able to tell you that, 'January is a rotten month anyway – all the book-sellers are stocktaking, and don't want to order any new books, especially if they've got Christmas overstocks to get rid of – whereas by February they're looking for important books like yours to give their New Year sales an impetus.'

Invoicing, Warehouse and Despatch
Once the sales people start selling the book, orders begin to flow into the publisher's office, where they are stored until the time comes for the preparation of invoices. Almost certainly other books will be published on the same day as yours, and the orders are collated so that the books due for publication can all be invoiced, packed and despatched together. Books ordered before publication are 'subscribed' and the total of such orders is 'the subscription' (terms which go back to the days when authors would look for wealthy patrons who would subscribe to their books, in advance, thus raising sufficient money for the author to afford the cost of having it printed).

The preparation of invoices used always to be done by hand, but in almost all firms nowadays a computer is used. The computer is also programmed to recognize 'stopped accounts' (those which the publisher will no longer supply – perhaps because they do not pay their bills) and other outlets with which, for one good reason or another, the publisher does not wish to do business, and it will also know the discounts normally applicable to each outlet.

Meanwhile the books have been delivered to the warehouse

from the printer and/or binder, on a date previously arranged with the warehouse manager, who must make sure that there is space for them near the packing benches. Later the books will be stored on racks, ready for repeat orders. Bulk supplies of slow-moving titles will probably be kept on the top racks, from which a fork-lift truck will be needed to remove them. They may well stay there until the book is remaindered or pulped.

The books are 'looked out' – that is to say, the requisite copies of each title on the invoice are brought together from the stocks – and packed, and then distributed so that, whether they go by post, rail or road, they will arrive in the bookshops in time for publication, but not too much before, since the booksellers do not want to have their stockrooms full of books which they cannot put on sale. It is important, of course, that the book should not be sold earlier in one outlet than another, especially if the shops are rivals in the same town, so publishers try hard not only to see that booksellers stick to the publication date, but that they themselves give the shops no excuse for not doing so. It is a tricky and complex job to get all the books out for the right date, especially as the warehouse will simultaneously be packing and despatching other, non-publication, orders, dealing with returns, answering queries, and keeping in regular touch with head office (most publishers' warehouses are separate from the administrative offices).

Publication Day

It is perhaps not surprising, with all these processes to go through, that the publication of a book is a lengthy business, usually taking at least nine months, and often longer. The actual production need not take all that long, and can indeed be speeded up, but it is very difficult to reduce the period required for an effective subscription (that is to say, selling the book into the bookshops and to wholesalers, at home and overseas, prior to publication). Bear in mind too that the various departments of your publishing house are dealing not just with your book but, at their various stages, with all the books that they will be publishing during the next nine months and often far ahead of that. And they will have their other problems too, of general administration, staff changes, office accommodation and the like.

When publication day comes, you might expect, as I did when I first entered publishing as a boy of eighteen, that the place would be humming. I envisaged presses thumping away in the basement, green-eye-shielded editors frantically answering three telephones at once and passing scribbled messages to a stream of messengers scurrying in and out. The images came, I suppose, from newspaper offices as depicted by Hollywood. In fact, publication day in a publisher's office is like any other day – if anything, quieter. All the work on the books coming out that day has been done, and the books themselves are in the shops waiting for customers. Occasionally, with a roaring bestseller, the publisher's phone may start to ring with repeat orders, but even that is more likely to occur several days after publication, when the bookseller is certain that the stocks are reducing rapidly and that there is sufficient continuing demand to justify a re-order. If you are lucky, your editor may remember to write to you to congratulate you on publication, or may even take you out for a celebratory lunch, but don't expect it as a matter of course. If the editor takes anyone out to lunch to celebrate it is likely to be the author of the most important book to be published that day, but in any case she/he may have forgotten, in the pressure of work on books still far away from publication, that it is indeed publication day.

After Publication
What happens to your book after publication? Probably very little, unless it has a considerable success and reprints are required. The representatives will still try to sell the book, but it will now be part of the backlist, and although for the first few weeks after publication they will ask their customers for repeat orders, unless these come in regularly, the book will receive diminishing attention. This is sad, but inevitable – they have to devote the bulk of their energies to the new books which are coming out.

For a while at least, the publicity and promotion people will continue to be active, but unless something happens to revive public interest in you or the subject of your book, they will ultimately give up – there is nothing more lifeless than the majority of last year's books, unless of course you are in the happy position of having written a bestseller or a standard work, or of being a very well-known author.

(It is interesting, by the way, to compare these three categories. The bestseller will continue to be active for quite a long time, but even in this case – unless it is one of those extraordinary books like Stephen Hawking's *A Brief History of Time* which go on and on selling in the original hardcover edition – the activity is more likely to be in the area of subsidiary rights, such as bookclub and paper-back editions, foreign sales, and so on. The standard work is an interesting phenomenon, and one which can be extremely pleasing to the author, for although its sales may not be large, they continue with a remarkable steadiness, until the happy day when the publisher tells the author, or accepts the author's suggestion, that it is time for the book to be revised and updated, after which it can look forward to a new lease of life. The book by the very well-known author may, of course, be a bestseller or a standard work or both, but it is the author's persona – perhaps as a politician or a pop-star – which keeps the book active rather than the book itself.)

The subsidiary rights department will go on beavering away for a long time, and is often surprisingly successful with books that have otherwise been forgotten by everybody except the author.

If you are fortunate, your editor or someone else in the publishing house may give you some information from time to time about how your book is going, but in many cases authors have to wait until the royalty statement appears to know the best or the worst. You are not being kept in the dark deliberately, although it may seem so; it is largely a question of out of sight, out of mind – editors find that it takes all their time to deal with new books going through, and tend to forget all about the book which was published a couple of months ago, or think to themselves, 'I really must write to So-and-so,' but never actually do. It may also be, especially in some of the larger houses, that they really have little idea of how sales are going, since, absurd though it may sound, some sales departments tend to keep their information to themselves, only passing it on to the editorial department if it is either unusually good or completely disastrous. It is very frustrating for the author not to know how the book is doing, but if you ring up daily or even weekly after publication, you will probably be regarded as a considerable nuisance; on the other hand, if the publisher volunteers no information, you can reasonably ask occasionally and be justified in expecting a rather more detailed reply than, 'Oh, it's doing quite well – I think.'

When the royalty statement arrives, it may be rather less comprehensive than you might hope. The royalty arrangements are different on nearly every book, and many publishers use a kind of shorthand on their statements which makes them hard to understand. However, in recent years considerable improvements have been made in many publishing houses, and it is to be hoped that all publishers will follow suit. The Model Royalty Statement drawn up by the Society of Authors and approved by the Publishers Association is shown in Appendix II.

Although some publishers attempt to supply annual royalty statements only (and, alas, succeed in so doing), the tradition in the trade is for six-monthly statements, which appear three months after the royalty period has ended. Thus the statement for the period January 1st to June 30th in any year, is due on the following September 30th, and that for July 1st to December 31st in any year on the following March 31st. The three-month gap was a necessity in the days when all statements were prepared by hand, partly because of the complications and the variety of the information included on the royalty statements (the terms for many books, even by the same author, often differing from contract to contract), and partly because of the need to have all the statements ready at the same time (a reasonably large publishing house might have to prepare many hundreds, even thousands, of statements for every royalty period). It is many, many years since publishers first began to use computers in their accounts departments, but for a considerable time they nearly all claimed that it was impossible to write a programme which would cope adequately with something as complex as royalties. That is no longer true, and virtually all publishers have computerized their royalty calculations. In doing so, their last justification for the three-month delay has vanished. Since the payment of royalties may exacerbate their cash-flow problems, publishers will be reluctant to abandon the old practices, but authors will feel little sympathy for them and will hope that one day, in the not too distant future, quarterly and even monthly royalty statements will be sent out.

In the meantime, even with the help of computers, the royalty department is very busy immediately after the end of a royalty period. When the statements have all been sent out, the department is naturally less pressed, and then is a good time, if you find the statement baffling, or if you think the figures are wrong (and it pays to check them carefully, because mistakes do occur) to go to see the royalties manager and ask for help. You will probably be welcomed, because the back-room people in publishing rarely have the chance to meet the authors whose names are so familiar to them and will be pleased to get to know you.

By this time, you will perhaps be well on the way with your next book, and the whole process will begin again. If you are a beginner, this second venture should be in some respects easier, since you know what to expect – but be prepared for variations on the theme. One of the great pleasures of a publisher's life is that the work is rarely of a totally routine nature, but changes with almost every book. The differences between one book and another can mean pleasure or disappointment for the author, so be prepared.

6

Contracts

'Barabbas was a publisher,' said the poet Thomas Campbell, and many, many authors would agree with him that publishers are thieves, or if not thieves, at least totally unscrupulous in the way that they exploit authors. Publishers naturally reply that any such statement is blatantly slanderous of a profession which has high risks and low profit margins, and whose honest businessmen would not retain authors on their lists if they were as wicked as that. (The publisher Peter Grose adds a footnote: 'I always thought Barabbas was a much misunderstood man . . . .') Publishers would admit that there are some rogues among their ranks, just as there are in any profession in the world, but would claim that the villains tend not to survive for long, since authors, and particularly agents, soon find them out. As for exploiting authors, they might point out that it is always easy to level an accusation of unfair treatment at anyone who is in a buyers' market. There may be comparatively few wildly successful books to be found, but there is never any shortage of works which some publisher somewhere will consider publishable; if you, as the seller, do not like the terms which they, as the buyer, propose, they will probably be able to find a whole string of authors of books of similar potential who will happily sign on the dotted line and not feel that they are being exploited – on the contrary, will consider the publisher's terms generous.

One of the difficulties facing authors is that publishers' contracts vary from firm to firm, and from book to book within each firm. This is neither surprising nor evidence of sharp practice – one of the truisms of the book world is that every book is different. Equally, every publisher is different, and there are good ones and bad ones and vast numbers of them who are just average. Thank God it is so. Publishers will only be alike when they are all state-owned and state-

116

run, which Heaven forfend, when they will probably all be equally bad. You should not expect all publishers to behave the same way and to offer the same terms, any more than you should expect a first novelist to receive the same treatment as one with a worldwide best-selling reputation. Nevertheless, it is all rather confusing.

Moreover, precisely because publishers are perpetually in a buyers' market, they have been able, if not to exploit authors outra-geously, at least often to be niggardly towards them, and this has perhaps been particularly true in their refusal to share more gener-ously with the author in some of the rewards of a successful book (although royalty percentages have usually increased when the sales have passed certain levels). They have also been assiduous in maintaining that they alone should control every aspect of the publication, many of them refusing to consult authors on any matter concerning their books and neglecting to pass on any infor-mation about what was happening to them. An author was some-one who wrote a book, amended it in accordance with a publisher's wishes, and then disappeared smartly into limbo (in which state the publisher had no wish to disturb him or her) and got on with writ-ing the next book.

Apart from authors who are consistently in the bestseller class, in which case they or their agents will be able readily to obtain favourable contracts, the individual author has little chance of fighting successfully for improved terms, especially since it is not always easy for a novice to understand fully the wording of the agreement, not to mention the smoothness with which the publisher can say, 'This is our standard contract,' with the implica-tion that all the other authors on the list accept it without demur, or even more tellingly, 'This is standard practice throughout the trade,' a statement which the author will be in no position to contradict. Such a fight can only be won if all authors band together, or if sufficiently influential bodies fight on their behalf.

It is for this reason that the Society of Authors and the Writers' Guild of Great Britain produced in 1980 a form of contract, known thenceforth as the Minimum Terms Agreement. (It should be noted, by the way, that the MTA is an agreement between a publisher or publishers on the one hand, and the Society of Authors and the Writers' Guild, on behalf of their members, on the other. It is not between a publisher and an individual author.) In the MTA, the Society and the Guild set out not only to lay down standards on financial matters, such as the royalty rates and the various splits of subsidiary earnings which they considered acceptable, but also to allow authors the absolute right, rather than a mere privilege, to be kept informed of publishing plans for their books and to be consulted on such subjects as jackets, blurbs and publicity. The Society and the Guild tried to persuade the Publishers Association to adopt the MTA on behalf of all its members. The PA predictably argued that it could not bind its members in any way, but drew up a 'Code of Conduct', to which it hoped they would adhere. The Code was both bland and unenforceable. The Society and the Guild then set about persuading individual publishing firms to sign the MTA (or a form of it, for it was soon realized that each firm was likely to want to negotiate certain changes, differing from publisher to publisher, to the basic formula).

Progress, despite vigorous efforts, has been lamentably slow. By 1997 the list of firms which have signed is a short one, although it includes a number of distinguished, major houses. However, although the signatories are few, the existence of the MTA has undoubtedly influenced a large number of other publishers so that they have greatly improved many aspects of their dealings with authors. They will not all concede your *right* to consultation on the jacket design, for instance, but at least none will now look at you with horrified incomprehension if you ask for it, and many will in fact show you the design in advance and allow you to comment on it (whether they listen to your comments and act on them is naturally a different matter). The point is that progress is being made, and publishers are much more likely nowadays than in the past to look upon their relationships with an author as a partnership, and for that we must all be grateful to the Society and the Guild and those of their staff and members who have spent so much time in fighting for the MTA.

A typical MTA is reproduced in the next pages, followed by comments on various of its provisions which perhaps deserve special attention.

AN AGREEMENT

AN AGREEMENT made this   day of   19 between the Society of Authors and the Writers' Guild of Great Britain of the one part and   (hereinafter called 'the Publisher' of the other part WHEREBY IT IS AGREED AS FOLLOWS:

Scope of the Agreement

This Agreement confirms the minimum terms and conditions to be observed in all contracts signed on or after   19 ('the contract') between the Publisher and authors who are members of the Society of Authors or of the Writers' Guild of Great Britain (any such member being called 'the Author') in respect of any original literary work first published in the UK in volume form but excluding the following:

1 Illustrated books being either:

a) books in which the proportion of space taken up with illustrations is 40% or more; or

b) specialist works on the visual arts in which the proportion of space taken up with illustrations is 25% or more.

2 Books involving three or more participants in royalties.

3 Technical books, manuals and reference works.

B Nature of Agreement

1 The terms and conditions of the contract shall be no less favourable to the Author nor in any way detract or qualify the terms and conditions specified in Section C hereof, except in so far as may be requested or may in exceptional circumstances be agreed by the Author or his/her agent.

2 This Agreement may be re-negotiated on either party giving to the other three months' written notice expiring at any time after the fifth anniversary hereof. For the avoidance of doubt either party may wish to ask for specified terms within Clauses 10 to 12 of this Agreement to be reviewed on three months' notice if unforeseen changes in the trade seem to make this imperative (but this provision shall not be invoked more than once in any 12 month period).

3 The contract shall contain the words 'drafted in accordance with an Agreement with the Society of Authors and the Writers' Guild of Great Britain'.

C Terms of the Contract between the Author and the Publisher

1 *The Typescript and its Delivery*

(a) The contract shall specify full details of the work including its proposed title, approximate length, approximate number and type of illustrations, index etc., and may refer expressly to a synopsis, specified correspondence between the Publisher and the Author and any other relevant material submitted by the Author. There shall also be stated (without being binding on the Publisher) the number of copies the Publisher proposes to print initially, the proposed format (i.e. hardback and/or paperback) and the anticipated retail price(s). In the case of commissioned works, the planned print run and anticipated retail price(s) may alternatively be disclosed on delivery of the typescript. The Author shall deliver by the date specified in the contract two legible copies of the work, or one typescript and one disc with identical text and compatible with the technology used by the Publisher. The work shall conform to a reasonable extent with the synopsis or letter in which the Author described his/her intentions and as a result of which the book was commissioned and shall be of a standard which might reasonably be expected.

(b) Within 30 days of delivery the Publisher shall notify the Author if any changes to the script are required (or if the script is to be rejected). Within a further 30 days (or such reasonable longer period as may be notified to the Author) the Publisher shall specify the changes required (or provide detailed reasons in writing for rejecting the script). Should the Author be unable to amend the material as requested within a reasonable time, the Publisher, in consultation with the Author, may arrange for someone else to amend the material and deduct the agreed cost of this from payments due to the Author. If the typescript is rejected because of the Author's failure to comply with Clause 1 (a) he/she shall be liable to repay, if so requested, payments already received.

(c) Should the Author fail to meet the agreed delivery date, the Publisher may agree with the Author a later date or give the Author reasonable notice in writing to deliver the work and should he/she fail to do so the Publisher shall be entitled to terminate the contract in which event the part of the advance received shall be returnable and all rights shall revert to the Author.

2 *Warrant and Indemnity*

The Author shall warrant:

(a) that the work is original, that he/she is the owner thereof and free to contract, and that the work has not previously been published in volume form elsewhere; and

(b) that the work will not contain anything that infringes copyright or is libellous or obscene or otherwise unlawful; nor will it infringe third parties' rights; and

(c) that all statements purporting to be facts are true and that any recipe, information, formula or instructions contained therein will not, if the reader were reasonably to act thereupon, cause injury, illness or any damage to the user or third parties.

The Author shall indemnify the Publisher (and any licensees or sub-licensees) against costs, expenses, loss and damage resulting from any breach of the foregoing warranties or any claim alleging breach thereof (excluding any claims which are reasonably deemed by the Publisher to be groundless, vexatious or purely malicious).

The warranties and indemnities shall survive the termination of the contract.

The Publisher reserves the right to request the Author to alter or amend the text of the work in such a way as may appear to the Publisher appropriate for the purpose of removing any passage which on the advice of the Publisher's legal advisers (in association with the Author's legal advisers, if he/she so wishes) may be considered objectionable or likely to be actionable at law, but any such alteration or removal shall be without prejudice to and shall not affect the Author's liability under the warranties and indemnity on his/her part. If the Author declines in such circumstances to alter or amend the text, the Publisher reserves the right to terminate the contract and seek reimbursement of the advance.

3 Copyright Fees and Index

(a) The Publisher will discuss and agree with the Author the extent of quotations and illustrations to be provided. The Publisher will further discuss the likely costs of obtaining permissions for the use thereof (taking into account the territories for which permissions will be required). Unless otherwise agreed, it will be the Author's responsibility to obtain all necessary permissions when quoting material which is in copyright and the Author will give the permission documents to the Publisher. If the Publisher clears permissions on the Author's behalf, the costs will be deducted from the advance or paid on invoice if the full advance has been paid.

The Publisher will reimburse the Author any copyright fees for agreed illustrations or maps up to £250 (or such higher sum as may be agreed).

(b) If in the opinion of the Author and the Publisher an index is required, but the Author does not wish to undertake the task, the Publisher shall engage a competent indexer to do so and the costs shall be shared equally between the Author and the Publisher, the Author's share being deducted from the advance or paid on invoice if the full advance has been paid.

4 *Licence and Review*

(a) The copyright in the work shall remain the property of the Author who shall grant to the Publisher the sole and exclusive right for a period of 20 years from the date of first publication ('the initial term') to print, publish and sell the work in volume form in the English language (or in any language as the case may be) in the territories specified in the contract and to sub-licence such rights specified in Clauses 15, 16, 17 and 18 hereof as may be agreed in the contract. The Publisher will inform the Author of all sub-licences granted and supply copies thereof on request. In particular the Author will be fully consulted and have an adequate opportunity to discuss and comment (without undue delay) on all proposed major sub-licences, including but not limited to serial, paperback, book-club, American, film, television and merchandising deals.

(b) On every tenth anniversary of the publication date (or within a reasonable time thereafter) either party may give written notice to the other that it wishes specified terms of the contract to be reviewed, in which case those terms shall be considered by the parties in the light of comparable terms then prevailing in the trade and shall be altered (with effect from the date of the notice) to the extent that may be just and equitable. Failing agreement on what may be just and equitable the matter shall be referred to arbitration under Clause 27.

(c) If the work is in print (as defined herein) at the end of 17 years from the first publication, the Publisher may inform the Author in writing of the date that the contract is due to expire and invite the Author (or his/her executors as the case may be) to negotiate in good faith with the intention of reaching agreement on revised terms for a further period. The Author, if so requested by the Publisher, shall inform the Publisher of the terms offered (if any) by other publishers and the Publisher shall be given an opportunity to match such terms but the final decision shall rest with the Author.

(d) If, with the Author's consent (such consent not to be unreasonably withheld), a licence is granted by the Publisher extending beyond the initial term, the reversion of rights to the Author (if applicable) shall be without prejudice to the continuation of that licence and the Publisher's entitlement to the Publisher's share of the proceeds therefrom. But the Publisher shall not be entitled to extend or renew, without the Author's consent, any licence granted which is due to terminate after the initial term (unless and until a further agreement is reached under (c) above).

5 *The Publisher's Undertaking to Publish*

The Publisher shall publish the work at the Publisher's own expense and risk within 12 months (unless there are particular programming or other reasons for later publication) of delivery of the final typescript and any other material specified in the contract. The Publisher shall consult the Author about the publication date. Should the Publisher decline to publish the work for any reason other than the Author's failure to meet the specifications in Clauses 1 (a) and 2, the advance stipulated in Clause 9 (including any balance unpaid) shall be paid to the Author without prejudice to any additional compensation to which he/she may be entitled for breach of contract.

6 *Production*

(a) Subject to 6 (b) to 6 (g) below, all details as to the manner of production and publication and the number and destination of free copies shall be under the control of the Publisher who undertakes to produce the book to a high standard.

(b) The Publisher shall consult the Author and obtain his/her approval on editing and the final number and type of illustrations, such approval not to be unreasonably withheld or delayed. The Author shall be shown artists' roughs (or, if that is impracticable, proofs) of the jacket and shall be fully consulted thereon and on the blurb in good time before publication, but the final decisions shall be the Publisher's.

(c) No changes in the title or text shall be made by the Publisher without the Author's consent (such consent not to be unreasonably withheld or delayed). If the Publisher uses discs supplied by the Author, all suggested editorial changes shall be clearly indicated. After the work has been accepted no material change shall be made without the Author's approval. However, the Publisher may edit the work in accordance with its normal style of punctuation, spelling, capitalisation and usage.

(d) In ample time before publication the Author shall be sent a questionnaire or letter inviting him/her to supply personal information relevant to publicity and marketing, and to suggest who should receive review/free copies.

(e) The Publisher will disclose to the Author, on request, the size of the first and subsequent print runs.

(f) Within 30 days of publication the Publisher shall return to the Author the typescript of the work, if so requested.

(g) The Publisher shall ensure that the provisions contained in (c) above are included in any contract for sub-licensed editions of the work.

7 *Approval of Final Edited Script and Correction of Proofs*

(a) Any substantive changes to the text will be agreed with the Author in writing before the typescript is sent to the printers.

(b) The Author shall be sent two complete sets of proofs of the work. The Author shall correct and return one set of proofs to the Publisher within 15 working days (or such other period as may be agreed). The Author shall bear the cost of proof corrections (other than printers' or publishers' errors) in excess of 15% of the cost of composition, such cost to be deducted from the advance or royalties.

8 *Moral Rights and Copyright Notice*

The Author will be given the opportunity to assert the right to be identified as the author of the work in the manner recommended by the Society of Authors and the Writers' Guild of Great Britain and the Publisher will observe the moral rights conferred by the Copyright, Designs and Patents Act 1988. In particular, the Author's name shall appear prominently on the jacket, binding and title page of the work and in all publicity material.

A copyright notice shall be printed on all copies of the work and the Publisher shall ensure that an identical copyright notice and the Author's assertion of the right of paternity appear in all sub-licensed editions of the work.

9 *Advance*

(a) Unless the Author requests a lower figure, the Publisher shall pay the Author an advance against royalties and earnings of not less than the following percentages of the Author's estimated receipts from the sale of the projected first printings:

(i) 65% if the work is to be published by the Publisher only in hardback or only in paperback.

(ii) 55% if the work is to be published by the Publisher in both hardback and paperback.

(b) In the case of a work already completed half the advance shall be paid on signature of the contract and half within one year of signature or on publication, whichever is the sooner (or as may be otherwise agreed at the Author's request).

(c) In the case of a commissioned work one third of the advance shall be paid on signature of the agreement, one third on delivery of the final and revised typescript, and one third within one year of delivery of the typescript or on publication, whichever is the sooner.

(d) The provisions of (b) and (c) may be varied by agreement when the work is to be published first in hardback and then in paperback under the Publisher's own imprint, or in special circumstances.

10 *Hardback Royalties*

(a) *On home market sales in the UK and Irish Republic*

10% of the British published price on the first 2,500 copies, 12½% on the next 2,500 copies, and 15% thereafter except on works for children when the royalty will be 7½% rising to 10% after 3,000 copies. In exceptional circumstances involving long works of fiction being published in short print runs for libraries or works of drama or poetry being published in short print runs, the Publisher may wish to ask the Author to consider accepting a lower starting royalty for specified reasons.

The Publisher reserves the right to pay four-fifths of the full royalty on bulk sales of 1,000 copies or more at a discount of 50% or over, and on sales to non-trade outlets at a discount of more than 50% to pay royalties on the price received by the Publisher.

(b) *On overseas sales*

10% of the price received on the first 2,500 copies, 12½% on the next 2,500 copies and 15% thereafter, except on works for children when the royalty will be 7½% rising to 10% after 3,000 copies. If the Author grants the Publisher exclusivity in EU/EFTA countries royalties on sales in those areas shall be paid as if they were Home Market sales. If the work is published abroad in a separate local edition, royalties will be paid at a rate to be mutually agreed on the local published price.

(c) On reprints of 1,500 copies or less the royalties shall revert to the starting royalties, except that the Publisher may not invoke this provision more than once in 12 months without the prior agreement of the Author.

(d) *Cheap and other hardback editions*

The Publisher shall pay to the Author a royalty to be agreed on any hardback edition published at less than two-thirds of the original published price, on any 'special' hardback edition under the Publisher's imprint (e.g. an educational or large-print edition), and on any other edition not covered by (a) or (b) above.

11 *Paperback Royalties*

(a) Should the Publisher publish a paperback edition under one of the Publisher's own imprints the Publisher shall pay to the Author on home sales 7½% of the British published price on the first 40,000 copies and 10% thereafter, except on small reprints of 5,000 copies or less (but the Publisher may not invoke this provision more than once in 12 months without the prior agreement of the Author). The Publisher reserves the right to pay four fifths of the full royalty on sales at a discount of 52½% or more. The royalty on copies sold for export shall be 6% of the British published price.

On children's books the Publisher shall pay on home sales 5% of the British published price on the first 10,000 copies and 7½% thereafter, and on export sales 4% of the British published price.

(b) Should the Publisher license paperback rights to an independent paperback publisher, all moneys accruing under such sub-licences shall be divided in the proportion 60% to the Author and 40% to the Publisher up to a point to be negotiated and then 70%:30% thereafter.

12 *Returns*

The Publisher shall have the right to set aside a reserve against returns of 15% for hardbacks and 25% for paperbacks of the royalties earned on the first royalty statement (after first publication or reissue) and to withhold this sum up to and including the second royalty statement in respect of hardback books and the third royalty statement in respect of paperback books, following which all moneys shall be paid in full and the Publisher shall accept responsibility for any over-payments resulting from subsequent returns. These provisions shall be subject to review annually at the request of either party.

13 *Remainders and Surplus Stock*

If the Publisher wishes
(a) To sell copies at a reduced price or as a remainder, the Author will be given the option to purchase (within 28 days) copies at the

remainder price and will be paid 5% of the Publisher's receipts on other sales.

(b) To destroy bound copies and put the work out of print, the Publisher will notify the Author accordingly and the Author shall have the right to obtain free copies within 28 days of the notification. If the Author requires more than 50 copies, he/she will pay the delivery charges upon receipt of invoice. There shall be no disposals under this clause within one year of first publication.

14 *Royalty Free Copies*
No royalties shall be paid on copies given away free to the Author or others, review or returned copies, or those destroyed by fire, water, in transit or otherwise.

15 *Bookclub Rights*
Should the Publisher sub-license simultaneous or reprint bookclub rights the Publisher shall pay the Author as follows:

(a) On bound copies or sheets sold to the bookclub: 10% of the Publisher's receipts.

(b) On copies manufactured by the bookclub: 60% of the Publisher's receipts.

16 *United States Rights*
If the Author grants to the Publisher US rights in the work, the Publisher shall make every effort: either to arrange US publication of the work on an advance and royalty basis, in which case the Publisher shall retain not more than 20% of the proceeds if an agent is involved (inclusive of agent's commission) and otherwise 15%; or to sell bound copies, in which case the Publisher will use its best endeavours to see that the Author is paid royalties (the percentage[s] to be agreed) related to the US published price. If the Publisher is unable or does not consider it reasonably possible to secure a royalty, then and only then shall the Publisher offer copies or sheets for sale inclusive of royalty, in which case the Author will be paid 15% of the Publisher's receipts, unless the discount is 60% or more, in which case the Author will be paid 10% of the Publisher's receipts.

17 *Translation Rights*
If the Author grants to the Publisher translation rights in the work, the Publisher shall retain not more than 25% of the proceeds from

any foreign language edition if an agent is involved (inclusive of agent's commission) and otherwise 20%.

18 *Subsidiary Rights*

(a) If the Author grants to the Publisher an exclusive licence to handle the following rights on his/her behalf, the Publisher shall pay to the Author the following percentages of the proceeds (after the deduction of any sub-agent's commission in the case of merchandising) from the licensing of the following rights:

(i)   First (i.e. pre volume publication) serial rights: 90%
        Second (i.e. post volume publication) serial rights: 75%
(ii)   Anthology & quotation rights: 50% on licences of £100 or less, otherwise 60%
(iii)   Condensation rights – magazines: 75%
                            – books: 50%
(iv)   Strip cartoon rights: 75%
(v)   Single voice TV and radio readings: 75%
(vi)   Straight-reading rights for audio/audio visual use: 75%
(vii)   Merchandising: 80%
(viii) One shot periodical: 80%
(ix)   Large print rights: 55%
(x)   Other hardcover reprint rights: 60% (80% if publication is prior to or simultaneous with a paperback edition published under one of the Publisher's own imprints)
(xi)   Graphic novel rights: 75%
(xii)   Electronic rights: 90%

(b) If the Publisher wishes to act as agent for the sale of any of the following rights (for which there is no collective licensing scheme) and the Author so agrees, the Publisher shall pay 90% of the proceeds to the Author: TV and radio dramatization, film and dramatic rights, sound and video recording rights, mechanical rights. Any legal fees or professional charges incurred directly in connection with the sale of film or video rights will be charged against the gross income.

(c) Reprographic rights shall be handled for the Author and the Publisher by the Authors' Licensing and Collecting Society and the Publishers' Licensing Society respectively. Any other income from reprography not covered by collective licensing schemes shall be handled by the Publisher and the income divided 50:50. In relation to editions of the work published by the Publisher, these provisions shall survive the termination of the contract.

(d) Public Lending Right and all other rights not specified above shall be reserved by the Author.

19 *Authors' Copies*
The Author shall receive on publication 12 free copies of the work and shall have the right to purchase further copies for personal use at 50% discount provided payment is made with the order. Should a paperback edition be issued under Clause 11 (a), the Author shall be entitled to 20 free copies.

20 *Accounts*
(a) The Publisher shall make up accounts at six-monthly intervals and shall render such accounts and pay all moneys due to the Author within three months thereof.
(b) Any sum of £100 or more due to the Author in respect of sub-licensed rights shall be paid to the Author by the end of the month following receipt provided the advance has been earned.
(c) Each statement of account shall contain at least as much information as is given in the Model Royalty Statement agreed between the Publishers Association and the Society of Authors. The Publisher shall supply copies of statements received from sub-licensees, unless such statements contain information about other authors in which case information will be provided on request.
(d) The Publisher shall make no deductions from moneys due to the Author other than those provided for herein or as may be required by law.
(e) Following receipt of a royalty statement, the Author may ask the Publisher to conduct an internal audit. The Publisher will do so and report the results to the Author.
The Author or his/her authorised representative shall have the right upon written request to examine the Publisher's books of account (during normal working hours) in so far as they relate to the work, which examination shall be at the cost of the Author. If errors are found to the Author's disadvantage, the Publisher shall rectify the error (with interest at the prevailing rate), and if it is found that a sum exceeding £50 is due to the Author, the Publisher shall pay the cost of the audit.

21 *Actions for Infringement*
(a) It is agreed that if the Publisher considers that the copyright or any one or more of the Publisher's exclusive licences in the work

has been infringed and the Author upon receiving written notice of such infringement from the Publisher refuses or neglects to take adequate proceedings in respect of the infringement, the Publisher shall be at liberty to take such steps as the Publisher considers necessary for dealing with the matter and if the Publisher desires to take proceedings shall be entitled to do so in the joint names of the Publisher and the Author upon giving the Author a sufficient and reasonable security to indemnify the Author against any liability for costs and in this event any sum received by way of damages shall belong to the Publisher. If the Author is willing to take proceedings and the Publisher desires to be joined with him/her as a party thereto and agrees to share the costs then if any sum is recovered by way of damages and costs such sum shall be applied in payment of the costs incurred and the balance shall be divided between the Author and the Publisher in proportion to the Author's and the Publisher's share of the costs.

(b) The provisions of this clause are intended to apply only in the case of an infringement of the copyright in the work affecting the interest in the same granted to the Publisher under the contract.

22 *Revised Editions*

If the Publisher and the Author agree that the work should be revised or updated, the Author, subject if reasonable to the payment of an agreed advance, will undertake such revision. In the event of the Author being unable by reason of death or otherwise to edit or revise the work, the Publisher may procure some other competent person to edit or revise the work, subject to consultation with the Author or his/her executors. The expense thereof shall be deducted from all moneys payable to the Author under the contract.

23 *Change of Imprint/Assignment*

(a) The Author shall be consulted in advance about any proposal to transfer the rights and licences in the work from one of the Publisher's imprints to another.

(b) The Publisher shall not assign the rights granted to the Publisher in the contract or the benefit thereof without the Author's written consent (such consent not to be unreasonably withheld).

24 *Termination*

(a) If the Publisher fails to fulfil or comply with any of the provisions of the contract within one month after notification from the Author of such failure or if the Publisher goes into liquidation (except a voluntary liquidation for the purpose of reconstruction) or has a Receiver appointed, the contract shall automatically terminate forthwith and all rights shall revert to the Author.

(b) When either all editions of the work published by the Publisher are out of print or when over a two year period average annual sales have fallen below 200 copies in hardback or 2,000 copies in paperback, the Author may give notice in writing inviting the Publisher to decide whether to reprint, reissue or publish a new edition of the work, as the case may be. Within 6 weeks the Publisher shall notify the Author in writing:

(i) That the Publisher does not intend to reprint or reissue or publish a new edition of the work, in which case the contract shall terminate automatically and all rights granted shall revert to the Author when stocks are exhausted or within 6 months whichever shall be the sooner; or

(ii) That the Publisher will reprint or reissue the work, in which case it shall do so within 8 months of receiving the notice from the Author; or

(iii) That the Publisher wishes to issue a revised edition, in which case the provisions of Clause 22 will apply.

The work shall be considered out of print if fewer than 50 copies of the hardback and 150 copies of the paperback remain in stock (as to which the Publisher will inform the Author). The rights shall not revert until any money owed by the Author to the Publisher has been paid.

(c) Termination under (a) or (b) shall be without prejudice to:

(i) Any sub-licences properly granted by the Publisher during the currency of the contract, and

(ii) Any claims which either party may have for moneys due at the time of such terminations, and

(iii) Any claims which the Author may have against the Publisher in respect of breaches by the Publisher of the terms of the contract.

25 *Advertisements*

The Publisher shall not insert within the work or on its cover or dust jacket any advertisement other than for its own works without the Author's consent and shall use its best endeavours to see that a similar condition is contained in all sub-licences.

26 *First Refusal*

The Publisher may ask the Author for first refusal on his/her next work, in which case the Publisher will make any offer for the next work within 3 weeks of receipt of a synopsis or within 6 weeks of receipt of a complete typescript as the case may be.

27 *Disputes*

Any dispute arising in connection with the contract, which shall be interpreted according to the law of England, shall be referred to a single agreed referee (under the informal disputes settlement scheme of the Publishers Association) on terms to be agreed between the parties informally. Failing agreement about the appointment of a suitable referee the matter shall become subject to arbitration in accordance with the Arbitration Act 1950 or any amending or substituted statute for the time being in force.

COMMENTS ON THE MINIMUM TERMS AGREEMENT

A Scope of the Agreement

Note that only those authors who are members of the Society of Authors or the Writers' Guild are entitled to the full benefits of the MTA (a good reason for joining) and only from those publishers which are signatories.

Note also that the terms of the MTA do not apply to highly illustrated books, to books involving three or more participants in the royalties, or to technical books, manuals and works of reference. It is unfortunately impossible here to advise the authors of excluded books on the terms which they should try to obtain, but of course the main principles of the MTA still apply. If in doubt about what is or is not an acceptable contract for such works and if you do not have an agent, you can if you are a member seek advice from the Society of Authors or the Writers' Guild.

C Terms of the Contract between the Author and the Publisher

Clause 1 The Typescript and its Delivery

Sub-clause (a). Note the requirement that the typescript 'shall conform to a reasonable extent with the synopsis or letter in which the Author described his/her intentions ... and shall be of a standard which might reasonably be expected'. Legally it might be quite difficult to define exactly what 'reasonable' and 'reasonably' mean, but the spirit of the words is crystal clear, and if all authors abided by them there would be far fewer publishers wanting to include a provision for 'acceptance' of the typescript in their contracts. If a clause is included which makes the publisher's obligation to publish subject to the acceptance of the book (and this is sometimes merely implied by the wording that part of the advance is payable 'on delivery and acceptance') then the agreement has turned into nothing more than a promise to consider the book for publication. The Society of Authors strongly advises all authors not to accept an 'acceptance' clause, arguing that publishers have the means, by insisting on receiving detailed synopses and specimen chapters before commissioning a book, of satisfying themselves that the author is competent to write it. However, believe it or not, not all the rogues are on the publishing side of the book business, and every publisher can cite cases in which, despite the most careful precautions and sometimes involving well-established authors, books turned out to be unpublishable when delivered. Publishers really do feel that they need some protection against the incompetent or unscrupulous author. As a matter of fact, the majority of books which have an acceptance clause do eventually get published by the house whose contract it is. And publishers who use the acceptance loophole to protect themselves from the obligation to publish a poor book may argue that if the acceptance clause is to go they will have to take fewer risks in commissioning books, and that will mean fewer commissions. However, even if that is the end result, authors should do their utmost to resist the inclusion of an acceptance clause, and should suggest instead the wording used in the second paragraph of Clause 1 (a), the point of which is to ensure that the grounds on which a publisher may reject a typescript are as clear and circumscribed as possible (e.g. failure by the author to meet the agreed specifications), and do not allow of rejection simply because of a downturn in the market, for instance, or a change of editor.

Sub-clause (b). If the publisher does ask for alterations, authors should listen carefully. Publishers don't usually suggest changes for changes' sake, but in the hope of improving the book and its sales. Accept the criticisms if you can, but, as I have said elsewhere, fight for your work if you really believe that you are right. Most good editors recognize that there is a point beyond which the competent author should not be pushed – it is his/her book, not the editor's, and he/she should be allowed the final say. Incidentally, if you are a bestselling author, do try not to get so grand that your publishers don't dare to make editorial comments in case you take umbrage and yourself off to another publisher. However good you may be, an informed comment from an experienced editor is always worth having, and you should let your publisher know that you welcome constructive criticism and will not be upset by it.

Clause 2 Warranty and Indemnity
Publishers' contracts vary widely in the scope of their warranty and indemnity clauses, which are often a cause of strife. When signing an agreement, beware especially of any mention of the author's responsibility to indemnify the publisher against expenses resulting from any threat of action, even if it is not pursued. There is really no reason why the innocent author should be expected to bear such costs, which should surely be part of the publisher's normal expenses.

Do take the warranty clause seriously. If you have the slightest fear that your book might infringe another author's copyright or might be libellous or might contain some other unlawful material, tell your publisher about it. The result may be a refusal to publish your book, which will be a blow for you, but less of a blow than a subsequent expensive legal action against you; on the other hand, the publisher may set your fears at rest, or help you to clear any obstacles in the way of publication; or the firm may be willing to assume any risks in the matter, in which case you should obtain from them a written statement to the effect that they accept full responsibility for the publication of the material about which you have warned them.

Sub-clause (a). The warranty that 'the work has not been previously published in volume form elsewhere' would clearly not apply in some cases (if your book had appeared first in the United States, for instance), but this would be a simple matter to clear with the publisher.

Clause 3 Copyright Fees and Index
This clause, or part of it, is one of the minor triumphs of the MTA. Many publishers in the past and still today would refuse to pay any of the author's expenses in respect of copyright fees, except perhaps by increasing the amount of the advance, which, unless part of it remained unearned, meant in practice that the author was still paying the whole sum. Others would not go beyond sharing the costs. It is therefore splendid to have a commitment on the

publisher's part to contribute up to £250. But note that this applies to the fees for illustrations and maps, and not to quotations of copyright text, which remain the author's responsibility to clear and pay for (see p.209). However, it is sometimes possible to negotiate with the publisher on this point. Whatever the contract says, it is as well to have in addition a separate document setting out exactly what has been agreed between the author and the publisher regarding copyright fees.

Almost all non-fiction books require an index. Before blithely agreeing to supply one for your book, you should be aware that the preparation of an index is a skilled job, and unless you feel really competent to undertake it you should consider using a member of the Society of Indexers. They can usually provide someone who is reasonably au fait with your subject, which is a great advantage. The downside is that professional indexers don't come cheap (precisely because theirs is a skilled job). If you decide to prepare your own index it will certainly be worth getting hold of *Book Indexing* by M.D. Anderson (Cambridge University Press).

Clause 4 Licence and Review
Sub-clause (a) This is undoubtedly the most controversial clause in the MTA, and most of those publishers who have signed an agreement with the Society of Authors and the Writers' Guild have balked at its inclusion. Hardcover publishers have been in the habit of buying rights for the full term of copyright. No one ever thought of working in any other way until the Society and the Guild began to argue that this is a restriction of an author's freedom, pointing to the fact that hardcover publishers normally grant sub-licences for a limited period only, and what is sauce for the goose should be sauce for the gander too. Why do publishers restrict the licence period when they sell subsidiary rights? So that at the end of the period they can either get the rights back, and perhaps sell them elsewhere, or renew the licence, if the sub-licensee has been doing an effective job, in either case probably obtaining better or more appropriate terms. Circumstances change, and the terms of an agreement which were fair and reasonable when it was signed ten or twenty years ago may now seem very unfavourable. Publishers fear of course that if their own licence period is limited (and a ten-year period would be even more desirable from the author's point of view than the twenty years specified in this clause) not only might an ungrateful author at the end of that time go to another publisher while the book was still sell-

ing well, but an unscrupulous rival publisher might tempt the author away with outrageously better terms.

The Society and the Guild have been rather more successful with Clause 4 (b), and most publisher-signatories of the MTA have accepted the possibility of revising the terms of the original contract under wording which still gives them a good chance of retaining the book on their list. It seems finally to have dawned on the more enlightened publishers that they have little to fear if they treat their authors well (i.e. as partners) and do a good job with their books.

Sub-clauses (c) and (d) apply of course only if sub-clause (a) has been accepted by the publisher.

Clause 5 The Publisher's Commitment to Publish

The commitment from the publisher to publish the book within a reasonable time after delivery of the typescript is an essential part of an agreement, and it should be a definite date (e.g. within 12 months of delivery of the typescript) rather than something vague like 'within a reasonable period'. It is of course subject to negotiation if there are legitimate factors which will delay the book's appearance – indeed, it may sometimes be advantageous for the book to be held up for a while, so that, for instance, its publication can coincide with some event which will give it greater publicity – but in the event of late publication, or non-publication, due solely to the publisher's dilatory attitude, the penalty of having to pay the balance of the advance should concentrate the accounts department's mind wonderfully, not to mention the fact that the author may be able, if the publication date in the contract is not adhered to, to cancel the agreement if that seems desirable.

While agreeing that it is fair to pay the balance of the advance if they decide not to go ahead with publication although the author is not in any way in breach of the contract, some publishers will ask that if the author succeeds in placing the book with another publisher, their own advance or part of it should be repaid. This should always be resisted. If the publisher cancels the contract then there is a penalty attached, and what happens to the book thereafter is no business of the defaulting company.

Clause 6 Production

The whole of this clause marks a great step forward in author/publisher relationships. Not so many years ago it was unheard of for an author to be consulted over the blurb, the jacket design and the like, publishers kept the size of their print runs as the darkest of secrets, and quite ruthless copy editing could be carried out without the author's consent. It was little wonder that many authors felt that they were being treated by publishers as second-class citizens. Fortunately, and largely as a result of the MTA, and the efforts of the Society, the Guild and agents, attitudes have greatly improved. However, there are still some unenlightened publishers around, so if you are offered a contract which does not include provisions similar to those in this clause, fight for them.

Like the rest of Clause 6, sub-clause (d) is good from the author's point of view, but it can cause some disappointment. Publishers don't always follow up the author's publicity suggestions and even when they do rarely spend as much money on publicity as the author would hope.

Clause 7 Approval of Final Edited Script and Correction of Proofs
Sub-clause (a) is really an extension of Clause 6 (c), but is welcome nonetheless.

Sub-clause (b). The more usual percentage of the composition cost above which the author pays for proof corrections has been 10%, so it is another achievement of the MTA to have increased the figure to 15%. Proof corrections are devilishly expensive, so the prudent author avoids any likelihood of a charge by making sure that the final typescript is as perfect as possible. In the case of topical books, where changes may have to be made at the last minute, special arrangements regarding alterations in proof should be made in advance with the publisher.

Clause 8 Moral Rights and Copyright Notice
The publisher's commitment to the insertion of a notice regarding the Moral Right commonly known as 'the right of paternity' is essential since the passing of the Copyright, Designs and Patents Act of 1988 (see p.206).

Clause 9 Advance
Sub-clause (a). Publishers who do not subscribe to the MTA appear to pluck a figure out of the air when deciding what advance to offer. In fact, the figure is usually based on an expectation of earnings from the first printing, but the amount offered may be a small proportion of the sum, since from the publisher's point of

view there is little point in paying out any more than is necessary to keep the author quiet. Setting out a firm percentage would seem to be a fairer method of calculation. However, while some authors may feel that it is important to obtain as large an advance as possible (in order to ensure that the publisher puts in the maximum effort), others believe that it is more important to fight for respectable royalties than to worry about the advance – and I think that in most cases they are right. Believe me, adding an extra £250 or even £2,500 to the advance is not actually going to make a great deal of difference to the publisher's efforts.

Sub-clause (d). The sort of variation that you may encounter, if the publisher is going to bring the book out both in hardcover and paperback, is payment of the advance as to one third on signature of the agreement, one third on hardback publication (or within one year of signature, if that is sooner), and one third on paperback publication (or within one year of hardback publication, if that is sooner). Publishers are quite often fairly flexible about how advances are paid, and will listen if the author wants to speed up payment (perhaps because of being broke) or delay it (perhaps for tax reasons).

Clause 10 Hardback Royalties
Sub-clause (a). Royalties offered to authors vary enormously, some not rising above a basic rate at all, others jumping at widely different points; some start at lower percentages than those recommended in this clause, while if you are in the bestseller class, even if you cannot expect to get a 25% royalty as top authors used to do before World War II, you will probably start off at a rather nice 15%. Some publishers may argue that to increase royalties after 2,500 copies and again after 5,000 copies will mean that the retail price of books will have to be increased. Not true. If the home sales have reached 2,500, let alone 5,000, the publisher should be making quite enough money to afford the extra percentage on additional sales. On the other hand, publishers do have increasing difficulty in publishing books economically if the initial print run is likely to be small, and it seems reasonable that they should have the freedom to negotiate terms which are a little less favourable to the author in such cases.

The abandonment of the Net Book Agreement has resulted in some books being sold to the trade and other outlets at very high discounts, and in such circumstances publishers now ask authors to share part of the burden by accepting a reduced royalty. The theory is that because these high discounts result in vastly increased sales, you will benefit overall. Of course, you probably need to be in the bestseller class to be affected, and if you are, you will have the clout to decide whether or not to accept the clause – some megastars have refused to do so. Even non-bestselling authors should take great care with the small print concerning royalties on high discount sales – some publishers see this as an area in which they can recoup some of the money that they are having to give away to the big bookselling chains, or on premium deals, and that is not fair to the author.

Sub-clause (b). It has long been accepted that on export sales publishers should pay a royalty based on the price they receive, rather than on the published price of the book, because the discounts that they give to overseas buyers are often very high. In the home market booksellers used normally to receive much lower discounts – rarely more than 35% for hardcover books – but now that discounts of 50% or more are commonplace, it may not be long before publishers abandon the published price as the basis for royalties altogether, and pay royalties on both home and export sales as a percentage of the price received. It makes a lot of sense from the publisher's point of view, because the calculations involved are much simpler. Authors need to be wary of this approach, ensuring that the percentages are worked out so that their earnings are not reduced. If the publisher's average discount over all sales is, say, 45%, then an 18.2% royalty would be necessary to be the equivalent of a 10% royalty on the published price. Additionally, it will undoubtedly make it much more difficult to check the accuracy of the publisher's royalty statements, since the author will have to take on trust not only the number of copies sold but what the publisher's receipts were.

Sub-clause (c). You may wonder why a lower royalty should be payable on a reprint when the origination costs of the book should have been absorbed by the first printing. The simple fact is that the start-up costs of a reprint are so high that unless the print quantity can be raised above 1,500 copies the whole thing may not be economically viable, especially if burdened with a 12½% or 15% royalty.

Clause 11 Paperback Royalties
Sub-clause (a). Another achievement of the MTA is the acceptance by publishers of the idea that the royalties on paperbacks should

rise after a given quantity have been sold. It is also interesting to note that recent MTAs include wording to cover small reprints of paperbacks – some years ago a quantity of less than 10,000 would have been unthinkable in the mass paperback market – and to allow for books sold at a very high discount.

Sub-Clause (b). For many years it was standard practice for hardcover publishers to retain 50% of all royalties received on a sub-licensed paperback edition, and their arguments for doing so were that if they had not published the book in the first place, the paperback edition would not have appeared; that they had invested money in building up the author's reputation, publicizing the book, securing reviews for it, and so on, and that if they had not done so the paperback publisher would not have been interested in it; that the growth of paperback sales had eradicated their ability to sell cheap editions of the hardcover book, making their initial risk that much greater; and that without a substantial share of the paper-back income, they would be unable to publish many new books, and especially fiction. However, thanks largely to the concerted efforts of authors' agents, the concept of the invariable 50:50 split virtually disappeared some years ago. Hardcover publishers have survived, and new books have continued to be published – even fiction – although it is certainly true that new novelists find it diffi-cult to get into print unless their books have a potential paperback sale. A 60:40 split, rising to 70:30 should be regarded as standard.

Clause 12 Returns
The Society of Authors, the Writers' Guild and agents used to be implacably opposed to the idea of royalties being withheld against returns from the bookshops of unsold books. However, the realities of life have to be faced, one of them being that the practice of send-ing out books on a 'sale or return' basis has become the norm. Books supplied on sale or return are entered in the publisher's ledgers as sales, but may be nothing of the sort, since the book-sellers and wholesalers have the right to return for credit any copies that they have not sold after a given period. Suppose a publisher has sent out 1,000 copies of a book on sale or return; they are counted as full sales and royalties on them are paid to the author at the end of the accounting period; but in the subsequent royalty period, 250 of those books are returned for credit, which means that the author has been paid royalties on books which have not been sold. This will not matter if a further 250 or more firm

sales are made, because the returns can be offset against them, but often no more sales are made. Equally, it would not matter if authors were prepared to refund any royalties paid on books which turned out not to have been sold, but in practice, although the advance is supposed to be the only non-returnable payment, publishers have long come to accept that any moneys paid to authors are almost always lost to them for ever. The problem of returns has become more acute with paperbacks – not surprisingly, perhaps, since they are so dependent on exposure for their sales. So the principle of a reserve against returns has become generally accepted. You may find that your publisher will ask for more than the 15% reserve for hardcover editions and the 25% for paperbacks specified in this version of the MTA, but you should resist giving in on this point.

In some happy cases it will be clear that the book is selling so well that there is no real justification for the reserve against returns, or that at least the percentage retained could be reduced. On the reverse side of the coin, the publisher may feel, if the book is producing disappointing results, that the reserve is too small. These two possibilities are the point of the wording which allows for an annual review of the matter.

Clause 13 Remainders and Surplus Stock
Another minor triumph of those in the Society and the Guild who have negotiated the MTA is to have persuaded some if not all of its signatories to pay a royalty on remainders. Publishers have resisted doing so for years, arguing that they should not have to add to their losses (remainders are usually sold to remainder merchants at less than the cost of manufacture). Since the books eventually reach the public at prices considerably above the cost of manufacture, it seems only fair that the authors should get something out of the deals, however little.

Many agreements in the past contained clauses which did not allow publishers to remainder or pulp books until two years after publication. Publishers argued that a large number of the books concerned could be seen to be unmitigated disasters within six months of publication, and that they should be free to dispose of them then. Twelve months seems a reasonable compromise.

Clause 15 Bookclub Rights
Sub-clause (a). 10% of the publisher's receipts is a much fairer

share than the small royalty (usually 3¾%) on the bookclub's price to its members, which is often specified in publisher's agreements.

Clauses 16, 17 and 18   United States Rights, Translation Rights, Subsidiary Rights
The author's shares specified in these three clauses are at least equal to and in many cases higher than it has been the normal practice of hardcover publishers to pay. It is perhaps worth pointing out that many of the rights covered by the clauses may or may not be granted to the publisher. Agents will normally retain the rights for the US, Translation, First Serial, Strip Cartoon, Single voice TV and radio readings, Straight-reading for audio/audio visual use, and Electronic, and those rights listed in sub-clause (b). However, an author who does not have an agent should probably allow the publisher to handle such rights, since publishers are usually better equipped to deal with them than most authors.

It is worth underlining yet again the importance of Electronic Rights. Technology has developed so rapidly that many authors are not yet aware that before very long their work, if successful, will appear as a matter of course in electronic form. If a publisher will not accept at contract stage the idea that the author should receive 90% of any proceeds from the sale of these rights, then it is essential at least to insert wording to the effect that the split of moneys will be agreed between the author and the publisher prior to the sub-licensing of the rights.

Reprographic rights should always be granted as specified in sub-clause (c), and Public Lending Right should always be retained by the author. The reference to 'other rights not specified above' in sub-clause (d) sounds rather casual, but could be of considerable importance to the author as technology speeds into all kinds of previously unimagined methods of communication. Some contracts suggest that the publisher should control any unspecified rights and that the split of income resulting from them should be negotiable. It is much better for the author to reserve the rights. As a general principle, if any new rights are sold, the author should receive either all the resulting moneys or not less than 90% of them.

Clause 19 Authors' Copies
Standard practice has been for the author to receive six copies only of a hardcover book. The provision of six extra free copies is one of the least costly things a publisher can do to keep the author happy.

It is good too to see a specified discount at which the author may buy additional copies, which is preferable to covering the matter with such phrases as 'at best trade terms' or 'at the lowest trade price'. The downside is that the author must pay for such copies immediately, rather than charging them to the royalty account, but this seems a small penalty in return for the generous discount. Although the clause refers to the purchase of copies 'for personal use', and does not include the wording 'not for resale' (which used to be standard), it is always advisable if you want to sell copies of your book to obtain the publisher's permission to do so.

Clause 20 Accounts
Sub-clause (b). The retention of sub-licence income, after the advance has been earned, until the next royalty statement is sent out, rankled with authors for years. Most publishers will now agree to a clause such as this.

Sub-clause (c) Publishers used to be very reluctant to divulge information about print runs and often failed to pass on any details from sub-licences. Moreover, in many cases their royalty statements were notoriously difficult to understand, and therefore frequently impossible to check for accuracy. The use of a form such as the Model Royalty Statement (see p.246) solves most of these problems, but may not protect you from inaccurate accounts, which can, as a result of human error, emanate from the most respectable of publishing houses. If you have serious doubts about the accuracy of your royalty statements, most contracts have a clause similar to sub-clause (d) which you can invoke. But do make sure that you have real grounds for suspicion – the simple belief that your publisher should have sold more copies of your book (which is naturally just as good as any of those titles on the bestseller lists) than the statement says is not really enough.

Clause 22 Revised Editions
Not all publishers will offer a new advance when asking an author to produce a revised edition of a book. Perhaps they should, but the author can be consoled with the hope that the book will earn far more royalties in its new form than it would have done if left to become totally outdated.

Clause 23 Change of Imprint/Assignments
Sub-clause (a). Since so many publishers nowadays own a number

of different imprints, it seems fair that the author should be consulted about a proposal to transfer a book from one imprint to another.

Sub-clause (b). The inclusion of this clause is an important protection for authors, preventing the publisher from assigning the rights in the author's work to a third party to whom the author might have reasonable objections.

Clause 24 Termination
A well drawn termination clause is very necessary in all agreements between an author and a publisher. It should be specific regarding the reversion of rights to the author, but so many different circumstances can attach to a book that it is advisable, if termination takes place, to insist that the publisher should state in writing exactly what the situation is (for example, which rights have reverted to the author, which sub-licences are still operative and how moneys accruing from them will be dealt with, and so on).

Clause 25 Advertisements
In the years before World War II it was not unusual for publishers to sell space in their books to advertisers, and it would never surprise me if they were driven to do so again in order to subsidize their publications. It is to be hoped that any such advertisements would be in good taste and not such as to upset the readers of the book or to damage the author's reputation, in which case the author would surely not withhold consent unreasonably.

Clause 26 First Refusal
The majority of publisher's contracts carry an option clause. If it specifies in detail the terms on which the publisher will be able to buy the author's next book or uses a phrase like 'on the same terms and conditions as the present agreement', it is legally binding. Authors should not accept such a clause, which could be very damaging to their interests. The option 'on terms to be agreed' is far less dangerous, since it probably commits the author only to the submission of a new book for the publisher's consideration, and allows for the rejection of the publisher's offer if that seems a wise course of action. Even better is wording such as is used in Clause 26. In practice, publishers should earn the right to see an author's next book. If they behave well towards their authors and make a success of their books, the authors will probably want to continue

to be published by the same firm, and in such a case the publishers are indeed entitled to expect loyalty.

Additional Points

The clauses in the MTA on which I have not commented are those which seem to me both self-explanatory and largely uncontroversial. There are, however, two further points which I should mention.

The first is to explain why lower royalties are offered for children's books. Children's books are normally priced very much more cheaply than adult books, although their illustrations may make them quite expensive to produce, so the publisher often works on smaller margins. Moreover, room usually has to be found in the costings for a fee or royalties paid to the artist who supplies the illustrations.

The second point concerns that phrase which occurs quite frequently, 'such consent not to be unreasonably withheld'. When your publisher allows you to comment on the proposed jacket design for your book, or asks you to agree to change the title, try to remember that she/he has a certain expertise which you should respect. If you are really unhappy, let the strength of your feelings be apparent, but don't have a row about anything – more will be achieved by not being unreasonable.

I now turn to more general comments.

Let me remind you that the publishers who have signed MTAs have done so only after negotiating acceptable changes with the Society and the Guild. If you are a member of the Society or the Guild and are offered a contract by a publisher who is a signatory, it may therefore not conform exactly to the version printed in this chapter. In any case, every book is different, and every publishing agreement is likely to be different in some respects.

Do remember that this is a *Minimum* Terms Agreement. It may be possible to improve on it in some instances. The other side of the coin is that, in certain circumstances, the publisher may wish, despite being a signatory, to offer you slightly less good terms (although of course convincing arguments for them will have to be presented to you). Any agreement must to some extent be a matter of give and take, but before either side can give and take there must be full understanding of what any changes may entail and why they are necessary. This is one of the reasons why it is so important to establish a friendly personal relationship with your publisher, and just as publishers should try to understand authors' problems and something of their circumstances, so authors should try to understand something about publishers' work and the difficulties they encounter. It is worth remembering that although your publishing house is a business, it is staffed by human beings, and human behaviour can often be extremely mysterious. The more you understand of what makes your publisher tick, the easier it will be to reach agreement.

Although the contract between an author and a publisher is a legal document, meaning, if it is well drawn, exactly what it says, and is usually intended to last the length of the licence it covers without amendment, it is not sacrosanct, either at the time it is drawn up or later. The fact that a publisher has sent you a contract does not mean that its details cannot be altered before you sign, and you should never be afraid to ask for changes in the terms – publishers are very unlikely to withdraw an offer just because you politely query a few matters. Even if you and your publisher do not see eye to eye over some specific point, it may be possible to make an arrangement whereby the matter can be reviewed in, say, three years' time, and this is a course of action which is particularly advisable in such cases as when a publisher decides to switch from paying royalties on the published price to paying a percentage of net receipts – you might decide to see how it works before committing yourself to it for ever. Equally, all kinds of problems or changing circumstances may occur during the writing or during the publication process or long after the book has come out which demand an alteration to the agreement, and there is no reason why you cannot negotiate changes. You can't just tear the contract up, unless you have real cause, but you may be able to amend some of its terms.

You might think, by the way, that if you have an agent you have no need to worry about the MTA, because the agent will see that you get the most beneficial agreement possible. A good agent will certainly do a good job and take care of all sorts of little things which you yourself might overlook. Moreover, most agents use their own tried and tested form of contract. But it's rather interesting that a well-known agent is on record to the effect that the MTA is a better agreement than those drawn up by many agents.

In general the effect of the MTA is both to protect authors' rights and to increase their rewards. Even the most curmudgeonly of publishers might admit, if forced to it, that it was about time that authors were given a little more say in the publication of their books, and would probably also agree that, except in the case of major bestsellers, few authors are at present well paid. So why haven't more publishers signed the MTA? A few say that there is no point, since they already give their authors contracts with terms which are at least as good as those specified in the MTA, but I beg to doubt whether many houses can justifiably make that claim – and if they do always offer such good terms, why don't they sign anyway? I suspect that some others feel that authors, once given the right of consultation, will pester them constantly and make their lives hell (recognizing, perhaps, that the authors might be paying them back in their own coin). More importantly, and I think this is probably the main sticking point, many publishers genuinely believe that they cannot afford the additional financial benefits which the MTA gives to authors. Pleading poverty, they will point out that the only place where the extra money can be found is in the pockets of the book-buying public. Warming to the subject, they will say that most publishers could make more money by closing down their businesses and simply investing the capital in stocks and shares or with a bank. So the extra cash will have to come in the end from the people who buy books, and higher prices will mean fewer sales. And that in turn will mean fewer new books published, and not-yet-established authors will find it even more difficult to get into print. We have heard all that before, and it has ceased to impress. The books published by those firms which have signed the MTA are not noticeably higher in price than those from non-signatory houses, and the signatories are flourishing (or if they are not, there are other reasons than the MTA for their troubled situation).

Supposing that your publisher does not accept the MTA, and puts to you a contract which seems, to say the least, to be ungenerous, is there anything you can do? Unless you are a well-established author you have very little clout, but you can try a bit of gentle haggling. You will have to make your own judgement about how far the haggling can go, for if you press too hard the publisher may simply withdraw the offer and go to an author who will accept the offered terms without argument. But publishers who have got to the stage of preparing a contract are likely to be fairly deeply committed to the book, and the person with whom you are dealing may have a little latitude on the terms. The publisher's position is often like that of someone attending an auction – he/she will have worked out in advance how much can be spent (or what terms can be offered on your book), but the full amount does not have to be bid at once. If the article being auctioned can be obtained (or your book signed up) for less than the planned maximum expenditure, the bidder will have done well, but won't necessarily be very unhappy about it if, instead, the whole amount has to be paid out.

Your problem with an agreement may not be concerned with terms so much as simply to understand what it means. Often the legal jargon is less than clear to the lay mind, and if, as sometimes happens, the publisher's form of agreement has been poorly drafted, it may not even make sense, or you may find that it contains two totally contradictory clauses. If you have no agent and are not a member of the Society of Authors or the Writers' Guild, what can you do? The first option open to you is simply to ask the publisher to explain everything which you do not understand. If you are still in doubt, another possible answer is to consult other authors, and if you do not know any, you might consider joining your nearest writers' circle, which will almost certainly include among its members some published authors with experience of publishers' contracts. Or you can consult a solicitor, but with the greatest respect to the worthy firm which deals with the sale of your house and the making of your Will and other such everyday affairs, it is worth going to a firm which specializes in literary matters, for your family solicitor may be as baffled as you are by some of the technicalities of the business, and may miss the points which should be queried and cause irritation by quibbling over matters which really are standard trade practice. Of course, you may be lucky enough to have a family solicitor who already knows something about publishers' contracts, or who is clever enough to work it all out accurately or diligent enough to find out the essential points from others. The main thing is that you should pay for advice only if you are sure that it is going to be good and informed advice, and the cheapest way of making certain might be to join the Society of Authors or the Writers' Guild.

One last important point needs to be made. Much needed though a Minimum Terms Agreement has been, and just though its provisions are, there are many cases where an author should not feel guilty at accepting lesser terms. It is a matter for your personal judgement according to circumstances; your publisher may be exceptionally generous in certain respects and mean in others, and you may decide that the good more than makes up for the bad; or you may be aware that the market for your writing is so competitive that you are lucky to be published at all; or you may take the view that your publisher is so active on your behalf that it is better to receive a smaller royalty or share of subsidiary moneys than it would be to get better terms from a publisher who would sell far fewer copies or rights; or you might be content with a low advance, knowing that it means that royalties are payable all the sooner. Those who have struggled to get the Minimum Terms Agreement accepted would undoubtedly say that every time you accept any terms which are worse than those laid down, you are letting down every other author and allowing the continued exploitation of authors. That is true. Authors should stick together, because it is the only way of improving their lot safely and permanently. Nevertheless, it is impossible to legislate for the circumstances surrounding the publication of every book and the relationship between every author and publisher. You have to make your own reasonable judgement.

7

Author/Publisher Relationships

Authors v. Publishers

Relationships between authors and publishers are often difficult, and have been so over a long period of time. The list of authors who have written nastily about their publishers is lengthy and distinguished. Why there should be quite so much acrimony is hard to explain – not all publishers are ruthless exploiters of their authors – but I think there are four main reasons for it: firstly, authors always see their work as being of high quality, and therefore expect, or at least hope, for far more sales than the publisher usually achieves; secondly, very few authors understand much about publishing; thirdly, authors, as a group, are trusting, not to say gullible; and fourthly, there seems to be an almost natural antipathy between authors and publishers.

The first point is pretty obvious. As for the second, in his biography of the founder of Penguin Books, *Allen Lane: King Penguin*, Jack Morpurgo wrote:

> Publishers are convinced that most authors are ignorant of the techniques of the publishing craft and suspect, often with justification, that many sustain this ignorance by a lofty conviction that comprehending the technical and commercial practicalities of publishing is somehow beneath their dignity and an unnecessary distraction from their prime duty, to set words, ideas or narrative to paper. Understanding the means whereby their handsomely embellished paper is to be reproduced, promoted, distributed and made profitable – to both publisher and author – is a process to which they need only give such thought as is, in their opinion, unavoidable.

> Alas, it is true, and a better understanding of the publishing business would save many an author from becoming disgruntled. It has

to be said, however, that the faults are not all on one side. Publishers as a whole – even those editors who work closely with their authors – tend to have little idea of what goes on in a writer's head. Even members of the general public are aware that the author's life is a lonely one – they have frequently been told so – and some of them are even prepared to believe the nonsense, put about mostly by the more pretentious authors, that it is 'agony' to write; editors, on the other hand, are often willing to accept, as the general public does not, that writing, although not 'agony', is hard and intensive work, and they are aware of the loneliness. But that is often as far as their understanding goes. They recognize that almost all authors are incapable of judging their own work, but do they see just how personal to authors their books are, and therefore how hurtful even the most well-deserved criticism can be? Do they understand that almost all authors feel wretchedly insecure, terrified of rejection or of not maintaining the standard both in writing and in sales of their previous work?

The third point refers to gullibility. Authors who would take the greatest care in the selection of any other person who is to perform some service for them will happily place complete trust in a publisher of whom they know little or nothing, and will expect that publisher to behave with perfect efficiency, despite the fact that nothing else in this modern world, alas, can be relied upon to do so. We are all used to trains that run late or are suddenly cancelled, to garages which fail to cure the faults in our cars, to builders who take longer than promised to finish their work and then charge more than their estimates. We grumble and pretend to be surprised when it happens, but we have been expecting the worst all the time. Most authors, however, seem rarely to be prepared for anything less than perfection from their publishers, and when inevitably they are disappointed, they are not only shocked and angry, but usually very ready to believe that the publisher's failings are deliberate and perpetrated in a kind of personal attack. No wonder that a breaking point in the relationship can easily be reached.

Coming to the fourth point, publishers would probably be shocked to learn that an astonishingly large number of authors see them (not, perhaps, as individuals, but certainly as a group) as The Enemy, but it seems almost natural that they should, just as we expect there to be conflict between unions and bosses, teachers and pupils – even husbands and wives. In fact, the reasons for this enmity are not hard to find. Authors feel weak and defenceless when facing the power of the publisher; their books are accepted or rejected apparently on a whim; they see their editors working in well-appointed offices, driving company cars, lunching regularly in expensive restaurants, and they contrast all this with their own starving-in-a-garret-type lives. It all adds up to a somewhat unfair view, but it has been compounded ever since the publishing trade began by the condescending attitude which many publishers adopted, or seemed to adopt, towards their authors – an attitude which seemed to be saying, 'Think yourself jolly lucky that I have graciously decided to publish your book', 'Yes, do come and talk about it, but don't expect me to give you my full attention, because I'm a Very Busy Person', 'Don't expect me to explain what is going on, because publishing is a Mystery, the secrets of which are revealed only to the privileged people who work in it' and 'For heaven's sake don't bother me with your trivial little problems, especially if they are totally unfounded complaints about the way my firm operates'. A belief that this is how publishers think and behave is widespread, and even the most rational of authors will have held it at times. It is undoubtedly partly responsible for the campaign which produced the Minimum Terms Agreement. In case any publisher is still in doubt, let me say that the MTA is not just about authors getting a slightly bigger slice of the financial cake, it is not just about authors being consulted about the publication of their books, it is not even just about the recognition that authors are essentially partners with their publishers – it is all those things, but it is also about authors not being patronized, not being condescended to, being treated as human beings, with respect.

Even for an author whose publisher has signed the MTA, or at least accepts its spirit, there will probably be problems in the relationship, and these will almost certainly be exacerbated by a failure to communicate – strange in a business so concerned with words. It is usually the publisher's fault. In all the years that I dealt with authors I found them to be almost always understanding and co-operative when I took the time and trouble to explain what was happening. At one stage of my career, when I joined a large company as Editorial Director, I promised myself that I would write regularly to all my authors to give them the latest news on their books – where we had got to in production, what luck we were having with subsidiary sales, how the book was selling, and so on. It never got done, alas, because there was just too much pressure of other work. And that reminds me to say, by the way, that you should not try to interpret the silence of your publisher as being significant or meaningful. No news is good news doesn't necessarily apply – nor does the reverse. It may be just that she/he is jolly busy.

Despite failures in communication, there is no reason why publishers and authors should not be friends, especially since they are both basically devoted to same cause, provided that, as in most human relationships, there is a certain amount of give and take on both sides. The most difficult thing for an author to understand is that the publisher is also concerned with other books and other authors, and that the author's own book may be one among, say, three hundred that the publisher is working on during the year – it is one three-hundredth part of the publisher's year, which is also, of course, taken up partly with administration and financial matters and all sort of concerns other than authors and their books; the most difficult thing for the publisher to remember is that the book represents many months or years of work by the author, and that it is at the moment the author's entire world.

If your publisher is not as friendly towards you as you would like, you may be justified in feeling that he/she is, at the least discourteous. But do remember that friendship is two-sided, and make sure that you are not being kept at a distance because of your own attitude. A publisher who likes your work should be interested in you as a person, and in your plans and your problems, but you should equally be prepared to be understanding, and to enter the relationship with neither too aggressive nor too defensive an attitude. If some of the things that worry you are just brushed aside, be aware that to the publisher they are probably commonplace – almost all authors are discontented with their sales, disappointed that their books have not been widely advertised, feel that their publishers are not making sufficient effort for them, suffer from writer's block, are short of money. The publisher has heard the same stories many times before and will hear them many times again, and will sometimes have difficulty in being as sympathetic as you would like.

The Difficult Author

There may be more than a slight lack of friendliness in the relationship, and you may, for instance, suspect that the publisher is deliberately avoiding you if every time you phone you are told, 'I'm sorry, she/he's in a meeting.' Of course, it may be true. Publishing used to be an autocratic business with decisions taken by the head of the house or by those individuals to whom authority had been delegated; nowadays it is much more a question of management by committee. Your publisher may indeed be in a meeting, to discuss editorial matters, or jackets, or publicity and promotion, or sales plans, or budgets and five-year financial plans, or staff salaries – not to mention the possibility that the meeting is with another author.

On the other hand there may indeed be a wish to avoid speaking to you. Why? Possibly because no decision has yet been reached on your book, or the editor is having difficulty in persuading others in the firm to be enthusiastic about it, and is reluctant to tell you yet again that you have to be patient. Or perhaps your book is being rejected, and being a coward, he/she prefers to tell you by letter rather than on the phone. Or maybe your request for this or that piece of information has been forgotten until you ring, and she/he is unwilling to expose the failing. All very unsatisfactory from your point of view, but also very human, and perhaps if you try very hard you can find enough of the divine in yourself to forgive.

However, if you are told constantly that the person you want to talk to is in a meeting, and if additionally your phone calls are never returned as promised, and in general it seems that considerable pains are being taken to avoid any contact with you, then either you have landed yourself with a rotten publisher, who probably has a rotten secretary into the bargain, or perhaps you are a Difficult Author. Difficult Authors are those who, among other unpleasant habits, phone daily (usually to say that their books are not available in such-and-such a bookshop), expect to be received immediately if they call unannounced at the publisher's office, ask their publishers to undertake any of their research which they find too difficult, believe that it is their publishers' responsibility to make their hotel and theatre bookings, instruct the publisher to obtain books for them from other publishers at trade discount, rewrite their books at proof stage, demand that the part of the advance due on publication should be paid now, although the book is not even half way to completion, and above all, argue over everything from a changed comma to the date chosen for publication, and who constantly complain. If you are that sort of author (and, believe me, there are plenty of them around, even if they don't all perpetrate every one of the horrors I have listed), be prepared for your publisher not only to be permanently in a meeting, but also to reject your next book, not because it is a poor one, but simply because life is too short to make it worth putting up with you.

'I recognize myself as a Difficult Author,' you may bravely say, 'at least in part. But the reason that I argue and complain constantly is simply that my publisher is both rude and extremely inefficient. Nothing gets done unless I badger.' Well, maybe you're right. But there are ways of badgering. Some people find it easy to be aggrieved, and if you are one of them, then however justified your complaints may be, your attitude may succeed only in antagonizing the one person who might be able to put right whatever is wrong, and increasing harassment on your part may lead only to greater inefficiency.

The Publisher's Inefficiency

There are of course times when authors should complain, and forcefully too. Publishers are undoubtedly often incompetent, and when they make stupid mistakes or fall down on promises, you are entitled to be angry. Why should publishers so often be inefficient? There are, I think, several factors to be considered. First of all, because every book is different, with its own peculiarities and problems, there is no universal formula which can be applied to the solution of its individual difficulties, and this clearly multiplies the opportunities for human error. Secondly, publishing is a pretty complex business, involving in all its many processes not only a large number of people and many skills, but also quite a few sub-contractors, and this makes it particularly vulnerable to Sod's Law ('if anything can go wrong, it will'). Thirdly, the expansion of the trade has led to additional inefficiency – and this point needs more detailed explanation.

For many reasons, publishers' output has increased dramatically compared with the numbers of books published, for example, between the two World Wars. Back in 1936 the book trade was shaking its collective head over the fact that more than 14,000 new books were being published every year – far too many, and an obvious recipe for disaster. Nowadays we produce well over 100,000 new books a year – more than 275 new titles every day, including Sundays and Bank Holidays. (Some observers dispute these figures, which they say are distorted by the inclusion of books imported in minimal quantities from foreign publishers for distribution in the UK, but even if these titles are ignored, the numbers are huge.) The reading public has also increased, of course, partly as a result of higher educational standards, partly because people have more leisure, and partly because paperbacks have made books far more acceptable than they used to be (many people still think of bookshops as elitist and would not think of going into one, whereas no-one could be snooty about the paperbacks in the newsagent's racks), and there is therefore an increased demand. But one of the main causes of the ever-rising total of new books is that publishers live in a totally different economic world from that which existed between the Wars. Many years ago, sweated labour in the printing and binding trade made it possible to make a profit with small numbers of even comparatively unsuccessful books, and a large profit on bestsellers, especially at a time when Britannia not only ruled the waves, which was important in terms of overseas markets, but sat firmly on inflation. Overheads were low, and so was taxation. Moreover, it was economically viable to print only a small quantity of sheets of a book, and to bind only part of that print run (further small quantities could be bound quickly and cheaply), and if a small reprint were needed, it could be obtained almost overnight; if the print quantity failed to sell out, the publisher had the 'safety net' of being able to produce a 'cheap edition', which was simply the original edition with a reduced price, and to go on reducing the price, but still making a profit, until the edition was sold out. Nowadays, manufacturing costs have risen substantially, because workers are better paid (which affects also the cost of basic materials), part production (binding only some of the printed sheets) is no longer economically viable, and the market for cheap editions has been replaced by paperbacks. Moreover, despite the public belief that books are very expensive, in fact retail prices have never rocketed sufficiently to keep pace with the financial pressures on the publishing business or even with inflation. All these factors have reduced the publisher's ability to make money on a small output, and the readiest answer to the problem has been to publish more in the hope that, although less profit is made on each title, greater volume will maintain the firm's overall results. (It is this philosophy, incidentally, which has regrettably turned books into 'product', and which has often led to the sometimes stifling rule of the accountants.) The more books that are published, the more occasions there are for incompetence.

At the risk of labelling myself as an old, politically incorrect grouch (which I undoubtedly am), who believes that the country is going to the dogs (which it probably is), I will fearlessly express the view that, despite better education for all, yet another reason for inefficiency is that the general standard of work produced by junior staff in offices these days is often very much lower than it used to be before the Second World War. Many people seem more concerned about job definitions and whether or not they get luncheon vouchers, than with the quality of their work. They don't care. And those who do care, especially in the higher ranks, are frequently so overburdened that to their despair they cannot give the attention to detail that they would like. This is where the inefficiency comes from, this is why computers are fed with inaccurate information, this is where the muddle is swept under the carpet – and this is where the sack may bring a charge of wrongful dismissal. And of course, it is all a situation which lends itself admirably to the Peter Principle of eventual promotion beyond the level of the employee's capacity.

Before you start thinking that I am rubbishing all publishers, let me say that there are some who run their businesses with great care and attention to detail, and who can very, very rarely be accused of inefficiency. If they can do it, why can't they all? So, whatever the cause of a publisher's incompetence may be, if you do encounter it you should certainly complain. But do make sure that it really is incompetence and that it really is the publisher's fault – the absence of your book from bookshops, for instance, to take a very common cause of complaint, may not be due to the publisher's failure, whatever the booksellers say (see p.185).

Sometimes a breakdown in author/publisher relationships can lead to a serious dispute. If this happens in your case, you should seek expert advice at an early stage, and it is available, if you are a member, from the Society of Authors or the Writers' Guild.

Authors and Editors
So far in this chapter, I have referred almost always to the author/publisher relationship, but in most cases it is more likely to be specifically an editor with whom the author has contact. A publisher's editor is not merely someone who purchases books from authors and then passes them on to be turned into printed books, but is in most cases truly an editor, in the sense of becoming involved in the actual writing of the book, perhaps as a critic who asks the author to make changes, perhaps even rewriting part of it him/herself. Not many authors manage to produce a perfect book,

and a good partnership between author and editor will often result in a very worthwhile improvement.

Few authors are capable of viewing their own books dispassionately, and even wives or husbands, whom so many writers credit in their acknowledgements as being their most helpfully severe critics, are often themselves too close to the work in question to see it plainly. A good editor is distant enough to have a clearer view, but at the same time is sufficiently in tune with the author's intentions to be sympathetic – and constructive – in making criticisms and suggestions for change. During the whole of my publishing career, I tried to follow the principle that in such matters the author's decision would be final – it was the author's book, not mine, and unless my criticisms were so fundamental that I felt I could not publish the book unless the changes I wanted were made, I would give way. But this bargain on my part was contingent on the author's willingness to listen carefully to my comments, to discuss them with me, and to be prepared to admit that I might possibly occasionally be right. I tried always to make it clear to the author that I was not interested in making alterations simply to justify my own existence or to boost my ego so that I could boast afterwards that the book was partly my work, but simply to make it a better book.

Some editors adopt a much more dictatorial approach, and many authors complain of their arrogance. It is very difficult to deal with this kind of high-handedness, especially when it comes from someone covering up uncertainties by an aggressive insistence on being right. Unless you can swallow this, your only course is to go over the editor's head to the editorial director, in the hope of getting a more sympathetic hearing. If that fails, or is impossible because the arrogant editor is in fact the highest authority in the company, then you have to choose between withdrawing your book and repaying any moneys you have received on account of it, or of letting it go through in a form which you dislike, and to do that will probably sour your whole relationship with the firm and make you dissatisfied with every aspect of the publication. There is not a great deal to be gained by having an ongoing angry relationship with your publisher, and it is much better to make a clean break. But of course it is easy to say that, and not necessarily easy to find another home for the book. And that thought brings me back to the plea that you should listen carefully to the editor's comments, and discuss them without heat. You may be able to persuade the editor to back down, or you may find that some of the suggestions are not as unpalatable as you first thought. Even arrogant editors are right sometimes. And if you stay with your publisher despite the disagreements, it may be possible to save yourself some of the trouble on your next book by discussing the project in much greater detail with the editor before you begin to write.

American editors tend to be far more insistent on working on an author's typescript than most of their British counterparts, and some authors find their editing very disturbing. It is difficult to know what to advise without going into specific cases, but in general the usual rules apply: plead your case as strongly as you can, having first considered seriously whether the editor might possibly be right, and if you get nowhere, then decide whether you want to stand on your dignity and cancel the contract, or whether you will hate the American edition of your book, but love the figures on the cheque.

It is worth repeating that the intentions of editors are always to improve the book. Nevertheless, they do have more than one duty. Whose interests come first with them – those of the author, of the editor, or of the firm? It's a difficult question to answer in black and white terms. Publishers understand very well that they are middlemen, dependent for their livelihood on authors, and in general they try to be sympathetic to writers and their work and problems. But if there is a conflict between their duty to an individual author and to themselves and their firm, they will naturally opt for the latter, and it would be foolish to pretend otherwise.

Of course, no alterations of any kind should be made to a book without the author's consent. Should you find at proof stage that your book has been altered, and that is the first you know of it, you are entitled to object most strongly. Even if the book is better for the alterations, you can accept the changes with gratitude, but still protest firmly that you should have been consulted. There is a vital principle here – that the author's work must not be altered without his/her consent – and all publishing agreements should carry a provision similar to that in Clause 6(c) of the Minimum Terms Agreement (see p.123). Most good publishers respect this principle, although they may feel that it should not be necessary to check with the author such minor changes as correction of typing errors, spelling and punctuation, or alterations made to bring the typescript into line with the publisher's house style. They may also correct obvious mistakes which appear to be unintentional on the author's part and which are probably due simply to a lapse of memory. But any of the minor alterations mentioned can infuriate the author, and it is my belief that the publisher should discuss the matter before any copy-editing of the typescript is done, and should come to some agreement about the extent to which the author wishes to be consulted about changes. If your publisher does not raise the matter with you, ask about it.

A question that arises frequently is the stage at which an author and editor should work together on a book. If you have sent in a completed typescript, there is obviously no problem, but if you are an established author on the list or have been commissioned, it is a very good idea to discuss the book as fully as possible with the editor before you begin to write, and perhaps to send in the early pages as you write them. Some authors hate to talk about their books in advance, and cannot bear to let anyone read a word of the book until it is finished, but if you can let your editor see the first few chapters, it may save a lot of grief at a later stage, because she/he may be able to point out where, if at all, you are going wrong, or how you might improve the book. Some editorial comments of this kind may irritate you because you are already aware of the problems and intend to do something about them at a later stage in the writing, but you will simply have to put up with that. One procedure to avoid is sending your book in chapter by chapter for criticism; since your editor will have read dozens of books between your submission of one chapter and the next, he/she will probably need, in order to remember the details, to re-read the first chapter when the second come in, and so on, which will be both unnecessarily time-consuming and boring.

If it is what you want, your editor will probably be willing to be adviser, sounding-board, critic, comforter, shoulder-to-weep-on, inspirer and friend, despite the fact that the most kind-hearted, considerate, undemanding human beings do sometimes undergo a transformation when they become authors – not necessarily in their everyday lives, but in anything which concerns their book – turning into egotistical, thoughtless, ruthless monsters – often pleasant monsters, for most of the time, but monsters nevertheless. Publishers can be just the same, of course – it's part of the human condition.

If you become friendly with your editor, beware – and the closer the relationship, the more need there is to take care – that you do not become the kind of monster who demands too much. Editors do have a life of their own to lead, and when they are out of the office may be very glad to get away from books (even yours) for a while. So phone the office rather than the editor's home if you want to talk business. And a word of thanks now and then will be much appreciated.

It always seems to me a pity when authors who live a long way away from their publishers never get to meet their editors. A face-to-face encounter is so much more helpful in establishing a relationship than any amount of telephone calls and letters. The cost of travel may be prohibitive for some authors to visit their publishers even once (although of course the expense can be claimed against tax), but if you have any opportunity to visit the city or town where your publisher works, do make a point of calling, writing first to make an appointment.

Editorial Titles

Some editors are called simply 'editors', while others have elaborate titles which may be very confusing. The titles used and the responsibilities of their bearers differ from company to company. There are two main editorial functions: one is the acquisition of new books, and the other the checking and preparation of authors' typescripts before they are sent to the printer. The functions may overlap, or both may be performed by the same person. In general, the former have titles such as 'Acquiring Editor' or 'Commissioning Editor' or 'Sponsoring Editor', although some may use a title referring to the section of the list which they handle, such as 'Science Editor' or 'Children's Books Editor'. One publishing house refers to 'Structural Editors', meaning that they not only acquire books, but work with the authors on any necessary major changes. Those whose functions lie in the second group are most often called 'Copy Editor', but 'House Editor' and 'Line Editor', although sometimes descriptive of very slightly different functions, come to much the same thing.

Many editorial titles are used only within the publishing house, and as far as the outside world, including the author, is concerned, the designation will often be restricted to 'Editorial Director', 'Senior Editor', 'Managing Editor' (if used accurately this title should suggest that its bearer is the person who allocates editorial work, whether acquisitional or copy-editing, among the personnel in the editorial department) or plain 'Editor'. If the title and the responsibilities of the person with whom you are dealing are not clear to you, then it is worth asking. It is always easier to work with people if you know what they do and do not do. Moreover, your editor will probably enjoy explaining it all to you – most of us respond readily when someone shows an interest in the details of our work.

Which Editor?

How do certain editors get involved with this or that book and its author? If the book is clearly of considerable importance, coming from an established author or from an agent, the editor who works on it will almost certainly be one of some seniority and experience. In a general publishing house most editors have certain special interests, so if your book falls into a specialist category, it will go to the editor responsible for that part of the list. Other books or authors may have been 'discovered' by an editor, who will probably continue to deal with the books concerned, and with subsequent work from those authors.

For a new author of a non-specialist book the process is often somewhat haphazard. Many books may be allocated at an editorial meeting pretty arbitrarily: 'This looks like an easy one – you'd better take it Mr Junior'; 'Who wants to read this book on prostitution in Edwardian London? It seems to be very popular in approach, so we won't send it out for an expert reading until we've looked at it in house. Who wants it? No one? Then you'd better glance at it, Ms Senior – you've got less of a load this week than the rest of us.' Naturally, this process results sometimes in books being handled by rather unsuitable editors, but the editorial director of the firm will usually keep an eye on things and give the book to someone else if it is obvious that the original editor is not the right one for the job.

Can editors judge books which are not to their personal tastes or are on subjects in which they are not expert? Good editors can at least recognize the merits or failings of such books. They cannot always eliminate their personal feelings, but they try to be representative of the average reader and to judge by the standards of the genre. They are, after all, professionals, doing a job, and not reading simply for pleasure. So you may well find someone whose literary idols are of the calibre of, say, Proust, working happily and successfully as an editor of pulp fiction (well, perhaps that is an exaggeration, but the principle holds good). As for expertise, as I have said elsewhere, most publishers use expert outside readers to check the accuracy and validity of specialist books, but the experienced editor will at least be able to judge something of the quality of the book and its likely appeal to the public, and some editors, in the course of working on a number of such books, become, if not experts, at least very knowledgeable on the subject.

The Author's Loyalty to the Publisher

Should you stay with one publisher all the time? It may be of course that you are prolific and/or versatile, in which case you may need more than one publisher. Too many new books by one author appearing on the same publisher's list can, unless you are particularly well-known, sometimes hamper each other's sales. Such authors sometimes use pseudonyms and often have a number of publishers. In the same way, if you write on a variety of subjects, you may need to be published by different houses specializing in your different kinds of book. It will be as well to keep your first publisher ('Publisher A') informed of your other plans, and indeed you may wish to make it clear that you will continue to give that firm first offer of all the books in the genre with which it first began to publish you, whereas your books of a different kind will be offered to Publisher B, and a third variety to Publisher C. If A, B and C all know where they stand in relation to you and your work, there should be no cause for dissension.

For the average author, however, unless you are very dissatisfied with your publisher, and if that company wishes to go on publishing your books and you continue to write the kind of thing which is suited to its list, then undoubtedly you should stay where you are. Publishers sometimes feel that many authors show far too little loyalty. The publisher may have brought out the author's first few books, including perhaps work which was not of the finest, gradually building up the author's reputation, and then he/she produces an important book which finally establishes his/her success and goes off to another publisher who reaps the benefit of the first publisher's work and faith. Usually, the author is wooed and flattered by the second publisher, who offers not only a larger advance, but promises more publicity and promotion, full consultation, etc. Beware of such offers. Many an author has moved to a different firm only to find that the change was not really worthwhile. On the other hand, if for some reason you are unhappy with your present publisher and you get a good offer from elsewhere, of course it is right to move, but I think it is fair first to discuss the matter with your current publisher, presenting your reasons for discontent quite frankly and offering the opportunity for the firm to put right whatever it is that you are complaining about. If the publisher cannot solve the problems, then there will probably not be much resistance to your leaving, for no publisher can work to the best advantage with an unhappy author. But again, you may find that you have exactly the same complaints about your new publisher – or that the problems have become even worse. This certainly happens with some authors who change publishers with alarming regularity, and one may wonder whether the reasons for their dissatisfaction lie more with themselves than with the publishers. Of course, no publisher is perfect, but no author is perfect, either.

When Your Publisher Leaves You
It is much more shattering when it happens the other way round, as it were. Here you are, having had a dozen books published by the same house, and suddenly they turn around and say that they do not want to go ahead with your new book, which they may even admit is just as good as its predecessors. The only explanation you get is that the market for your kind of book has declined to a point where it is no longer economic to publish your work. Sorry, and all that. The literary agent, George Greenfield, revealed something which your publisher may be reluctant to tell you (partly because it may reflect on the firm's abilities, and partly because it is not very flattering to you) when he suggested in his memoirs, *Scribblers for Bread*, that an author who has published six novels without steadily increasing sales is unlikely to achieve better results with subsequent books, so that the publisher will probably not wish to continue to bring out that author's book. Of course it does not always apply, but if it fits your case, then your only hope is to find another publisher who has perhaps a more vigorous sales approach, or lower overheads, or some other quality or set of circumstances which will allow the firm to take you on in the belief that it will do better for you than your previous publisher. But it is going to be quite difficult to find such a publisher, because all the optimism and enthusiasm for your work could wither away once the details of your past publishing history are revealed. Not a very hopeful outlook. Your other alternative is to write a much better book – a suggestion which may not be a lot of help, I'm afraid. Another idea, which might be more rewarding, is to change to a different genre, and perhaps adopt a pseudonym into the bargain. It would mean beginning your career as an author all over again, as

it were, but it might make success attainable for you.

Do study the market. It could be that the reason why your publisher has declined your new book is simply that it is of a kind which has gone out of fashion. No doubt the publisher will tell you if this is so, but it is also something that you can and should find out for yourself by checking in bookshops and libraries, and studying the *Bookseller*, and indeed by talking to your publisher before you embark on a new book. Reading can also be recommended – all writers should read voraciously, because you can learn more about writing from other people's successes and failures than by any other method – and if you read a fair amount of contemporary writing, it will help to keep you abreast of the trends and styles which are currently wanted.

The Publisher's Staff

In writing of author/publisher relationships, I have emphasized the role of the editor, who is likely to be the person in your publishing house with whom you deal most of the time. But it is as well to meet others who will be working on your book if you can – among them I would single out the sales director, the marketing director, whoever is in charge of publicity and promotion, the production manager, the person who prepares the royalty statements, the subsidiary rights manager, and the sales representative who covers the area where you live. It does no harm either to make contact with the managing director. Indeed, the more people in your publishing house that you know, the better, and you should feel free to contact any of them direct if you have a query or complaint which falls within their sphere. Since, however, your editor is your prime colleague, it is worth making a point of keeping him/her informed about any dealings you may have with other members of the staff. It saves the wires from getting crossed.

8

Complaints and Questions

The publisher has lost my material
Given the fact that several hundred typescripts flow in and out of most publishers' offices every year, it is surprising that they do not get lost more often, especially since publishing tends to be physically a rather untidy business. If the typescript has been lost, not too much harm will have been done, although it may be very inconvenient, provided you still have a copy; a publisher with any sense of responsibility will pay for it to be replaced or at least contribute part of the cost, despite the fact that the form letter or card acknowledging receipt of your book probably states somewhere that the firm accepts no liability for the loss or damage of your material while in its possession. If you have a word processor, your work should still be on disc and it is an easy enough matter to run off another copy (although I still think the publisher might pay both for the paper and something for the inconvenience caused). The loss or damage of other materials, such as illustrations, transparencies, or perhaps goods of some value which are to be photographed in order to illustrate the book, is a much more serious matter, since they may be extremely costly or impossible to replace. The best solution is to take out an insurance against loss or damage. Circumstances will probably differ in each case, but broadly speaking, if you are sending the material to the publisher unsolicited, the responsibility for insuring valuables is yours, but if the publisher has asked for them, the firm may be willing to pay the premium, but should in any case, in my view, be prepared at least to share in the cost. It would be wise to discuss the matter in advance if possible, leaving the publisher fully aware of what sum

could be considered reasonable compensation in the event of loss or damage.

My book has been rejected for political reasons

If you write a book which takes a political position, or attacks or defends certain views, the book may be rejected solely because of this aspect of the contents rather than because of any lack of quality. Some naïve authors believe that publishers have no right to turn down such a book and that it is their duty to publish any book which is adequately written and saleable. Not true. Publishers still, fortunately, have freedom of personal choice. If you receive such a rejection it suggests that you have not done your market research. Choose another publisher whose existing list demonstrates that the firm's policy is likely to be in accord with the views propounded in the book.

I put up an idea to a publisher who rejected it and then immediately commissioned another author to write a book on the very same subject

Are you absolutely certain that the publisher pinched your idea? It seems to be a curious fact that a number of people often have exactly the same idea at about the same time, and it is possible that the publisher had already commissioned the book in question before your suggestion arrived – in other words, the rival book got in first.

Since ideas are not copyright, authors are often afraid that, if they suggest a project to a publisher, or if they send in a completed typescript, it will be unscrupulously snaffled. The publisher Stanley Unwin commented on this fact, saying: 'An illusion seldom entertained by competent authors is that the publisher's readers and others are waiting to plagiarise their work. I think it may be said that the more worthless the MS, the greater the fear of plagiarism.' Publishers in general do not steal ideas. However, it is possible that some time after rejecting a submission an editor may dredge the idea up from his/her subconscious, believing it to be completely original. Active editors conceive a large number of books and get their inspiration from hundreds of different sources.

If you can prove your point to be true, then you undoubtedly have a case against the publisher, but you will have to have watertight evidence – dates and correspondence relating to your submission of your material and its rejection, and similar evidence of the publisher's dealing with the other author.

My hardcover publishers also control a paperback company and other concerns which utilize other subsidiary rights. They want me to give them all those rights, but wouldn't it be better for me if the competition had an opportunity to bid for them?

Many authors would think you lucky to have this automatic interest in the subsidiary rights of your book. If you are really unhappy about it, you should take your book elsewhere – there are still several publishers who do not have any direct links with the users of subsidiary rights. In today's difficult conditions, however, you should probably accept the offer with gratitude, especially since your publishers should be willing to give you a full royalty on the paperback edition, whereas if you go to an independent hardcover house you will be expected to share the sums which come from the paperback publisher.

If your main worry is that you might expect a much larger advance to be paid if the book were sent out to all the paperback houses for them to make their bids, you might try asking the publishers whether they would accept a 'topping right' arrangement, which would mean that they had to submit the subsidiary rights to other concerns, but would have the right to buy them themselves by topping, or improving on, the best bids they received. This ploy can usually be used, however, only by authors who are in the bestseller class and therefore have the clout to make publishers do things they don't really want to do.

My contract bears no resemblance to the Minimum Terms Agreement

Unless your book is in one of the categories specifically excluded (see p.119), the contract should not be all that different from the MTA, even if the publisher is one of the diehards who has refused to accept its terms. If you have not yet signed the contract, there is time to alter it, and you should be able to get at least a few improvements made. Your best course is to join the Society of Authors or the Writers' Guild, either of which organizations will tell you what changes are those for which you should fight hard, and give you good advice about how to put your arguments to the publisher.

My publishers have offered an absurdly low advance for my book
I understand how little payment it may seem in relation to the amount of work you did to produce the book, but the publishers are probably being realistic rather than mean. Unearned advances are a major factor in driving publishers towards bankruptcy. You might get a better advance elsewhere. On the other hand, your publishers might spend the money they save on better promotion of your book, because it's not just a matter of saving money, but of spending wisely. On the other hand again, they might not.

I suspect that you are also worried that because the advance is low, the publisher won't put any effort into the book. Certainly, more attention will be given to the books on the list on which a fortune has already been spent and which will have really large print quantities, but publishers are actually just as eager to sell the books like yours which have more modest costs and potential sales. Ask the publishers for a larger advance, and you may get a bit more. If you don't, console yourself with the thought that you will start getting royalty moneys sooner.

My publisher has put an unrealistic delivery date in my contract
Alter it, then – telling the publisher that you are doing so, and why. Most publishers will be reasonable about such matters, unless your book is to be published to coincide with some event – an anniversary, for example – in which case you may just have to meet the required delivery date, or give up the whole idea of writing the book. Whatever the problem, discuss it with the publisher, and together you may find a way round it.

My publisher wants to break my contract
The fundamental points in a publishing contract are that the author has written or agrees to write a book and the publisher undertakes to publish it. There are many side issues which may give rise to breach of contract by either party, but they are insignificant in comparison with a decision by the publisher not to proceed with the publication of the author's book.

The publisher may have many possible reasons for such a decision. Sometimes it results from recognizable failings on the part of the author: perhaps the completed work differs substantially from the synopsis on which it was commissioned, or is much shorter or longer than the extent specified, or the author has been so tardy in delivering it that the market for it no longer exists, or the book is

clearly libellous. The publisher can hardly be blamed in such circumstances. In any case, all is not necessarily lost, since the author may
be able to avert disaster by doing extra work on the book.

The agreement may be rather more arbitrarily rescinded on the
basis of failings, either real or imaginary, on the author's part, if
there is an 'acceptance' clause in the contract (see p.133), and it is
often very difficult to argue in such cases, since the publisher's
personal taste and views are involved.

Contracts are sometimes broken because the editor who bought
the book has left the firm, and there is no longer anyone working
there to care about the book. Everyone in a publishing firm should
care about the book. Everyone in a publishing firm should care
about all the books on the list, of course, but in practice some books
get published because a single person is enthusiastic about them,
and if that person leaves, those who take over may be indifferent
or even hostile to those books. 'I always thought we were crazy to
buy that,' the new editor may say. 'We only took it on because So-
and-so was madly enthusiastic about it and bullied everyone else
into believing in it.' Of course, this kind of thing does not affect all
the books on the list of an editor who leaves the firm, many of
which will have wide support from the rest of the staff, and tends to
happen only with books which would be borderline prospects in
any publishing house. In the United States editors seem to move
very frequently from one publishing concern to another, but they
often take their authors with them, so this question does not arise
on the other side of the Atlantic to the same extent.

Publishing is a business which requires a considerable amount of
capital investment; consequently it always tends to have cash-flow
problems and to suffer when interest rates are high. A recession
during the 1980s had a major effect upon British publishers: a
number went out of business, and almost all those who survived did
so by reducing, as far as they could, their output of those contracted
books which they considered to be the more doubtful propositions
in terms of profitability. The cancellation of contracts became
commonplace, even for authors who had been published for many
years with apparent success. Those publishing houses which came
through that period of crisis did so in most cases in a leaner,
tougher condition, and seemed in a better state to withstand any
future difficulties of the kind. However, even in the slightly calmer
waters through which they sailed in the 1990s, publishing firms
continued to founder. Publishing is a risky business. There is usually

a large publishing house, or a conglomerate, eager to gobble up failed businesses, but not all such giants are willing to take over all the firm's contracts. Moreover, there may be redundancies in the editorial department, with the result that you may lose your book's champion. So contract cancellation is always a possibility, for one reason or another – and not a particularly remote one, either.

What is the author's course of action when it happens? The first thing is to ask whether anything can be done to alter the publisher's decision, such as cutting the book to make it more economic, or making other changes. It is worth asking, but the publisher's reply is likely to be a firm rejection of all salvaging recipes, since any such possibilities have already been considered and discarded.

You are now left with two alternatives. You can insist, possibly with the threat of legal action, that the publisher comply with the terms of the contract and publish the book. In general, this is not a course to be recommended. It is extremely difficult, if not impossible, to force publishers to publish a given book, and if they cannot finally escape from doing so, they will almost certainly print a minimum quantity and make only sufficient effort at selling it to recoup their costs. The author/publisher relationship will be permanently soured. Few authors who force their publishers to bring out a book can rejoice in the results.

The second alternative is to be compensated by the publisher. Some publishers may try to persuade you that their liability should be limited to any part of the advance already paid, but this is hardly fair, and you should demand at least the balance of the advance and preferably a total sum (including any advance already paid) equal to the amount that the book might have been expected to earn for you at least on the first printing. It helps if your contract specified the number of copies which the publisher intended to print, since that will give a good indication of what the sales might have been. Each case is different, and it is impossible to lay down any hard and fast rules about the amount of compensatory payment which is fair, but if you have no agent, you should seek professional advice, either from the Society of Authors or the Writers' Guild, if you are a member, or from a good solicitor.

In any case, as well as compensation, or even if the fault lies with you and you are not entitled to any money (and indeed may have to pay back sums which you have already received), you should obtain from the publisher an official letter confirming that all rights in the book in question have reverted to you and that the publisher has no further claim on you whatsoever. You should also ensure that all material supplied by you to the publisher is returned. You are then free to place the book with another house if you can. Some publishers, when paying compensation, ask that the sums paid shall be returned if the book is placed elsewhere, but you should resist any such suggestion (see p.136).

In extreme cases – if, for instance, the firm is already bankrupt – you may not get any compensation, but you should still make a claim, and also be sure that you get your rights back. Once you receive notification that the firm is going into liquidation, you should write to the receiver or administrator and demand that rights should revert to you forthwith; if you don't do this, you may find that the receiver is treating your rights as assets and may sell them off in a way which would be highly unsatisfactory from your point of view.

You may feel in all these situations that you are in the apparently unhappy position of a David taking on Goliath – or even several Goliaths. There you are – one lone author, with little of the essential background knowledge, and possibly without the means to pay for legal advice – facing a large company and all its resources, and you may be dealing with high-powered executives whom you don't know, rather than with your friendly editor. Don't be intimidated. Those executives know that, unless you are the one who is at fault, that they are in fact in a weak position, and they are probably almost as unhappy about it as you are. Be firm, be tough, stand on your rights.

One other circumstance might be mentioned: the occasion when your publisher declines to publish your book on the grounds that it 'will do your reputation no good', but, on the assumption that it will be up to your usual standard, wishes to publish your next book. To put the book on one side may mean that you have lost the work of a year or more, and you have the choice of listening to what is said and allowing yourself to be convinced, or of parting company with that publishing house and taking the book to another. Before you choose the latter course, you will have to decide whether your relationship with your present publisher is worth preserving, despite the rejection, and that may depend not only on the way you have been treated in the past, but also on whether you believe that the verdict on this present book could possibly be right. It would be in order to ask to see the reports on it, and if you are not fully convinced, perhaps to ask that the book should be sent to another reader, possibly without your name on the typescript, in order to get one more independent judgement, although of course such a report would have to be very favourable to outweigh the previous adverse comments.

My publisher wants to reduce my royalties
As an alternative to cancelling the contract, some publishers ask authors to take a lower royalty or a smaller share of subsidiary rights than those specified in the contract. (This complaint does not, of course, refer to the clause in many agreements which says that the royalty payable on small reprints 'shall be at the minimum rate', but to an overall re-writing of the contract to the author's detriment.) The author in this situation is facing a nasty dilemma: refusal to accept the lower rates may result in the publisher cancelling the agreement altogether; acceptance means lower earnings and the setting of an unhappy precedent not only for the author's future dealings with that publisher, but for other authors and their publishers too. Publishers are often quite adept at using the ploy, 'Ms Scribble and Mr Copperplate have already agreed to similar terms,' to make you feel that you are being unreasonable if you demur.

The only answer is to find out all you can about the circumstances, including if possible details of the publisher's costings and expected profit, and then to make a judgement. If you insist on a full royalty, will the publisher really either cancel the contract or lose sales because the book's retail price is too high? And supposing you agree to reduce your earnings, can you be sure that the publisher is also suffering to some extent? What effect will it have on your future dealings with that firm? What are your chances of selling the book to another publisher? When you have considered all the factors, you can make your mind up. If you decide to accept lower rates, at least make sure that you have it in writing that your agreement to the revised terms is not to be taken as a precedent.

Why are royalties so low? I have been told that manufacturing costs amount to about 20% of the retail price, the bookseller gets an average of 45%, and the publisher expects to take a gross profit of 25%. Why should the author be satisfied with a mere 10%?
I understand your point of view (the figures you give, incidentally, are pretty rough and ready, but let's accept them for the sake of

argument). Now, if the author's royalty is to be increased (and I assume you are talking of at least doubling it), where is the extra money coming from? The manufacturing cost is a constant – books with long print runs may be cheaper, but short-run books are more expensive, so it averages out. Booksellers will not take less than the average 45% discount, which they already say is insufficient for their survival, let alone prosperity. Out of their 25%, publishers have to pay their overheads, which involves the salaries of their staffs (a major proportion), publicity and promotion, rent, rates, heating, lighting, telephone, postage, and so on, not to mention the fact that the Treasury will be taking its share in the form of taxes; the publisher also expects to make a net profit (and why not?). So, I repeat, where is the extra money to come from? Let me ask another question: who pays the author's royalties? Answer: the publisher. Wrong. The publisher merely passes on a share of the money paid by a member of the public who buys the author's book. And it is that member of the public who will have to find the money to pay higher royalties. What is more, if the royalty is to be increased from 10% to, say, 20%, but leaving the manufacturing price and the publisher's profit at the same cash figures, that doesn't mean an increase in the retail price of the book of only 10%, but (because the bookseller's cut is based on the retail price) an increase of about 25%, which is something that the book's purchaser might not be willing to stand.

Some authors do, of course, get a basic royalty of more than 10%. They are usually the big names, whose books can be guaranteed to sell in very large quantities. The manufacturing price of such long-run books is lower as a percentage of the retail price and the publisher will also be prepared to take a smaller percentage (because the actual return in cash terms is satisfactorily large), so the higher royalty can be paid without passing the cost on to the book-buying public. Even if you are not in the bestseller class, if your book is reasonably successful you will probably move from the basic 10% to a higher royalty rate when your sales have reached a level specified in your agreement, and the rate will probably jump again when you have passed a second target figure.

One cost which I did not include in the publisher's overheads is that of unearned advances. You might be surprised to learn how many books do not earn anything near as much as the publisher paid out in the form of an advance. One publisher reports that this occurs so frequently that, if you include those unearned sums, he is paying authors what amounts to an average 17½% royalty. You may think that this simply indicates that he is not very good at working out what the advances should be, but it isn't as simple as that. So why does he so often pay a larger advance than he should? Because he is under pressure from agents and authors, because he always has competitors who may be even rasher than he is in calculating the size of an advance, because he is sometimes over-optimistic, because sales are always unpredictable. I do not know of any publishing firm which never pays too large an advance to any of its authors, and many publishers would say that unearned advances are the rule rather than the exception. It's a crazy business.

My editor has left and I don't know anyone at my publisher's now
When an editor, or any other member of the publisher's staff, leaves the firm, that person's work is naturally passed over to a successor, or sometimes shared out between a number of people. Whoever has taken over responsibility for you and your book should write to you so that you know who you are dealing with, and should perhaps suggest a meeting so that you can become acquainted. Sometimes, however, this is not done – perhaps because your new editor is so overburdened with the additional responsibilities that, even with the best of intentions, there seems to be no time to stop and write, or perhaps because publishers are human and, as with any other group of men and women, include some who are lazy or inefficient or discourteous, or all three.

If after a while you have heard nothing except that your former editor has departed, write to the head of the company, and ask to be put in touch with your new editor. You shouldn't have to do this, but it's better than just sitting at home waiting for a word which may never come. Then, when you have written or spoken on the phone, if your new editor makes no suggestion of a meeting, propose it yourself.

It may happen that when you meet your new editor, you don't get on very well together – we all meet people from time to time to whom we are not sympathetic. In this case I suggest that you write a tactful letter to the editor's superior in the publishing house, asking if there is anyone else that you could deal with. If you make it clear that you accept that there may be faults on both sides, no one's feeling will be badly hurt, and a change may be possible. Of course, your new contact may now be the only editor in the firm, or perhaps is also the managing director. Your only solution then is to grin and bear it, or to find another publisher.

My editor, who doesn't seem to understand my book, has asked me to make editorial changes to it of which I strongly disapprove
You obviously need to have a cards-on-the-table talk with your editor. When you do so, remember that editors are entitled to their opinions and that their aim is to enhance the chances of success for the books they deal with. Listen carefully to what is said, and be ready to concede any valid points. At the same time, the editor must remember that it is *your* book, and as its creator you are entitled to feel very strongly about how it should or should not appear. If at the end of the talk, you have got nowhere, and the editor is still asking for these radical changes, you can either refuse to make the changes, or you can carry them out. If you choose the latter course, the argument is over. If you refuse to make changes you may find that the editor collapses and accepts the book the way you want it to be; you must also be prepared, however, for a refusal to publish the book as it stands. And the next stage after that sounds to me like a nasty law case.

My publisher has made editorial changes to my book without asking me
I hope you are referring to what might be termed fairly minor alterations – correction of typing errors, punctuation and spelling, and amendments to bring the text in line with the publisher's house style. Publishers regularly make such changes in authors' typescripts before they are sent to the printer, and since extraordinarily large numbers of authors cannot spell, know little about punctuation, are frequently inconsistent and often inaccurate, the service that copy editors provide in these respects is something to be grateful for. Even so, you should be consulted about even the most minor of alterations. If you happen to be meticulous in such matters and indeed feel strongly about your commas and full stops, or if you are deliberately breaking the rules for effect, it is as well to discuss the matter at an early stage with your editor, and to put a note at the front of the typescript, addressed to both copy editor and printer, asking them to respect your intentions and not to alter your work.

If the editorial changes go beyond the scope of normal copy editing, and particularly if the basic structure or emphasis or spirit of the book has been seriously tampered with, or if you strongly disapprove of even the minor changes, you should protest in the strongest possible terms, and you will be within your rights to insist on the reinstatement of your original version, even at proof stage. Nothing should be done to your typescript without your consent.

My editor is insisting that I change my work so that it is politically correct

Like many things which originate in the United States, political correctness, when taken to extremes, can often be manifestly absurd. However, the basic idea is now widely accepted, and as long as it does not go too far, you probably have to fall in line, as I have tried to do in this book. It is perhaps particularly necessary to avoid the old practice of using masculine pronouns to refer to both men and women when one is writing about a business like publishing, in which women nowadays play a very important part. The problem is that 'he or she', 'him or her', and the other pairs of alternatives are clumsy constructions, and can become quite irritating if they have to be repeated frequently. The difficulty can often be overcome by using plurals ('the publishers' rather than 'the publisher', which then allows you to use 'they', 'them'. 'their', etc), and in other cases the masculine or feminine pronouns can be avoided altogether by a fairly simple re-arrangement of the wording. If you do use the alternatives, it is a matter of personal preference whether to use the form 'he or she' or 'he/she'. You should also consider 'she or he' or 'she/he'.

I get no editorial help

It has long been said that British editors are over-reluctant to help their authors to improve their books (or are perhaps incapable of doing so), whereas American editors go to the other extreme and often virtually rewrite books which had no need of such treatment. If your editor does not help you, it may be simply that she/he does not see anything wrong with the book (which means either that the book is perfect as it stands or that the editor isn't a very good one), or knows that something is wrong but cannot put a finger on what it is, or cannot clarify the problem sufficiently for you to under-stand exactly what she/he means; or it may be that the editor expects you, as the author, to have a more dispassionate view of your work than in fact you have, so that if you are told, for instance, that the whole thing needs a bit of cutting, or that such and such a part needs strengthening, you will understand what is meant without needing further details. If that is the problem, you can try asking for a fuller explanation. If you don't get this kind of help, and if you are certain that you really do need substantial assistance with your writing, your only course is probably to change publishers if you can, or perhaps find one of those literary agents who enjoy working with authors on their books.

Of course, one other possible reason why you do not get editorial help is that you have demonstrated in the past that you don't really want it. With some of their authors, especially the more successful ones, editors have to tread very delicately, knowing that the least hint of criticism will be greeted with anger, abuse, hysterics, the sulks, argument, or at the very least will be totally ignored, despite the fact that the author begged for comments and advice.

Can the publisher change the title of my book?

Everyone agrees that the title is extremely important, and the only problem is to recognize what constitutes a good one. We can all pick them out after the event, but not always beforehand. The story has often been told of the publisher Stanley Unwin consulting booksellers about a book which he was going to publish and which had already earned itself some reputation in Europe. Many advised him to change the title, saying that 'expedition' was an old-fashioned word to use for a true adventure story, and that no one would be able to remember or pronounce the second word of the title. He refused to change it. The book was of course *The Kon-Tiki Expedition*.

As a general principle, it should go without saying that a title should not be changed without the author's approval, but in this business the old adage that two heads are better than one is often true, and if a publisher wants to change a book's title, and is prepared to explain sensibly the reasons for doing so, the author should be prepared to be convinced. It is one of those matters about which publishers believe that they have considerably more expertise than authors. They're not always right, but most of the time they probably are.

My proof corrections have not been followed

When your publisher sends you proofs to correct and you mark them up, using all the standard signs, making sure that all your corrections are totally unambiguous, it is very disappointing to find sometimes that in the finished book the corrections have not all

178

been made, or that new errors have occurred. By all means protest to your publisher if this happens, but it is unlikely that anything much can be done about it, at least until the book is reprinted (if it ever is). Why are corrections ignored, and why do new errors appear? It is possible that certain corrections may not have been noticed (perhaps two pages of the proof were turned at once); as for the new errors, they can occur in the process of correcting the original mistake, especially if a considerable rejigging of the words or paragraphs is necessary.

Another cause of complaint is when printing errors are not corrected in a reprint, despite the fact that the author has given the publisher a list of them. What can you do about it? Little, except perhaps to find out beforehand, if you can, when your publisher is going to reprint the book again, and then send the production manager a repeat list of the corrections in good time with a plea to ensure that they are carried out.

My publishers have deducted an enormous sum from my royalties, which they say is the cost of proof corrections, although I didn't make all that many changes

You are quite lucky to have the amount owing deducted from your royalties rather than being asked for an immediate cheque. If a publishing contract contains a clause saying that the author must bear the cost of proof corrections, apart from printer's errors, by the amount by which those costs exceed 10% (or in the MTA 15%) of the cost of composition of the whole book, it sounds very generous. You might think you could alter 10% (or 15%) of the book without incurring any charge, but in fact the cost of carrying out proof corrections is extremely high, and comparatively few changes can soon mount up to 10%, or even 15%, of the original composition cost. Moral: get your typescript to as near a perfect state as you can and don't start improving your book at proof stage unless it is absolutely essential to do so.

If the corrections were needed to take account of changes in the subject matter of your book which had taken place between the completion of the typescript and the arrival of proofs, so that you were engaged in effect in an updating process, the question should have been discussed with your publisher at the earliest possible moment, so that some plan of action and agreement about how the extra costs would be handled could be made.

It is a terrible hassle to get the illustrations for my book, and permission to use them, to say nothing of being extremely expensive. Surely this should be the publisher's responsibility?

It seems to me that in most cases the obtaining of illustrations and of permission to use them should be the author's responsibility rather than the publisher's (and the same applies to quotations from other authors' writings, to the preparation of an index, to any extraneous material which is not your own work, unless perhaps such things were not in your original concept of the book and have been added entirely at the publisher's request). Yes, it is a hassle, but it's part of being an author. You may be able to get some professional advice about these matters from the publishers, but the actual work is down to you.

Regarding the cost of illustrations, the basic MTA suggests that the publisher should be prepared to contribute up to £250 towards the permission fees. You may have to argue to get that much, but you should not have to take responsibility for all the payments. As for textual permissions, index costs and the like, it is always worth discussing the matter with the publisher, who may be prepared in some circumstances to share the expenses. But always resist as firmly as possible if the publisher suggests increasing the advance to cover the extra costs, which means in effect that you will be paying the fees. The advance and any payments by the publisher for permissions should be kept entirely separate. Whatever arrangements are agreed between you and the publisher, the whole matter should be decided before the contract is signed, and the details then incorporated in the agreement or in attached correspondence. See also p.209.

I have masses of good illustrations available for my book, but my publisher refuses to use more than a few

There are three factors which may have come into play in this case. Firstly, it may be a question of simple economics – adding more illustrations means adding to the production costs of the book, which would perhaps result in a higher retail price than the publisher believes the book can stand. Secondly, some of the illustrations may not be suitable for reproduction – a faded old photograph may be all the more interesting because of its condition when you hold it in your hand, but when it is reproduced in a book can look of very poor quality. Thirdly, it may be an editorial decision not to include certain illustrations – the editor may feel that they are far less interesting than you believe them to be, especially, perhaps, if they are family photographs, which will probably mean much more to you than they would to the general public.

The jacket design is a travesty of my book
If the jacket is factually incorrect, you have every reason to protest, and the publishers should listen, although they may not do anything, since final control is in their hands.

The most frequent complaints about jackets concern fiction when the artwork does not follow your descriptions of the characters or the scene portrayed. Good jacket/cover artists understand that they should reflect the contents of the book with a fair degree of accuracy, but many feel that they have a licence to adapt in order to make what they consider a better picture, and this is why, for instance, your blue-eyed blonde heroine may turn up on the jacket looking like a Spanish señorita. Why doesn't the publisher make the artist change the painting? Usually because to do so would seriously delay publication of the book – but that, it seems to many, is a poor excuse. Other problems arise from a practice of some publishers of buying stacks of artwork with no particular book in mind; when a jacket has to be prepared, the art director looks through the available artwork and chooses something which is often no more than vaguely appropriate. It's a poor way of working, and the author is entitled to make a strong protest.

My book has been very badly produced, on poor paper and in small print
Publishers insist that the manner in which they produce books is their responsibility alone. Sometimes, in their efforts to economize and keep the retail price of the book down, they go too far, and the result is a very unattractive volume. It is hard to say whether this will affect sales, unless the book is quite ludicrously unpleasing or is physically difficult to read. Books can be very beautiful objects, and some people collect them as such, but the majority are bought simply to be read, whatever they look like.

My publisher keeps delaying the publication of my book
The most frequent causes of postponement of publication are an unforeseen delay in the manufacturing process – the printer may not have kept to the schedule, the paper for the book was discovered to be faulty, or there has been a strike – or because editorial

work on the book has taken much longer than anticipated. Books are sometimes delayed because the publisher believes that a later publication date will be beneficial to the sales. If the publisher can give you a reasonable explanation of what has caused the delay, then you can only accept it with as good a grace as you can manage, remembering that most publishers are only too eager to get their books out, because it is only then that they can begin to recoup the moneys spent on them. If the delay is not explained to your satisfaction, you have few courses of action open; you may be able to sue for breach of contract, or you can, after protesting, go away to lick your wounds – and that's about all.

My biography of X has been delayed so long by my publisher that another author's biography of the same person has come out first and taken all the attention and sales
A very difficult problem. Delays happen for all sorts of reasons, and some books seem to be jinxed in this respect, while others may go through all the publishing processes remarkably quickly. Perhaps the other publisher knew of your book and speeded publication of the competitive biography in order to pre-empt you. If you become aware of a rival book early enough before publication, you should warn your publisher (who is often surprisingly ignorant about what the competition is doing, publishing often being a very inward-looking business) in the hope that it will be possible to get things moving more quickly with your own book. Occasionally rival publishers will agree to publish books on the same subject at the same time so as to be fair to both, but not everyone agrees that this is a good idea, and many houses will attempt to steal a march if they can. There is not much you can do about it, except to accept the fact that this is a business in which luck or ill-luck plays a tremendous part.

My book has been wrongly categorized by my publisher
It is easy enough for a publisher to put all the fiction on the list together, but few other categories are really distinct – some biographies could be described as 'history', and do you put a book about how to paint watercolours under 'art' or 'crafts' or 'hobbies'? Some books are very difficult indeed to slot into neat categories. It doesn't seem to me to matter very much as far as the publisher's catalogue is concerned. Any good bookseller will be able to work out what a particular book is about and to put it where it will be found

by customers for it. In the past there have been some extraordinary stories about the absurd way that books have been placed in bookshops by ill-educated, ill-trained young assistants – misled by titles, a book like *Wild Swans* could end up in 'ornithology', or *The Golden Bough* in 'gardening'. But I think those days are over, even in the big chain stores – at least, I hope so.

No one will buy copies of my book at the ridiculously high price the publisher has put on it
Well, I hope you're wrong. But publishers don't fix their retail prices arbitrarily, and take into account not only the costs but the size of the market and what they believe it will bear. A really good book, which is authoritative, and especially if it is on a subject which is comparatively unusual, will often be given what seems to be an exceptionally high price. The publisher does this in the belief, usually justified, that those people who are interested in the subject will not care about the cost because so good a book will be essential in their eyes.

My publisher made a great to-do of consulting me about publicity and promotion, but did not follow it up
The probable reason for failing to follow up the author's suggestions is lack of money, but without a written undertaking from the publisher to guarantee that specified publicity will be given to the book, there is nothing much you can do in these circumstances, unless you have the money and the facility to provide your own publicity. If you do decide to do anything like that, tell your publisher first, just to make sure that you do not duplicate efforts.

There is one other point to be made here, and it is an important one, since it can apply to a great many aspects of the author's relationship with the publisher's staff. When an editor, or a publicity manager, or a royalties clerk, or the managing director, or the postperson talks to an author, there is usually a desire to be friendly and to please the writer, and it is therefore very much easier at the time, especially for the inexperienced, to promise the author anything he or she wants rather than possibly having a row by saying 'no'. Without wishing to add to the mistrust which so often unfortunately exists between authors and publishers, I would caution you to take a grain of salt with what your publisher tells you, especially if the person concerned is comparatively junior. If you have doubts, ask for a commitment in writing. Whatever it is may still not be carried out, but you would then have legitimate grounds for complaint and for asking that the situation should be remedied.

My book is not advertised, and of course, since it has not been advertised in them, none of the national papers has reviewed it

As has already been said, few publishers will concede that press advertising actually sells books, and the literary editors of national newspapers would strongly deny that the space devoted to a particular publisher's book is directly related to the amount of money which the firm spends in advertising its wares in that paper. Only a tiny number of books receive reviews in large numbers. Space for noticing new books in newspapers and other media is strictly limited and since many literary editors believe that the most important part of their function is to see that 'important' books (i.e. literary works and books by authors with well-known names) are reviewed, the chances of notices for less obvious candidates, especially for popular fiction, are poor. However, this is mainly true of the national press. Provincial and local papers are often more ready to put in notices of books which are not necessarily either literary or by famous writers. Why not have a word with the editor of your local rag? Your publisher should have done so, but you, as a local resident, may be more persuasive.

All my reviews have been unfavourable

Don't expect your publisher to do anything about this. A protest to the literary editors of the papers concerned will do nothing (except perhaps harm). If the reviews are inaccurate, you may wish to write to the paper pointing out the reviewer's errors, but this frequently results only in a reply in which you suffer still more. Obviously you cannot let a gross distortion of the facts about your book go by, but on the whole it is probably wisest to suffer bad reviews in silence, if you get them, consoling yourself with the thought that any publicity is better than none (it ain't necessarily so, of course). You might also stop to wonder whether all the unfavourable notices are in fact justified.

Shouldn't my publisher send me copies of the reviews of my book?

Publishers are not usually contractually obliged to send their authors copies of reviews. Most of them subscribe to a cutting service (which authors can also do if they are wealthy enough to feel it worthwhile), and can often be persuaded to make a photo-copy of reviews or to send the author duplicates if they have them. Some publishers send the author all the reviews a certain time after the publication of the book, clearing their files by this method. If your publisher does not send you reviews, then all you can really do is ask whether it would be possible for you to have them.

My book is not available in bookshops

Every publisher is constantly bombarded by letters and phone calls from authors complaining that their books cannot be found in bookstores – particularly in the author's local bookshop – or that their friends have not been able to buy copies. Sometimes this is the publisher's fault, but not always. There is nothing that compels any bookseller to stock any given book, not even the fact that the author lives in the same town. All the publisher and his represen-tatives can do is to try to persuade the bookseller to order copies. If the persuasion fails, then you and your friends are going to be disappointed.

Of course, publishers are occasionally to blame – they lose orders, they supply the wrong books, they sometimes take an unbe-lievably long time to invoice and despatch books, they make all kinds of human errors – but this sort of thing does not happen often, and by and large they do not refuse to send books to book-sellers without good reason. Books lying in warehouses do no good for publishers, but only cost money. Believe it or not, publishers do actually want to sell books, not only because they can then recoup their outlay and pay the author's royalties, and their wages and overhead expenses and perhaps make them a profit which will enable them to stay in business, but because successful publishers attract new books and new authors, and the one recipe for success is to sell books in large quantities.

Don't, therefore, immediately blame your publisher if your book is apparently not available in the bookshop. The sales people may be tearing their collective hair over the situation just as much as you are. The distribution of books, the full penetration of the potential market, is the greatest problem any publisher has to face, not exclud-ing such perennial favourites as cash flow and Difficult Authors. What is the potential market for a book, and how do you reach it? Let us take a typical example. You have written a book on Pig-Sticking, and you tell your publisher of the huge demand there will be for it. 'There are five thousand members of the Pig-Sticking

Society for whom it will be required reading,' you say. 'Then there are some ten thousand occasional pig-stickers in Britain and the overseas markets, who are less committed, but still interested – let's say that half of them will buy the book. At least a thousand copies will go to people in the Anti-Pig-Sticking League, who will want to read it so that they know what our latest thinking is. Add in your own standard market, through bookshops and libraries, and it seems to me that you will end up with a print quantity of at least 15,000 copies.' The publisher tries to disillusion you, explaining that the vast majority of your totally committed pig-sticking enthusiasts will not in fact buy the book, but will borrow it, either from each other, or more likely from the public library, which is also where the members of the Anti-Pig-Sticking League will undoubtedly go, if they bother at all. Pressed by you, the publisher may agree that there is in fact a specialist market potential, but will say that realistically it will probably not amount to more than two thousand copies. Even then there will be a problem in reaching the prospective buyers. A leaflet and an order form which can be passed to a bookseller could be sent to them all, but there is little likelihood that many of them will take any action (the average response to a mailing shot is not much more than 1%), and if they are persuaded to go to a bookshop, the bookseller may have declined to order the book in the first place, and the customer, put off by not finding it readily available, may decide to give up the idea of buying it. Or perhaps the publisher has decided that he will no longer supply the bookseller to whom that customer goes, because the bookseller neglects to pay the bills, or indulges in early selling (putting a book on sale before its publication date), or for some other valid reason. As for general sales, there may indeed be a market, but a very small one indeed.

But why should the bookseller be so reluctant to order the book? Well, perhaps the last time that something similar came along, the bookseller was persuaded to take a dozen copies, because the author lived nearby and swore to having at least twelve friends who had promised to buy the book. One of the friends did buy a copy from the bookseller, and two others borrowed that copy, one bought it from a different shop, three got it out of the library, two decided to wait in case a paperback came out, and three never intended to read it anyway. The bookseller was left with eleven unsold copies. That was all right, you might think, because the books had been supplied on sale or return and the unsold copies could be sent back to the publisher for credit. 'Yes,' the bookseller would reply, 'but while the books were in my shop they were taking up space that I could have devoted to other books that would have sold. Sale or return arrangements help me, but they are the lesser of two evils – especially since returning the unsold books to the publisher is a time-consuming chore. I do my best to order only those books that I am sure of selling.'

A fact which does not make the life of the publisher's sale manager any easier is that authors seem always to believe everything that booksellers tell them. Good booksellers do not lie, but others, more prone to human weakness, may decide that it is simpler to deal with a dissatisfied customer, especially in the case of an author, who does not want to buy copies of the book, but simply to see that they are on display, by putting the blame on the publisher, saying that the order hasn't been filled or even that the book is out of print. And we have all met the incompetent bookseller's assistant who seems to have no knowledge of the wares in the shop or any desire to sell books, and who will say anything which will get an awkward customer out of the shop. If you have a complaint about your book not being available, ask your publisher whether what you have been told is true, before you go off the deep end. And it will help if you can name the bookshop concerned, and report accurately on what has been said.

I do not want, on the other hand, to put all the blame on booksellers, large numbers of whom do a very good job. Imagine being faced with over 100,000 new books every year, plus the necessity of keeping stocks of backlist books and standard works such as Bibles and dictionaries. Small wonder that they do not stock all books. Naturally, the larger the bookshop the better chance there is of finding your book in it, although this does not necessarily apply to the large chains, some of which have a policy of not dealing with small publishing houses, especially if they are producing books of restricted local interest. On the other hand, many small independent booksellers survive because of their willingness to order any book for you, and their ability, if they have a good wholesaler, to supply it quickly in most cases.

It is particularly galling, of course, when your book is not available in the shops for some special occasion, especially as such events do often help to sell books and are ephemeral in nature, so that the sales won't be achieved when the books eventually arrive, as they frequently do, two or three days after the whole thing is over. There is nothing you can do except to complain loudly and hope that your publisher won't be so inefficient in future.

You may wonder, in your exasperation, why on earth it should be so apparently difficult to get books speedily from the publisher to the bookshop, sometimes taking five or six weeks. Firstly, it may be that the bookseller has not sent your order off immediately, not because of inefficiency (although that could be a reason for delay), but because it makes economic sense for everyone concerned, even the customer, who may have to avoid paying a surcharge on a single copy order, if the bookseller lumps together the orders he receives for books which have to be ordered from one particular source. Next there is the question of delays in the post, which we all suffer from time to time, especially with second-class mail. When the order arrives in the publisher's office, it will have to take its place in a queue of orders waiting to be processed, and similarly, when it reaches the warehouse, it may not be possible to deal with the order immediately. At any one of these stages additional time may be lost if weekends happen to be awkwardly placed in relation to the progress of the order, and holidays and illnesses can also cause delay. Nevertheless, some publishers manage to be far more efficient than others in processing orders. Why? Well, it may be that the efficiency is produced by employing many more staff and using up-to-date equipment in both the office and the warehouse, and by always using first-class post, and by other such practices which can speed the processing of orders, but that sort of efficiency can sometimes prove very expensive, and always has to be measured in cost-effectiveness. The truly efficient publishers have better management and staff – it's as simple as that.

The solution to all these problems is to write an enormous bestseller. It will also remove most of the other causes for complaint and questions dealt with in this chapter. Since for most authors that is just a dream, some more practical advice may be in order. Do let your publisher know if your book is not available in the bookshops, but try to do so in a friendly rather than a complaining way, and don't keep on and on about it. If something has gone wrong, the sales department is probably well aware of it, and is doing everything possible to put it right.

If all else fails, most publishers will allow their authors to buy copies of their books for sale to their friends or to people they encounter at conferences and other events, such as poetry readings. There is a standard clause in most authors' contracts which allows the author to buy copies of the book at trade terms, but it usually says, *not for resale.* If you buy your book from your publisher at trade terms you must therefore seek the firm's permission before selling them. Such sales will presumably be at full retail price and you will make a profit; remember that you will have to declare such earnings to the Inland Revenue. You should also, if your publisher agrees to the arrangement, use it with care, making sure as far as possible that you do not take sales away from a bookseller by so doing. If any of your local booksellers steadfastly refuse to stock your book, it might be as well to let them know that you propose to sell copies yourself.

My publishers are pathetic. I've just had my royalty statement which shows that my first novel has sold only 673 copies, and they only printed 1,000 anyway.
Alas, that sort of disappointing sale is not unusual nowadays for first novels by unknown writers.
In fact, that's quite a good figure.

My previous books have always sold more copies
This does not mean necessarily that your publishers are making any less effort – indeed, they may be trying harder than ever in the past. The plain fact is that, except for bestsellers, the market for hardcover books is a declining one.

My publisher calls my book a bestseller, but it has sold only just over 10,000 copies
Bestseller standards vary according to the genre of the book. To sell 10,000 of a book aimed at a smallish market which could not normally be expected to exceed, say, 2,500 copies, would justify calling it a bestseller, whereas for popular fiction a much larger figure would be required. In any case, publishers sometimes use the term, whether they should or not, to impress the trade, the public and the author.

I have the feeling that my publisher is interested only in selling to libraries
You may be quite right. Some books, particularly in the field of popular fiction – romances, westerns, and so on – are published virtually exclusively for the library market, and the publisher makes little or no effort to sell the titles to bookshops, simply because it is obvious that bookshops won't order the books.

Bookshops in this country, especially outside London, sell very little fiction, and that applies to so-called 'literary' novels as well as to 'entertainment' fiction. Apart from the work of a limited number of bestselling authors, fiction sells in hardcover almost exclusively to libraries. You need to be realistic. If your publisher sees your book as one for the library market and makes no effort in other directions, that may be the best course for your book. The publisher is also possibly a specialist in that kind of publishing (although there are far fewer such firms than there were ten years or so ago), so before you rush off to another house which does try to sell to outlets other than libraries, make sure that you are really going to be better off. Of course, you should be able to earn some Public Lending Right moneys when your book is borrowed from the libraries, and perhaps you will eventually join the ranks of quite a large number of successful writers who started their careers with precisely this kind of publishing experience.

My publisher's firm is so small that the books on the list are not distributed by the major chains
A problem indeed, for the publisher as well as the author, and one to which I can offer no solution. If your book is of a very specialist nature, it may not matter a great deal that it is not available in the major chains, provided that your publisher knows how to sell it in its own market, but if it is a general book, its chances may well be damaged. The really small firm may be able to attract splendid authors, may have a marvellous editor, may publish beautifully produced books, but almost always will have selling and distribution problems (any author who tries self publishing will meet similar difficulties – the real killer is getting the books where the buying public will see them). There is always the hope that the small firm will get bigger (as many have in fact done in the past) or will produce such stunning books that the chains have to take its output. There is also the consoling thought that if the major chains do not stock the books in question, it opens the field for the independent bookseller, who may therefore be more enthusiastic about them than would otherwise be the case.

My publisher refuses to reprint my book
Publishing is a chancy business. No one can predict for certain how a new book will perform – whether it will sell as expected or in excess of or below its target. Fixing print quantities for books is a

gamble. Many factors are considered: the publisher's experience with books of a similar nature, the editor's enthusiasm, the reaction of subsidiary rights buyers prior to publication, the jacket or cover, advance orders from bookshops, and of course some kind of estimate of the book's potential based on the marketing department's researches, and so on. It is very difficult to get the answer right. More often than not publishers are over-optimistic and print too many copies, and have to remainder or pulp the surplus, losing money on such copies. In an effort to avoid such overstocks publishers will sometimes print too few copies. The book sells out on publication or shortly thereafter, and the author is then dismayed when the publishers refuse to reprint. Why should they do so? Usually because the information that they gather from their sales representatives and from bookshops leads them to believe either that, although the publisher may be out of stock, there are plenty of copies of the book in the shops, or that the unsatisfied demand is not large enough to warrant reprinting, which cannot be done economically for anything but a large quantity, often virtually as big as the original print run. Although the origination charges for setting the book in type, designing the jacket, etc., have all been met, the cost of starting up a reprint is so high that a large printing is needed if the unit cost per book is to be kept to a level which will allow sales to be profitable. This is one of the reasons why authors whose sales have brought them to a higher scale of royalties are asked to revert to a minimal royalty on 'small' reprints of 1,500 or sometimes 2,000 copies or less. The more elaborate the book, especially if colour illustrations are involved, the more costly the origination of the reprint will be.

Sometimes the sales reports will suggest that there is sufficient demand to justify a reprint, but that it will take many years before the entire quantity is sold, and the publisher may regretfully have to decide that the required capital just cannot be tied up for that length of time.

Knowing all this does not console the author who sees lost sales (and the publisher will not be happy about it, either), but at least there is the likelihood that the publisher will be more receptive to the author's next book than if the first one had been over-printed.

I have been asked to revise and update my book, but the publisher has not offered me a new advance

The MTA suggests that advances should be paid for revisions, but most publishers' contracts simply say that the author agrees to update the book if necessary, and make no mention of payment for the work. But an updated, revised edition should generate a whole lot more sales for a book which might otherwise have died of old age, so you should have the pleasure of continuing royalties. Lucky you. And the amounts you receive may go up too, because the book's retail price will probably be increased.

My book is to be remaindered

When the sale of a book has stopped or has petered down to almost nothing, the publisher will either pulp or preferably remainder the unsaleable balance of the edition. Apart from the problem of whether or not the author receives any royalties on remainder sales (see p.141), the author is often angered, feeling that the book has been remaindered within too short a period of original publication. The MTA gives the publisher the right to remainder a book twelve months after publication, which is a reasonable date to put in the contract, but it seems to me that justice in this matter depends to some extent on the kind of book involved. If one is talking of a serious work of non-fiction which is not essentially topical and ephemeral, it is entirely fair for the author to ask that it should not be remaindered until a minimum of two years after its first publication, unless the publisher can demonstrate that the book has stopped selling completely, and that there is no likelihood of an improvement. If, however, we are considering fiction, it is an unfortunate truth that the majority of novels are moribund six months after publication, and often before that. If the publisher wishes to remainder your novel within a comparatively short period, although you might ask for it to be kept going for a few months longer, or perhaps for only a part of the stock to be remaindered, so that copies would still be available through normal trade channels, it seems reasonable to me for you to consider the request favourably. A renewed sales effort to dispose of the overstocks just does not work, unless there is some outside influence to affect matters, such as the release of the film of the book; booksellers, faced with thousands of new books appearing every month, will not look kindly on the attempt to sell them a novel which they first considered six months or more ago, and which cannot be said to have exactly leapt off the shelves.

Authors are rightly incensed when their books are remaindered without their knowledge. If the book is to be remaindered the author should always be informed and have the opportunity of buying copies at the remainder price. If this does not happen, a vigorous protest has sometimes forced the publisher to buy back from the remainder merchant the copies that the author wants.

Of course, if your book is remaindered, there is nothing to stop you buying copies at the remainder price and then selling them at the full retail price shown on the jacket or cover, or at any price which will give you a good profit. If you give talks, or go to writers' gatherings such as the Summer School at Swanwick, you will certainly be able to dispose of copies. You should, of course, report the profit you make to the Inland Revenue as part of your income. However, be careful about how many books you buy, making sure that there's a real chance of getting rid of them within a reasonable length of time.

When your book is remaindered, you should check whether it is a full or a partial remainder (see p.44). If the publisher has no remaining stock, you are entitled under most publishing contracts to have all the rights in the book returned from the publisher to you, with the possible exception of those relating to any active sub-licences.

I was not told of the bookclub sale until the royalty statement arrived

You are right to feel annoyed. It's bad-mannered and stupid of your publisher not to have told you something like that, especially as it was good news. Protest, and ask that nothing similar should happen in the future.

Incidentally, some authors are very much opposed to bookclubs, because they believe that bookclub sales work against bookshops. It is fairly noticeable that most of the authors who refuse to let their books appear in club editions are those who regularly produce bestsellers. While admiring them for defending bookshops, one cannot help thinking that it is always easier to stand on one's principles when one doesn't have to count the pennies.

My publisher has sold electronic rights in some of my old books and wants to take 50% of the income. Is this fair?

No, it jolly well isn't. Contracts which were signed some years ago make no mention of electronic rights, and some publishers take advantage of this to try to get a large share of the proceeds. You should receive 90%.

My publishers have sold their own edition of my book in the United States rather than selling the rights to an American publisher

This situation normally applies only to highly illustrated books, especially those which have a number of pages in full colour, since the only way in which the book can be made economic is for the British and American publishers to work together so that a double-sized print quantity can be ordered. Books of British origin are manufactured in such cases by the British publisher, who usually sells the sheets to the American publisher at a fairly low price which is inclusive of the author's royalty, and the same thing works in reverse with books of American origin. Sometimes foreign language editions are also involved. The reward to the author on these deals is minimal, but it is often true that if no such arrangement could be worked out, the book would not be published on either side of the Atlantic, and this is why in many cases the British (or American) publisher will not sign a firm contract with the author until an American (or British) publisher has agreed to join in the deal.

It is the same principle on which packagers work (see p.28). The author will probably earn more money on a packaged book, but it is not always easy to persuade a packager to take on your book – they prefer to dream up their own ideas and to choose the authors that they want to write for them.

If there is no cost problem and the book is a perfectly ordinary one, the British publishers have presumably tried to sell American rights. Having failed, although they are unlikely to have much success in the States with their own edition of your book, a few extra sales are better than nothing.

No effort has been made to sell subsidiary rights in my book

Are you sure? If your publishers have really made no effort to sell subsidiary rights, they are either fools or incompetent, and you should leave them as soon as possible if you can find someone else to take you on. But do try to find out first whether it is simply that, despite considerable industry on their part, all the subsidiary rights buyers to whom they have submitted your book have rejected it. Paperback publishers, bookclub editors, serial editors for magazine and newspapers are all faced with an embarrassment of riches, and reject far more books than they accept. For instance, although there are several bookclubs, only one in every fifteen of the books which might be suitable for a club is likely to be taken.

If your book has not sold any subsidiary rights, you may have been unlucky, or it may be that your book is just not good enough, but it doesn't necessarily mean that your publishers haven't tried. If you ask them, they may be able to tell you to whom they have submitted the book and possibly whether any reasons for the rejection have been given, and this may be useful information for you to bear in mind when writing your next book. They may also tell you why they have *not* submitted your book to this or that potential subsidiary rights buyer. If, for instance, the editor of a paperback house has repeatedly told your publishers that he/she is not currently interested in thrillers, your publishers would be foolish to submit your thriller – unless it is of such outstanding quality that they can say to the paperback editor, 'I know you don't want thrillers, but this is so brilliant that you must read it.' If the paperback editor knows that your publishers would not say that unless the book really were extraordinarily good, then an exception might be made, and it might be considered. But if the book is as splendid as that, your publishers will have had no difficulty in selling it to one of the other paperback houses anyway.

My publisher turned down a subsidiary rights offer as not good enough; it has now been withdrawn, and no other offer has come in

Bad luck. For the publisher, too. I keep telling you it's a gambling business.

I am an internationally known, bestselling author. My hardcover publisher has been taken over by a conglomerate which has its own mass-market paperback concern. They are going to revert all the paperback rights in my books from the house which has successfully published them for years, and with whom I have excellent relationships, so that they can publish them under their own imprint. And they are doing this without consulting me

I am not surprised that you are angry. Unfortunately, for many years in the past it was standard practice to give hardcover publishers full control of paperback rights, without any need to consult the author about their sale or reversion, let alone any right of veto. Legally, you probably have no recourse; morally, however, you are entitled to make as big a fuss as you can, and if you shout loudly enough you may be able to shame the conglomerate into behaving properly. At the very least, of course, you will change your hard-cover publisher for your future books (that will larn the conglomerate!), and make sure that every contract you sign gives you the right of approval of any deal concerning subsidiary rights.

It is unfair that I have to wait so long for my share of subsidiary rights income

Publishers who sell subsidiary rights receive moneys from those to whom they sell, and then divide them according to the proportions set out in the contract between themselves and the author. Now, it is standard practice that the advance originally paid by the publisher to the author is against all sums due under the contract, which means that the author receives no extra payment until the advance has been earned, whether by royalties on the original edition or from the author's share of subsidiary rights, or a combination of the two. Let us suppose that the publisher has paid an advance of £1,000, and has sold subsidiary rights for a sum of which the author's share is £600. £600 of the original advance has now been earned, but that money will not be paid to the author, nor will any further sums be payable until the remaining £400 of the advance has been earned. This is not unfair, especially since publishers frequently take into account their expectations of receipts from subsidiary rights when calculating how much the original advance should be.

What is less fair is the practice of some publishers of retaining the author's share of subsidiary rights money *after* the original advance has been fully earned until they next send a royalty statement to the author. This could mean that for a considerable time moneys due to the author are kept and used by the publisher. Supposing that after the advance has been earned your publisher receives moneys from subsidiary rights of which your share is £500. If the royalty accounting periods end at 30th June and 31st December, and if it so happened that these payments reached the publisher on 1st July, the £500 could be retained until the following 31st March, when the royalty statement for the six months ending 31st December would normally be rendered to you. Fortunately pressure from authors' organizations and agents has made the practice far less common than it used to be. Any publisher who still retains moneys in this way may be legally entitled to do so by the terms of the contract, but it is a morally reprehensible procedure. It should be noted, however, that the MTA makes provision for such moneys to be passed to the author within one month only when they amount to £100 or more.

I have just discovered that a large company has made several dozen photocopies of my book and distributed them among its staff. Can they do this?
No, they can't – at least not without permission. It's illegal to do so in the case of any copyright material. Check that your publishers have not made any special arrangement with the firm concerned (if they have, they should have told you about it). Unless such an arrangement exists, your publisher should then give all details to the Copyright Licensing Agency, which will be happy to follow the matter up, and if necessary take legal proceedings.

The hardcover edition of my book is out of print, and the publisher refuses to reprint, but is still taking a cut of the paperback royalties
Most publishing contracts include a clause which allows the publisher to retain rights provided that any sub-licensed edition of the book is in print, even if the original edition is not. A reprint may be impossible to contemplate, for even if the book is still selling in the sub-licensed edition, the market for the original edition may now be non-existent or too small to justify a reprint. In these circumstances some publishers will occasionally agree to increase the author's share of the subsidiary income, but very few will release all rights to the author, arguing that they took the initial risk with the book, and if they had not done so the subsidiary rights in question would not have been sold at all, and it was they who conducted the negotiations for the sale, all of which is a valid justification for them taking their share, and will remain so throughout the life of the sub-licence in question. Legally, unless your contract does not have the kind of clause referred to above, you have no cause for redress. Morally, it depends somewhat on the kind of sums involved. If the publishers have already received a very substantial amount in the form of their share of subsidiary rights, then perhaps they have less justification for still taking their full percentage than if the moneys involved are small. But that's a difficult one to argue.

My royalty statements are late and inaccurate
In these days of computers there is no excuse for lateness – except,

of course, the usual one that the computer has broken down. There is also no excuse for those publishers who allow themselves the luxury of producing only one royalty statement annually – protest most strongly if you encounter shabby treatment of that sort.

As for inaccuracy, the occasional mistake is probably inevitable, simply because human beings are concerned with the preparation of the accounts, and human beings are fallible. One of the functions of an agent is to check royalty statements carefully, and those authors who don't have agents must do it for themselves, and bring any errors to the notice of their publishers. If the inaccuracy is serious, most contracts allow the author to examine the relevant parts of the publisher's account books. And if you don't understand your royalty statement, ask your publisher to explain it to you.

I have just read about an author who has signed a deal with a publisher giving him a million pounds for his next two books. I'm green with envy

So am I. Enormous advance payments to certain authors have been with us for some time now, and seem to be a phenomenon which has come about largely because of the need that the big publishing companies feel to attract major authors and simultaneously to show off their wealth and power. The publishers who spend these astronomical sums ('cheque-book publishing', as those who can't afford it are wont to describe it) have usually tried to take out insurance by selling various subsidiary rights for equally huge amounts, so that their risks are diminished. However, at the time of writing there is some indication that publishers are beginning to recognize that the mammoth advances are not always earned out, in which case they lose a lot of money, so there is a faint possibility that fewer such payments will be paid. In any case, I'm not sure that really do envy the author you mention – just think of the responsibility that sums like that place on him. On second thoughts, yes, I do still envy him.

When unknown but talented authors struggle to get into print, it is appalling that tennis stars, MPs, models, TV 'personalities' – anyone who has a famous name – can be paid huge sums for bad, or at best, mediocre novels, which they often did not write themselves

I quite agree. Alas, that's the way the world is.

My agent is useless

Then change to another agency, or (possibly with the help of the Society of Authors or the Writers' Guild) dispense with an agent altogether. But before you take either of these courses, discuss the whole matter with your present agent, making plain every aspect of your dissatisfaction. A conversation, or exchange of correspondence, can often solve any number of problems. You might find, for instance, that the failure to place your work is not due to lack of effort. And that advice to talk about what is worrying you to the person concerned applies to many of the other complaints in this chapter. You may discover that your complaints aren't really justified, or that things are not as bad as you thought; at the least, you should gain some understanding of the other side's point of view.

When books are discounted in the shops, more copies are sold, so since my book is not discounted, I am losing out. Why can't all books be discounted?

Books can be sold at less than the recommended price only if someone is prepared to make less profit than usual on each copy. Usually, three parties are involved: the publisher, who sells the book to the bookseller at a higher discount than normal; the bookseller, who takes a smaller profit on each sale; and the author, who gets a reduced royalty. The bookseller may regard discounted books partly as 'loss leaders' (i.e. as items which will bring customers into the shop where, with luck, they may buy something in addition to the discounted book), but the publisher, the author, and indeed the bookseller too are all really relying on substantially increased volume of sales to bump up their overall profits – they make less on each copy, but because they sell more copies they gain in total. It really works only with bestsellers, and of course publishers can better afford to offer high discounts on bestsellers because the production cost per copy is lower than that for most books because of the high print run, and because a bestseller is ordered in large quantities and bulk orders are economical to process. If all books were sold at discounted prices, many of them would no longer be economically viable. But if all books were cheaper, you might say, more would be sold, and print quantities would increase, and the economics would no longer be a problem. Unfortunately, it wouldn't work like that. As far as run-of-the-mill books are concerned, very substantial extra sales – probably at least double their present levels – would be needed to increase print quantities sufficiently to compensate for lower profit margins, and the reduction in retail price would have to be huge to achieve that.

My book was published six months ago, but already my publisher has lost interest in it

In most cases, a very high proportion of the sales of a book has been achieved before publication and for a few months after, and from that time on sales may virtually have ceased. Additional promotion and effort by the publisher will not stimulate additional sales, unless there is some justification for it, such as the release of a film based on the book. Even then, the new publicity may result only in the sale of those copies of the book already in the bookshops, without much re-ordering. Books which survive for a longer period usually continue to sell on their own momentum, and again additional attention does not often produce much effect.

Lack of interest in your book is also due in part to the fact that much of your publisher's time and attention are now being lavished on the new books on the list. Before publication and for some time after your book no doubt had its fair share of such interest and effort – now it is someone else's turn.

My book, which was a failure, was remaindered and is now out of print, dead and forgotten. Nevertheless, I've been advised to ask the publisher for the rights back. Why should I bother?

Because you should never give up hope. Get the rights back, and then see if you can re-sell them. You may not be able to pull off any major publishing deal, but you might interest one of the large-print publishers. Or perhaps a film producer will come across a copy of your book and decide that it would make a really smashing film.If any subsidiary rights in your book are sold now or in the future, you will have to share the proceeds with the publisher if the rights have not reverted to you, but if you've got them back, all the money will be yours. Another possibility is self-publication of a new edition. Anyway, reversion of rights is not a difficult thing to arrange – just write to the publisher and ask for confirmation that, since the book is out of print, all rights have reverted to you.

Whenever I complain to my publisher he just fobs me off with some unconvincing explanation

Either the publisher is incompetent and does not know the answer to your queries, and hasn't the courage to admit ignorance, or more likely is ashamed of the company's inefficiency and is trying to cover up. Loyalty to the firm and its staff may be preventing a confession that you are right and that your complaints are justified. Not only that, but to tell you the truth might mean that you would lose any remaining faith that you might still have in the publishing house. I think that honesty is always the best policy for a publisher when dealing with authors, but maybe there are exonerating circumstances. Perhaps you should also ask yourself whether by any chance you could be a Difficult Author, pestering the life out of your poor publisher with trivial complaints and queries.

My publisher is greedy

Very probably. If you think so, say so. Your publisher may be able to explain why she/he appears that way, and may even respond by being more generous towards you. But do remember that one of a publisher's function is to make the firm profitable, and that may mean saving as much money as is consistent with not losing publishing opportunities as a result of apparent parsimony. Any business person tries to strike the best possible bargain. Try a little haggling.

9

Legal Matters

Publishers' Contracts

The contract that you sign with a publisher is, of course, a legal document, and so is the correspondence with the firm which deals with any commitment on either side which is not covered by the agreement. These papers should be kept carefully in a safe place, and you should stick rigidly to all the terms and conditions in them – your signature on the contract is a statement of your acceptance of all the terms. If later you find that your contract is irksome in some respect or commits you to something which you cannot fulfil – the delivery date for the completed typescript of your book, for instance – talk to your publisher and seek permission to amend or waive the relevant part of the agreement. Get the permission in writing, so that there can't be any argument later.

The contract and any correspondence attached to it will be needed if you ever reach the unhappy position of being involved in a law suit with your publisher. You will certainly need professional advice in such a case. If you are already a member of the Society of Authors or the Writers' Guild such advice will be readily available to you from whichever of those bodies you belong to, but neither organization will provide assistance for a member in a legal dispute which was already in existence before that member joined.

Copyright

Copyright is granted by law to the creator of a work, giving that person the exclusive right to reproduce and publish it in whole or in part. The law of copyright is enormously complicated and the Copyright, Designs and Patents Act of 1988, while clarifying some matters, has left others in a confusing state of obfuscation, especially when an author writes for and at the behest of his/her employer, in which case the copyright usually belongs to the employer, although the concept of 'moral rights' (see below) may complicate the issue. Moreover, the European Commission has a long programme of copyright-related matters under consideration, and will undoubtedly recommend many changes in the years to come; most of their new regulations, fortunately, are likely to benefit authors rather than be to their detriment.

However, the average author fortunately needs to know only certain basic facts about copyright, which will be set out below, and if more detailed advice is required, it can be readily obtained from the Society of Authors or the Writers' Guild.

Your book (or, indeed, anything you write, or anything which you have created and recorded orally on tape or on a video) is protected by copyright as soon as it is committed to paper or recorded. Some authors feel it useful to establish the date of the work's completion, which can be done, for instance, by depositing a copy of it with your bank and obtaining a dated receipt, or by posting yourself a copy in a registered parcel which you then keep with its seals unbroken. The authors who do this are usually afraid that if they don't protect themselves and their work in this way it may be copied or stolen by an unscrupulous publisher. I must say I know of no professional author who bothers with such a performance. Most publishers give full respect to the copyright of any material submitted to them.

Copyright in a work published during the author's lifetime extends in the EU for seventy years after the author's death, and in most countries of the world copyright continues similarly to be protected after the author's death, although in some countries the term is shorter.

On publication, protection of copyright internationally is secured by the Berne Convention, which was first drawn up in 1886, has been frequently amended since (the latest changes attempt to provide the basis for copyright in the electronic age), and is still in force. Over sixty countries of the world adhere to it, now including the United States, which for many years refused to sign because of its own internal copyright laws. In 1952, under the auspices of Unesco, the Universal Copyright Convention came into being, and was seen as the major instrument providing international copyright protection. Resulting from this agreement, the copyright notice printed in book was standardized in the form of the word 'Copyright', the symbol ©, the name of the copyright owner and the date of the first publication. More recently, the Berne Convention has regained its status as the premier international agreement on copyright, and its latest version has virtually superseded the Universal Copyright Convention.

Unless the publisher is buying material outright, all publishing agreements should include a clause stating that published editions of the work will include a copyright notice in the author's name, and the publisher will see that it is printed in the work as a matter of course – publishers are just as keen as authors to preserve copyright in the books they bring out.

Unfortunately, many countries of the world, especially in the Far East, have little regard for copyright. In Taiwan, Korea and the Indian sub-continent, for instance, pirate publishers flourish, publishing books by European and American authors without authorization and without payment of royalties. Among the worst offenders is the Republic of China. If you learn of the pirating of one of your books, inform your publisher or your agent immediately. Often they will be powerless to do anything, because in some cases the pirates are actually encouraged in their illegal work by their governments, but at least you should keep them informed. The same advice applies, incidentally, if you discover that your work has been plagiarized or that your copyright has been infringed in any other way. Don't suffer in silence. However, before rushing too precipitately into action, you should bear in mind that while a direct quotation of your work may be a clear-cut case of plagiarism, it is rather more difficult to prove that similarities of plot have been pinched by one writer from another.

Unless there are very special reasons for doing so, you should never surrender the copyright in your work, but instead should grant your publisher a licence to publish and to control certain other rights, with clauses which will ensure that all rights revert to you if the publisher fails to carry out the commitments of the agreement. Some publishers frequently try to buy the copyright in an author's work, offering an outright fee which will almost certainly be more than an advance against royalties might be expected to be, and which may be large enough to be very tempting. If such an offer comes your way, think carefully before accepting. Once you have parted with your copyright, the publisher can go on producing the work, possibly in very large quantities, without paying you any additional money, and the outright sum you received may end up looking very small against the royalties that the work's sale would have brought in, even if those royalties had been on a low scale. And a publisher who has bought the copyright in your book is free to edit it, change it, abridge it, and indeed do anything at all with it, without consulting you or paying you any more money, no matter how much income it may generate. Parting with your copyright is not only foolish, but normally pretty irreversible – even if the firm to which you sold it goes out of existence you are unlikely to get your copyright back.

A sensible course of action, if you are asked to give up your copyright, is to take professional advice (from the Society of Authors or the Writers' Guild, perhaps), since there are some circumstances in which it may be an acceptable option. For instance, it is normal and reasonable to grant the publisher copyright when you are one of many authors contributing material to an encyclopaedia or a yearbook or some other reference book of that type. It would be impossible for publishers of such books to cope with licences and royalties and subsidiary rights for all the contributors. However, since the object of buying the copyright is to simplify the arrangements rather than to cheat the author, the better firms often pay additional fees if the book is reprinted.

Do remember, by the way, that just as copyright laws protect you, so they protect other authors, and you must not infringe their rights any more than they must play around with yours. See the section on Permissions below.

Some Miscellaneous Copyright Matters

The copyright in letters belongs to the person who writes them, not the recipient.

As for photographs, the copyright normally belongs to the person who took the photograph, unless it was taken in the course of employment and at the behest of the employer, who in such cases is the copyright owner.

There is no copyright in ideas. Many authors worry about this, fearing that their bright ideas will be stolen by unscrupulous publishers. There is rarely any justification for such concerns – as explained on p.167, the majority of publishers will never knowingly pinch ideas.

There is no copyright in titles either, nor in authors' names. You are entitled to call your book *A Brief History of Time* or *The Day of the Jackal* if you want to without infringing anyone's copyright. However, even if it appeared under your own name as author,

Stephen Hawking, in the first case, or Frederick Forsyth, in the second, could sue you for 'passing off', which is to say for attempting to con the public into buying your book in the belief that it was the famous one (even if that was not in fact your intention). And I wouldn't advise you to call yourself Jeffrey Archer or Catherine Cookson, for the same reason. If your name really is Jeffrey Archer or Catherine Cookson, you will need to use a pseudonym, however unhappy you may feel about it, or at the least to add an initial or a middle name and to call yourself, for instance, something like Jeffrey C. Archer or Catherine Jane Cookson.

As a final point, there is no copyright in generally accepted facts. See the section on Plagiarism below.

Moral Rights
Moral Rights were enshrined in law in the Copyright, Designs and Patents Act of 1988. There are four such rights, the most frequently cited of which are the first two, commonly known as the right of 'paternity' and the right of 'integrity'.

The right of paternity guarantees that the author will be identified in any use which is made of that author's work, whether in whole or in part. The right is, however, effective only if it has been 'asserted' by the author in a notice printed in her/his work. The following wording is suitable: *The right of (Author's name) to be identified as the author of this work has been asserted by him/her in accordance with the Copyright, Designs and Patents Act 1988.*

The right of integrity protects the author against the unauthorized distortion or mutilation of her/his work in any adaptation or other treatments of it. It does not have to be asserted.

The remaining two Moral Rights allow for the right of privacy, preventing the publication without permission of a photograph or film commissioned from the photographer for private or domestic purposes, and for the right of protection for an author against having someone else's work falsely attributed to him/her.

Most book publishers are willing to conform to the law as far as Moral Rights are concerned, but authors who work in other fields, like films and television, may not always find a similar willingness on the part of those who commission their work. Point out to such people that Moral Rights are actually part of the law of the realm, and they will simply take their commission to an author who either does not know the importance of retaining the rights, or does not care. Authors must stand firm, and shoulder to shoulder, on this issue.

Libel

The laws of libel are pretty complex, and it is not the province of this book to give a complete survey of them. However, some helpful points may be made.

First of all, the essence of libel is that it is damaging to the victim, so you are in no danger if you write about real-life people provided that you do not say anything unpleasant about them. You do not even have to be all that bland in your comments, as long as what you write does not damage the person's reputation or expose that person to hatred, ridicule or contempt. Of course, you have to be careful, because something which you may consider to be the mildest of criticisms may be thought by the subject of your remarks to be offensive in the extreme.

The next point to remember is that you cannot libel the dead. Even with this freedom, however, there is a danger, because a remark about a dead person could be considered by his/her living descendants to be libellous of them if in some respect it damages their reputations. For instance, if you were to write, 'Lord Blank came from a family noted throughout history for lechery, duplicity and total incompetence in high office,' you might be referring in your mind only to Lord Blank himself and his forbears, but his descendants might not be at all pleased.

There are several possible defences which an author can make to a charge of libel, the first and best of which is that the matter complained of is true. But you have to be able to prove it, and it is rarely a simple matter to do so, and can be very expensive if you have to do your proving in a court of law.

The next possible defence is one of 'fair comment'. This is what protects journalists from actions against them when they say rude things about public figures such as politicians and royals. You may still have to show that your 'fair comment' is a matter of opinion, rather than fact, and that you wrote in good faith and without malice.

A somewhat similar protection exists primarily for reports of judicial or parliamentary proceedings, and is known as 'privilege'.

And lastly, there is the defence of 'innocence', if you can prove that you had no intention of libelling the person concerned and did so by accident. This is normally concerned with fiction, and the defence would work best if you could show that you did not even know of the plaintiff's existence, and, even better, if you could demonstrate that you had taken some steps to find out if anyone of that name existed, but had not succeeded. Let us suppose that you have written about a fictional criminal medical practitioner for whom you have invented the name of 'Doctor Tobias Tiddleywink'. You are horrified when a real-life Doctor Tobias Tiddleywink turns up and sues you for libel. If you can prove not only that you had no personal knowledge of the existence of Doctor Tobias Tiddleywink, but also that you had checked in the BMA register and had found no mention of him (because he had only just quali-fied), you would have quite a strong defence. You would still, however, have to issue an apology, and your book might have to be withdrawn, and the whole thing would probably cost you a great deal of money.

You may have yet another answer. 'X won't sue,' you may say, 'because it's not going to be worth her while. She hasn't got the time for a court case, and if she did sue, she knows I haven't got the money, so even if she wins she won't get anything out of me.' Or you might suggest, 'Z wouldn't dare sue me. He knows that if he did, far worse things than I have written would come out in the trial.' Well, yes, but honestly I don't think any publisher could be blamed for being very wary indeed about either of those approaches.

The best answer is to avoid libel like the plague. If you write non-fiction, it is quite easy to recognize potentially libellous matter. It is more difficult with fictional characters. Some authors of novels, short stories, plays and other imaginative work believe that if they model one of their characters on a real-life person, all they have to do to avoid a charge of libel is to change the name. This is not so. If people who are libelled recognize themselves (and they probably will, despite the myth that your friends will never identify themselves with the characters based on them in your books), and especially if their friends and acquaintance can also recognize them, they will have a case against the author concerned, whatever the characters in the story or stories may be called. It is not even enough to change the physical appearance of such characters, although this may help, for it depends on how impenetrable the disguise is – if they and their buddies can still recognize them, you are not out of trouble. You may be a bit safer if you change every-thing – name, physical appearance, occupation and even sex – but you may still find yourself in hot water. Yet another danger lurks in the fictional presentation of certain public figures; if, for instance, you were to write a novel in which you showed a fictional

Chairman of the Coal Board in a very unpleasant light, the real-life holder of that office might have a case against you, even though you had changed his name, appearance and other characteristics. The moral is to make sure that all the characters about whom you write anything which might sound like libellous material are wholly imaginary, not even remotely based on anyone you know or have heard of, and if they happen to be in one of the professions, to check that there is no doctor or clergyman or lawyer or whatever it may be with that particular name.

The notice that appears in the front of many novels indicating that the characters in it are imaginary and bear no resemblance to any person, living or dead, is of little use. I doubt if it would even scare off someone who is thinking somewhat frivolously of suing (if anyone ever does such a thing), and it certainly won't deter any serious complainant.

If there is anything in your book which you consider to be of a potentially libellous nature,. you should bring it to the attention of your publisher. Additionally, if you are worried and your publisher does not do this, you can submit the book to a solicitor for an opinion, although it is as well to choose one who is a specialist in the field. Your publisher will know the names of suitable firms. It will be expensive, but perhaps less expensive than a libel trial, the costs of which are likely to be horrendous – more to be feared, in fact, than the possible damages.

Permissions

If you are quoting from someone's work and if it is in copyright, you must obtain permission to do so, pay a fee for the privilege, and always give details of where the quotation is taken from. Under rules known as 'fair dealing', a limited amount from a single author's work may be quoted without permission or payment, but exactly how much may be used is always a vexed question. Some time ago the Society of Authors and the Publishers association set out the following definitions of the length of extracts which would be considered to be covered by fair dealing: a single extract of up to 400 words from a prose work; or a series of extracts, each of which should not exceed 300 words, totalling not more than 800 words from a prose work; or extracts totalling not more than 40 lines from a poem (but the extracts should not amount to more than a quarter of the complete poem). Whatever the length of the extract, it is essential that the author and the source of the quotation should be identified. And your quotation must, by law, be used only in the course of criticism or review. In practice, few publishers or authors will complain if you use a brief extract to illustrate or underline a point you are making, but you must not take it for granted that you can quote in such circumstances without permission. Fair dealing does not cover your use of copyright material as part of an anthology which you are compiling, and for such use permission must always be sought and paid for.

Unless the extract which you are quoting is very brief indeed, it is always as well to apply in writing for permission to use someone else's material, approaching the publisher of the work and giving details of the use you intend to make of the quotation. The publisher will tell you in what form the obligatory acknowledgement of the source should be made and what fee, varying from nothing to large sums for a lengthy quote from an author of note, will be payable. Since the fees often vary considerably, it is a good idea to find out what they are before you make up your mind to use the pieces in question, and you should check with your publisher to find out exactly what permission you need to get – whether, for instance, you need World English Language Rights, or perhaps only British and Commonwealth rights.

Works written by authors who have been dead for more than seventy years are usually out of copyright, but there are occasional exceptions to this rule, and it is always as well to check.

Plagiarism

If you deliberately copy someone else's work, without permission or acknowledgement, pretending that it is your own, you are guilty of plagiarism, a crime for which you can be sued. If your book has been published and is deemed to contain plagiarized material, it will probably have to be withdrawn and fairly substantial damages will be payable to the author whose work you have stolen. 'Then how much of my research,' you may ask, 'can I use?' That depends on what you are talking about. If you are referring to facts, there is usually no problem, provided that they are generally known to and accepted by a large number of people – if you have checked the date of, let us say, the assassination of President Kennedy, and intend to use that information in your book, there is no question of plagiarism. However, if you quote a fact which is not widely known and which has been discovered and published by one person only, you may be infringing that person's copyright. If you are talking of more than a fact – if, for instance, you go on to describe Kennedy's assassination, using the actual words in the book you consulted, you will certainly be guilty of plagiarism. If you insist on making use of someone else's material, you will have to paraphrase – that is to say, you will have to put everything in your own words. And is that enough? No, almost certainly it is not. You can't get away with changing the words if you still use the same sentence structure, and the same kind of paragraphing, and all the same facts. In particular, you must avoid what might be called the stylistic idiosyncrasies of the author whose work you are using.

Plagiarism is, of course, not only a matter of copying another author's words and the way in which they are presented or of following too closely the method that author used to organize the material. You will also be guilty of the same crime if you use the plot of someone else's novel. That, you may think, must surely present a real problem, since it is well known that there is only a handful of basic plots on which all fictional material must be based. And you wonder how on earth the writers of romantic fiction can avoid plagiarism since all their plots are almost bound to have many similarities. Yes, but they aren't all told in exactly the same way, they don't all have the same characters, the subplots vary considerably, and the main theme of the story will twist and turn in different ways. It is still possible to be original in your treatment. But if you follow the pattern of another author's story too exactly, then it is plagiarism.

It is really a matter of common sense. Don't pinch other writers' ideas or work. Don't even 'borrow' from them. 'Borrow' in this context is simply a euphemism for 'steal'. But if you do use existing material, at least rework it so extensively that it has become truly your own – and so that it is not recognizable to the original author.

Supposing you plagiarize another author by accident. This is more likely to happen with a plot than with the actual words. It is certainly possible that two novelists could come up with the same basic story and could choose to tell it in exactly the same way. It is also possible for an author to have read someone else's book some time ago, to forget all about it, and then to dig it out of the subconscious in the belief that it is an entirely original idea. In the former case, if you can prove that you had never read the other author's book, you may get away with it – but that's a pretty difficult thing to prove. In the latter case, you're probably firmly guilty of plagiarism, even if it was not, as it were, premeditated.

Obscenity, Blasphemous Libel, Sedition and other Offensive Material

It seems unlikely that obscenity, blasphemous libel and sedition will cause an author much trouble nowadays, when anything goes and freedom of speech is sacrosanct. However, even in a liberal society laws do exist to protect people from the publication of offensive material (or what those who legislate consider to be offensive).

It is still, for instance, possible to be prosecuted for publishing pornography (especially if it has to do with paedophilia), and the police periodically raid bookshops, and court orders are given for the destruction of obscene material (and of course there is an outcry when some perfectly respectable books get caught up, as inevitably they do from time to time, in such a prosecution).

Equally, there are laws which prohibit the promulgation of blasphemous material. At the time of writing this protection is given in Britain only to the Christian religion.

The idea of sedition dates back to a time when all power was in the hands of the king, who needed to protect himself against any attempt by his enemies to topple him from the throne; in today's climate, arguments for the overthrow of the government, for the establishment of a communist régime or of a fascist dictatorship, or indeed for the dissolution of the monarchy can be put forward in books with impunity, but there are still restrictions, which come under the heading of sedition, against the publication of material which the government of the day wishes to remain secret.

Finally, everyone must be aware of the laws which are designed to protect the ethnic minorities against the abuse of racism. Other forms of 'political correctness', although not actually enshrined in law, have to be observed, at least until the point when they reach patent absurdity.

Awareness of what is offensive should prevent you from getting into trouble – or at least it should mean that if you have written questionable material you have done so with your eyes open, knowing the dangers that you are courting. Your publisher, and the printer of the book, will be in the same boat, of course. One of the troubles is that, in this context, what you have written needs to offend one person only to bring down the whole force of the law on the heads of all three of you.

Wills

Everyone should make a will, simply because it will save all kinds of hassle after one's death. But are there any special words of advice for authors? Your copyrights will continue for up to seventy years after your death, and may go on earning money, and, for tax purposes, your executors will have to have some assessment made (probably by the publishers concerned or by your agent, if you have one) of the value of these assets. If you do not mention them specifically in your will, they will form part of your general estate and be inherited by your principal heirs; on the other hand, you may wish to leave special directions as to the disposal of such copyrights and the income from them, and indeed of your Moral Rights (which can be bequeathed independently of the copyright). You might bequeath them to relatives, or direct that the income from some or all of your books should go to one of the charities for authors, such as the Authors' Foundation or the Royal Literary Fund, or perhaps to such an organization as the Society of Authors, or the Writers' Guild, or International PEN, or Book Trust. Equally, you could simply direct that a sum of money from your general funds should go to one of these bodies. If you are wealthy, you might even consider setting aside enough money to fund a prize (possibly to be administered by the Society of Authors). Whatever you decide to do, your solicitor should be able to draw up an appropriate clause in the will, but it is probably worthwhile to consult any organization concerned which will be able to give specific advice on the best form of wording.

10

The Rewards of Writing

Every now and then considerable publicity is given to the success stories of certain bestselling authors. Hearing of the fortunes that they make, it is no wonder that many people think that writing is an easy way of making money. Most of them never get beyond thinking about it, but if they do try to write they are likely to discover that it is much harder work and demands far more skill than they thought. And of course, it is not just a matter of putting all those thousands of words on paper – there is also the business of planning and construction (which is what we are doing, as all we authors know, when we are discovered apparently asleep at our desks).

But there is another shock awaiting those who think that writing is the simple key to riches, for if they manage to complete their books and get them accepted for publication, they will discover that the average author's earnings are pitifully small. Very few can make writing a full-time .career unless they have other means of some kind. The income is also almost totally unpredictable, often varying from book to book and from year to year.

Moreover, even if you begin with a moderate success, there is no guarantee that it will continue – you may fail to have another book published at all, and if you do apparently establish yourself by having five or six books published, unless you've arrived in the bestseller class, you may find thereafter that your publisher is no longer interested in you and your writing. It's a cruel world. Mind you, ordinary, run-of-the-mill authors do survive and go on having their books published, but few of them can look forward to making much more than pin money.

So what are the rewards of writing? First of all, and despite the fact that I hear some of my readers giving a hollow laugh, there is the reward of writing for its own sake. Some authors like to talk about the agony of writing, but that's a load of old codswallop, and although writing may be hard and requires considerable stamina and application, I have yet to find an author who really and truly finds the work an agony. On the contrary, most will admit, if pressed, to the pleasure it gives them. There is a sense of achievement in putting words to paper, a joy in the creativity involved, and there can sometimes be great happiness in reading something you have written and finding satisfaction in it, feeling that you have managed to express exactly what you were intending to say, and in the best possible manner.

When, earlier in this book, I commented cynically on the statement that everyone has a book in him/her by saying that it should usually stay there, I was really making a commercial judgement; 'everyone' more often than not has neither an interesting enough story nor the skill with which to tell it to make the book a likely candidate for publication. But my cynicism ignores that simple pleasure which 'everyone' may get just from writing the story.

Few authors, except perhaps for ardent diarists, and even they may have half an eye on the main chance, write only for themselves, but there can be additional rewards here, even if your writing remains unpublished, for it may give great pleasure to your family and friends. I think particularly of those autobiographies with which every publisher is familiar, which do not get published because their authors are unknown and their lives neither unusual enough nor distinguished enough to be of wide, and saleable, interest. Those stories will probably be of great value to the family, especially your descendants. Don't we all regret how little we know of our grandparents and the generations before them?

So if this is the kind of book you think of writing, do go ahead – write it for your own enjoyment and that of your family. Don't expect to be published commercially, although of course there is no harm in trying to interest a publisher, and if you succeed in that, you will have earned yourself a bonus. Or if you write poetry or science fiction or treatises on unpronounceable chemical compounds or a manual of Pig Sticking, or even an account of your package holiday in Playa El Populario, Majorca, or the hilarious story of your house-moving – whatever you write, don't let anyone stop you or discourage you, and above all don't be disappointed if you do not achieve publication. Remember there are other rewards in writing.

However, you are probably still interested in the financial question. Let us suppose that you have something to say, are equipped to say it, and that it is of book length. (By 'something to say' I do not necessarily mean that you have to have some sort of message for the world, but that you have a story to tell, or information to impart; by 'equipped to say it' I mean that you have a modicum of writing ability, can express your thoughts on paper, perhaps have some understanding of the shape and form that a book requires, and the stamina to complete it; and by 'book length' I mean that, unless it falls into a category such as children's books or poetry, where much shorter lengths are acceptable, the completed typescript would be at least thirty to thirty-five thousand words in length – and preferably nearer to sixty thousand words, or indeed more, unless it is intended for a series in which the books are normally of shorter length than that.) So you write your book, and then have the good fortune to find a publisher who agrees to publish it. What can you expect to earn from it?

I cannot tell you. You could make a fortune, or you might barely cover your expenses, or end up out of pocket. You are likely to receive an advance from your publisher which might be as little as £100, or a more reasonable £750 to £1,500. The advance could equally be in a much higher bracket if the publisher can envisage a really large sale, or if there is a reasonable certainty of making sales of subsidiary rights for substantial sums.

If the advance is low, you will have some chance of earning royalties which exceed it, and indeed some authors feel that there is little point in pressing for a few hundred extra pounds to be added to the advance, preferring to look forward to the royalties which will come in sooner. But you have to remember that for a book priced at £14.99, more than one thousand copies have to be sold at a royalty of 10% to earn you £1,500, and many books nowadays fail to reach that sales figure. If the paperback rights are sold, the paperback publisher will probably pay an advance of upwards of £750, but you will have to share those moneys with your hardcover publisher in proportions determined in your contract. Translations may bring in extra sums, and if the US rights in your book are sold, the increase in your earnings could vary from modest to substantial. But it is all extremely chancy, and if you end up making £3,000 out of your book you have been far from unlucky. When you consider the fact that you have spent a great deal of time and effort in writing the book, and that the income does not usually arrive in one nice cheque, but may be spread over a long period – even several years – it is plain that you are not going to be rich. Even if you multiply those earnings by ten, meaning that you have had a fairly substantial success, it will probably take at least four years from the time you began to write until you have received the whole of the £30,000, so it scarcely adds up to a princely annual income.

Most of your income from books will come to you under the terms of the contracts you sign with your publishers or other persons or organizations which you license to use your work in some way, and this applies whether you sign up directly or use an agent. There are, however, two important sources of money which may come to you without the intervention of either publisher or agent. These are Public Lending Right and fees collected by the Authors' Licensing and Collecting Society, more details of which can be found on pp.220–3.

Another possibility is that you might receive a grant if you apply for one and your work is considered to be of special interest. The Regional Arts Boards sometimes award bursaries, usually when an author is working on a book and needs extra funds for research purposes, and moneys are available for similar purposes from various sources, such as the Authors' Foundation, which is administered by the Society of Authors. If you have a good case, make an initial enquiry to your local Arts Board or to the Society of Authors. Grants can also sometimes be obtained from the Royal Literary Fund.

Then the many prizes which are on offer must not be forgotten. The 1998 *Writers' and Artists' Yearbook* takes no less than twenty-eight pages to list all the prizes available, and just about every conceivable kind of writing seems to be eligible for one or other of them. Many are for published work, and in such cases it is usually up to the publisher to enter the books, but there are also several which can be awarded to unpublished work, which obviously has to be submitted by the author. The most prestigious prize of all, and by far the largest, is the Nobel Prize for Literature, which of course is given only to the most eminent of authors when they have established over a lifetime's work an international reputation and one which is expected to survive (although it must be admitted that many of the past winners are now almost totally forgotten). In Britain the most important of the major prizes is considered to be the Booker, awarded to the novel which the panel of judges deem to be the best published in the year under consideration, and its nearest challengers in terms of value and public interest are the Whitbread Literary Awards (which include the Whitbread Book of the Year), the *Sunday Express* Book of the Year Award, the International IMPAC Dublin Literary Award (currently exceptionally generous at £100,000), the Orange Prize for Fiction (for women writers only), and the Betty Trask Awards. Other notable prizes include the AT&T Non-fiction Award, the Lloyds Private Banking Playwright of the Year Award, and the Smarties Book Prize for a children's book. Many of the other awards are, of course, highly prestigious in their particular fields, although the public at large hears less of them than of those I have mentioned.

It cannot be repeated too often that bestsellerdom is not always solely a question of your ability as a writer, important though that is, but also depends to a frightening extent on luck – the luck of choosing the right title, finding the right publisher, being published at the right time, receiving the right kind of publicity, finding the public in the right mood to respond to your work. Many potential bestsellers are published every year, of which a few make it to the top, and the others sink without trace – and it is a matter of luck. Certainly some publishers are more vigorous than others in forcing their books on to the bestseller lists, and some authors feel that it is a great advantage to be published by one of the big concerns because of the extra weight they can bring to bear and their flexibility and strength of resources; others believe that you get far more personal attention, and therefore perhaps a better chance of becoming a bestseller in a small publishing house. Whether your publishers are large or small, however hard they may try to make you into a bestseller, they will have to have a little bit of luck – no, a fairly large bit of luck – to succeed.

The element of fortune is something that, if you are wise, you should accept. Some authors are forever bemoaning their failure to hit the jackpot, frequently blaming their publishers for their lack of success, whereas others content themselves with making a nice little addition to their income by writing and publishing new books regularly, but without hankering too continuously for rewards that they are never likely to earn. They keep their envy of luckier authors in check, and allow their dissatisfaction to focus on the quality of their own work – and of course, no good writers are ever entirely satisfied with what they write. This is not to say that you should have no confidence in yourself and your writing. I think all writers should constantly tell themselves that their new book is the best that they have ever written, but that it won't make them a fortune. The first part of that may help to keep up your morale, while the second half should help to ensure that your bank manager loses no sleep over you.

Of course, there are many prudent authors who manage their affairs without ever falling into debt, and who take a realistic view of the potential earning capacity of their work. Even when their publishers greet their new book with wild enthusiasm and begin to talk hysterically of enormous sales and US and foreign language and subsidiary rights buyers queuing up for the chance to bid for the book, these sober, sensible authors, instead of cracking a bottle of champagne to celebrate, will take a large pinch of salt with all that is said, and wait to see what happens. If the publishers are right, the champagne will keep for the few months before they are proved so; if they are wrong, a good cup of tea or coffee will be much cheaper and almost as cheering. It goes without saying that I am just such a sensible author, and I am sure that you, who are reading this now, are another.

Remember that any income you receive from writing has to be reported to the Inland Revenue, and you will be taxed on it. If you are a professional author, it is almost essential to get a good accountant, and preferably one who understands something of the author's position vis-à-vis the tax authorities. There are many expenses that authors can legitimately claim, such as the cost of all necessary stationery, research expenses, including the purchase of books for that purpose, postage and telephone (including telephone rental), travel and motoring costs, secretarial charges (which can include some remuneration for your spouse or partner who takes messages, checks proofs, helps with your research) and so on. And you can set capital expenses, such as the cost of your typewriter or PC, against your writing income. Of course, all these costs must be incurred solely for the purpose of your writing, and in the case, for instance, of telephone rental, unless you have a separate business line which you use solely as an author, only a proportion of the charges will be allowable. You should keep all bills and receipts in connection with your writing for your accountant's use, and you will need detailed records of business telephone calls, car mileage and the like for your tax return. Many authors keep a separate bank account through which they pass only income and expenditure directly to do with their writing. Few publishers are qualified to give reliable tax advice, but agents are often knowledgeable on the subject, and the Society of Authors or the Writers' Guild may be able to help, but there is really no substitute for a capable accountant.

I referred at the beginning of the last paragraph to 'professional' authors. If you are writing in your spare time from another job, which provides your main livelihood, can you really consider yourself a professional author? It depends on your attitude. If your whole approach to writing is professional, the fact that it is a spare-time job is irrelevant. Being professional means dedication and perseverance and determination never to fall below the highest standards that you can attain.

It is possible that, however professional your approach may be, you will fall upon hard times. If this should happen, there are, alas, unlikely to be any long-term solutions to the problem, but some sources of temporary help do exist. For instance, the Society of Authors has a Contingency Fund, from which grants may be made in the event of sudden financial hardship, and equally the Royal Literary Fund is available for authors or their dependants who find themselves in difficulties, and in some cases for the provision of small pensions.

Public Lending Right
As long ago as 1951, John Brophy (at that time a popular novelist, but now, alas, largely forgotten), convinced of the unfairness of a system which gave authors no reward for the thousands of borrowings of their books from Public Libraries, proposed that authors should be paid one penny ('the Brophy Penny') every time one of their books was so borrowed.

The issue was taken up by the Society of Authors, which persuaded A.P. Herbert to spearhead a campaign to bring in the necessary law. Various schemes were drawn up, which succeeding Ministers for the Arts considered and altered or rejected, and the matter dragged on unsatisfactorily for year after year. In 1972, the formation of the Writers' Action Group, led by the late Brigid Brophy (John's daughter) and Maureen Duffy, brought a new vigour to the battle. All authors owe an enormous debt of gratitude to Ms Brophy and Ms Duffy, for without their determined leadership Public Lending Right would not have become law as soon as it did and in a form which was suitable to most authors. They did not achieve success entirely alone – they were supported by the

Society of Authors and the Writers' Guild, by individuals, by agents and other interested parties – but let no one take away the credit due to them. It was not easy – indeed, it took seven years of intense lobbying from the time that the Writers' Action Group was formed until an Act was finally passed in 1979 and Public Lending Right was brought into being. Authors would register their books with a central authority; all books borrowed from a number of libraries in various parts of the country would be recorded for a period of twelve months; from these sample figures would be extrapolated the supposed borrowings for the country as a whole; the government would provide an annual sum of £2 million, which, after the deduction of administration costs, would be divided among the authors concerned in proportion to the number of times their books had been borrowed. Various conditions were built in, such as restricting the most popular authors to a maximum payment of £5,000, and limiting the scheme to authors who were still alive.

When the necessary administration was in place, PLR finally came into operation in 1983/4, but the sum which the government made available remained at £2 million, the figure allocated in 1979, despite the fact that substantial inflation had taken place in the intervening years. Since that time various adjustments have been made to the scheme, mostly to widen the scope of those who may benefit from it, and the money has been increased (although the increases have never caught up with inflation). In that first year, 7,562 authors registered for the scheme, the rate of payment worked out at 1.02p per loan, forty-six authors received the maximum payment of £5,000, 5,327 received £99 or less, and 1,449 got nothing at all (each book had to earn a minimum of £1 before any payment for that book was made). By 1995 the number of authors in the scheme had risen to just under 25,000, the rate of payment was 2p per loan, 104 authors received the maximum payment (which some years previously had been increased to £6,000), 14,630 received £99 or less, and 4,744 got nothing (another early change had been that the minimum of £1 could be earned from the total loans of *all* an author's registered books before any payment was made, and this minimum has recently been increased to £5). A sum of 2p per borrowing is not a large amount of money, and although authors will agree that even the most niggardly payment is better than nothing, many will remember that the Brophy Penny was 1d in the old money and in purchasing power its present-day equivalent would be at least 10p, and probably more.

One of the provisions of the Act, and this has not been changed by any subsequent amendments, is that PLR payments belong exclusively to the author. Publishers do not receive any part of them, and neither, since the moneys are paid direct to the author, do authors' agents. When the Public Lending Right Bill was first passed, many publishers felt that their exclusion from any benefit was unfair, and they certainly had a valid point. However, the law is the law, and publishers generally have come to accept it without quibble. But if you should come across any attempt by a publisher or an agent to take a percentage of your PLR earnings, you should resist very firmly.

The responsibility for registering for PLR remains with authors. It is not undertaken by your publisher or your agent – you, the author, are the one who has to send details of your book or books to the PLR office. It is easy to do, and will cost you no more than a couple of postage stamps (one to get a form, and one to send it back when completed). Thereafter you can easily add any new books to your list. For full details write to: Public Lending Right Office, Bayheath House, Prince Regent Street, Stockton-on-Tees, Cleveland TS18 1DF.

The Authors' Licensing and Collecting Society
Set up by writers in 1977, this organization collects sums of money which are due to authors for certain subsidiary rights in their works (rights which are not licensed to publishers), but which for special reasons cannot be paid to the authors directly. The Authors' Licensing and Collecting Society (ALCS) then distributes the moneys to the authors concerned. Among such payments are fees for cable transmission of television programmes, and educational off-air recording fees, but the bulk of the money paid to the authors of books comes from two sources – public lending right in foreign countries, and photocopying fees.

Britain is not the only country to have PLR. It exists also in a number of EU countries and in some parts of the rest of the world. In Germany, to take one example, PLR is allocated to British authors, but cannot by German law be distributed directly to the authors; it is therefore transmitted to ALCS and passed by them to the authors concerned. As the principle of PLR becomes accepted throughout the world, more and more countries are likely to be making payments through ALCS to British authors.

ALCS is the joint owner, together with the Publishers Licensing

Society (PLS) of the Copyright Licensing Agency (CLA), which exists to license and collect fees, in respect of the photocopying of copyright material, from organizations such as schools, universities, industry, government offices and various professional organizations and societies. The moneys it collects are split between authors, represented by ALCS, and publishers. Its first payments, made in 1987/88 amounted to £1.4 million. The sums have increased year by year as, with the law behind it, the CLA expands its licensing to cover the ever-widening use of photocopying machines. At the time of writing, the total amount which the organisation has passed to authors and publishers has reached over £50 million. CLA is also watching with extreme care the developments in the field of electronics which could involve the storage and use of copyright material, and will be vigilant in its protection of the interests of both publishers and authors, and will collect and distribute any fees due.

To join ALCS, write to The Membership Secretary, ALCS, Marlborough Court, 14-18 Holborn, London EC1NA 2LE (tel: 0171 395 0600; fax: 0171 395 0660). The annual subscription is currently £5.88 (inclusive of VAT), but members of the Society of Authors and the Writers' Guild are entitled to free membership of ALCS, and are automatically entered on their books.

11

Organizations For Authors

Authors like to say, with an air of martyrdom, that being an author is a lonely business. In fact it is. It is not just that one tends to write in a private world, shut off by the act of creation even from one's family and friends; it is also frequently very difficult to know where to go for unbiased advice regarding one's dealings with publishers, and for the companionship of others whose problems and pleasures may be somewhat similar.

In the matter of advice, it is hoped that this book will be of some help, but it clearly cannot cover every problem that may arise. You may feel that you can rely on your agent for sound advice, but supposing that you want to find out whether she/he is behaving well towards you in the way that an agent should. And if you have no agent anyway, where can you go?

The Society of Authors
The Society of Authors, which has over 6,000 members, was founded in 1884, and exists primarily to further the interests of authors and to defend their rights. It therefore acts as an advisory body to its individual members, but also represents authors' interests in negotiation with government departments (over such matters as VAT and PLR) and with publishers, either individually or through the Publishers Association, and with any other bodies which may be concerned with authors and their work. It also administers various prizes and funds, and acts for the estates of a number of deceased authors. After a referendum of its members, the Society became, in 1978, an independent trade union. It is not affiliated to the TUC, and is completely non-political.

The Society offers free legal advice and, in some cases, representation to its members, but does make the rule that it cannot be involved in a legal dispute which is already in existence at the time you join the Society – in other words, if you are in the middle of a legal argument with your publisher, for instance, it is no use rushing off to join the Society of Authors and expecting it immediately to take on your case with all the attendant expenses. If you are already a member and were before the dispute began, that is a different matter.

The Society also offers free business advice to its members, and this includes two services in particular: the provision of information about publishers and agents, and the clause-by-clause vetting of publishing agreements. Medical insurance and pension schemes are also available to members, plus fringe benefits such as books and stationery for purchase at specially reduced rates. Although principally concerned with advisory and representational activities, the Society also organizes seminars and other events which combine the useful and the merely social.

The Society includes a number of specialist sub-organizations: Broadcasting, Children's Writers, Educational Writers, Medical and Technical Groups, and a Translators Association. It publishes a quarterly magazine, *The Author*, and it has available a most useful set of 'Quick Guides' to such subjects as Copyright, The Protection of Titles, Income Tax, Libel, Value Added Tax, Publishing Contracts, and Authors' Agents, and 'Guidelines' for Academic, Educational and Medical Writers. These leaflets are free to members, and available to others at a modest fee.

Full membership is open only to those who have had a full-length work commercially published or broadcast or performed in the UK or who have an established reputation in another medium. Associate membership is available if you have had a manuscript accepted for publication but not yet published and if you have had occasional items published, broadcast or performed. The annual subscription is a set sum (currently £70, with a small concession for those who pay by Direct Debit, and larger concessions in some cases for members under 35 or over 65). It includes free and automatic membership of the Authors' Licensing and Collecting Society (see Chapter 10). Full details may be obtained from The Membership Secretary, The Society of Authors, 84 Drayton Gardens, London SW10 9SB (tel: 0171 373 6642; fax: 0171 373 5768).

If you are not a member of the Society, but qualify for membership, I would earnestly ask you to consider joining, and for three reasons: firstly, the wider and stronger the membership the more power that the Society (and the Writers' Guild) can wield in negotiations with the government and with publishers; secondly, the reasonable deal that most authors receive nowadays from publishers is due in no small measure to the efforts of the Society over the past century, and I think joining can be regarded as a necessary expression of gratitude for that work, and of hope for future improvements; thirdly, the services which the Society offers are in themselves of considerable value, including of course the fact that if you are a member and have a book accepted by a publisher who is a signatory of the Minimum Terms Agreement you will be entitled to have all the benefits of that arrangement incorporated into your agreement.

The Writers' Guild of Great Britain
Founded in 1959, this organization was originally called the Television and Screenwriters' Guild, and although it now includes representation for all kinds of authors, and has a special Books section, it is still primarily orientated towards the film, television, radio and theatre writer.

The Guild's principal aims are twofold: firstly, to give individual advice and help to members on the whole range of issues involving their business life as writers, including legal advice, taxation and contracts; and secondly, to negotiate minimum terms agreements in each of the five industries using a writer's work. The Guild currently has agreements providing for protection for its members in film, television, radio, theatre and books. It publishes a monthly Newsletter.

Membership of the Writers' Guild of Great Britain is open to anyone who has had work published, broadcast or performed (using a somewhat complex points system for minor works), and to any writer who has had a contract offered, even if it has not yet been signed. The current annual subscription (which includes free and automatic membership of the Authors' Licensing and Collecting Society – see Chapter 10) is £70, plus 1% of that part of an author's income earned from professional writing sources in the previous calendar year. Full details are available from The Membership Secretary, The Writers' Guild of Great Britain, 430 Edgware Road, London W2 1EH (tel: 0171 723 8074; fax: 0171 706 2413).

The Writers' Guild of Great Britain and the Society of Authors work amicably and closely together on such issues as PLR, the MTA and reprography (reproduction by photographic means – primarily by photocopiers). Many of the members' benefits available from the Guild parallel those offered by the Society, and indeed there is a considerable area of overlap as far as operation of the two organizations is concerned. Amalgamation has been proposed, but while this would make sense in many ways, the two groups are sharply divided on some issues. One of these is that, although the Guild makes it clear that it is non-political, has no involvement with any political party and pays no political levy, it is nevertheless affiliated to the TUC and to other individual unions in the Entertainments industry. The Society is not so affiliated.

PEN – The World Association of Writers

This international organization was founded in 1921 to promote friendship and understanding between writers and to defend freedom of expression within and between all nations. The initials P.E.N. stand for Poets, Playwrights, Editors, Essayists, Novelists, but membership is open to any writer or translator (or indeed to anyone who works in virtually any capacity in the book business), provided that he/she is of good standing and subscribes to those principles. PEN Centres are spread throughout the world; each is autonomous and organizes various seminars and other events for its members, and many of the centres issue regular journals. An International Congress takes place every year. One of PEN's most important concerns (and indeed a good reason for joining) is with the plight of writers who are imprisoned or otherwise persecuted for daring to express views which do not coincide with those of the régimes under which they live. PEN Centres have campaigned for the freedom of such writers, and even when their efforts have met with failure, they have sometimes been able to pass greatly appreciated messages of encouragement to the authors – clearly something which deserves the support of every writer in the free world. Full details may be obtained from: PEN International, 7 Dilke Street, London SW3 4JE (tel: 0171 352 6303; fax: 0171 351 0220).

Book Trust

Worthy of support by all authors, Book Trust exists to promote books and reading in any and every possible way. While it receives the support of all branches of the book trade, it is in no way dependent on any of them, and for this reason and because of its charitable status is able to speak for books to bodies who might be suspicious of a commercial purpose or vested interest. Membership is open to everyone interested in books and reading. Book Trust has a useful information service about books published in the UK and USA; it arranges exhibitions; it has a Children's Book Reference Library and the Mark Longman Library, a collection of books about books, publishing and bookselling. The Trust administers various Literary Awards, notably the Booker Prize, and produces a wide variety of books, pamphlets and leaflets designed to make books more easily accessible to the public. Full details may be obtained from: Book Trust, Book House, 45 East Hill, Wandsworth, London SW18 2QZ (tel: 0181 870 9055; fax: 0181 874 4790).

Author–Publisher Enterprise
This organization exists to help and support self publishers. It runs courses, and provides information and advice about self publishing. For details write to: Author-Publisher Enterprise, 7 Kingsland Road, West Mersea, Essex CO5 8RB (tel: 01206 382558).

Writers' Circles
Many authors find congenial companionship in attending writers' circles. The membership usually comprises both regularly published authors and those whose work has not appeared in print, and standards of ability are liable to vary greatly within the group. A programme of lectures and social activities is usually arranged, but the reading of their new work by members to the assembled company, which is then free to criticize it, is always one of the main functions of a writers' circle, and can be very helpful, provided that you are not too thin-skinned. You should be able to find details of your local circles in the Public Library. A Directory of Writers' Circles is available from Mrs Jill Dick, Oldacre, Horderns Park Road, Chapel-en-le-Frith, Derbyshire SK12 6SY.

Writers' Conferences
Arising out of the writers' circle movement and as an extension of the functions of such groups, many residential courses for writers take place up and down the country. Some are run to make money for their organizers, and can be quite expensive, but those which are best attended are non-profit-making, with quite modest fees. The writers who go to these conferences find the diet of lectures from experts, discussion groups, brief instructional courses and

social activities very much to their taste; they include writers working in every genre, from journalism to poetry, from children's books to biography, from drama to all varieties of fiction, and they range in experience from complete beginners to bestselling authors. Many writers have been attending these conferences year after year for donkey's ages, and they do so at least in part for the pleasure of talking to others who share the same interest in all aspects of the writing business.

The most popular and longest-established of these residential courses is the Writers' Summer School, which takes place at Swanwick in Derbyshire for a week every August. Full details may be obtained from: Mrs Brenda Courtie, The New Vicarage, Parsons Street, Woodford Halse, Daventry, Northants NN11 3RE.

Other popular gatherings include:

Writers' Holiday, held at Caerleon in South Wales, in late July. For details write to Mrs D.L. Anne Hobbs, 30 Pant Road, Newport, NP9 5PR.

Southern Writers Conference, held at Chichester, West Sussex, in mid-June. For details write to Mrs Lucia White, Stable House, Home Farm, Coldharbour Lane, Dorking, Surrey RH4 3JG.

Scottish Association of Writers' Weekend Conference, held at Crieff, Perthshire, in April. For details write to Ms Anne Graham, 55 Grange Loan, Edinburgh, EH9 2ER.

Scottish Association of Writers' Weekend Workshop, held at Pitlochry, Perthshire, in October. For details write to Ms Anne Trevorrow, Old Quarterhouse, Darvel, Ayrshire KA17 0ND.

Scarborough Writers' Weekend, held at Scarborough, North Yorkshire, in October or November. For details write to Mrs Audrey Wilson, 7 Osgodby Close, Scarborough, North Yorkshire YO11 3JW.

South East Writers Association Weekend, held in Leigh-on-Sea in April. For details write to Mrs Marion Hough, 47 Sunningdale Avenue, Leigh-on-Sea, Essex SS9 1JY.

Annual Writers' Conference, held in Winchester in June. For details write to Mrs Barbara Large, Chinook, Southdown Road, Shawford, Hampshire SO21 2BY.

The Arvon Foundation

This organization offers people of all ages over sixteen the chance to meet, talk and work in an informal way with practising artists. There are three Arvon centres – in Yorkshire, Devon and the North

West Highlands. The centres provide a full programme of five-day courses in various fields of writing and related art forms. Full details may be obtained from: The Arvon Foundation, Lumb Bank, Heptonstall, Hebden Bridge, West Yorkshire HX7 6DF, or The Arvon Foundation, Totleigh Barton, Sheepwash, Beaworthy, Devon EX21 5NS, or The Arvon Foundation, Moniack Mhor, Kirkhill, Inverness IV5 7PQ. Incidentally, many of the Regional Arts Associations are willing in certain cases to subsidize would-be writers who wish to attend one of the Arvon courses, so it is worthwhile for such persons to contact the local Arts Association in this matter (for addresses, see below).

Creative Writing Classes
Creative writing classes (usually run under the auspices of local Adult Education authorities) are intended primarily for those who have not been successful in achieving publication, but many successful authors do attend them. Their value naturally depends on the ability of the tutor taking the classes, which in many cases differ from the average writers' circle only in that the tutor is there as a kind of superior authority when the members' work is discussed, although some of the time may be devoted to formal lectures and instruction from the tutor. Some people attend the classes more for the sake of a pleasant evening among fellow writers than for the instruction. Details are available from Adult Education offices and from Public Libraries.

The Regional Arts Boards
The Regional Arts Boards are sometimes able to offer bursaries to authors to assist them while they are writing books. They also often help to subsidize local literary events, visits of authors to schools, courses for would-be writers, etc., and several run a criticism service enabling authors to get a professional assessment of their work. Their addresses are:

East Midlands Arts Board, Mountfields House, Epinal Way, Loughborough, Leicestershire LE11 0QE (tel: 01509 218292; fax: 01509 262214).

Eastern Arts Board, Cherry Hinton Hall, Cherry Hinton Road, Cambridge CB1 4DW (tel: 01223 215355; fax: 01223 248075).

London Arts Board, Elme House, 133 Long Acre, Covent Garden, London WC2E 9AF (tel: 0171 240 1313; fax: 0171 240 4580).

North West Arts Board, Manchester House, 22 Bridge Street, Manchester M3 3AB (tel: 0161 834 6644; fax: 0161 834 6969).

Northern Arts, 9-10 Osborne Terrace, Newcastle upon Tyne, NE2 1NZ (tel: 0191 281 6334; fax: 0191 281 3276).

South East Arts Board, 10 Mount Ephraim, Tunbridge Wells, Kent TN4 8AS (tel: 01892 515210; fax: 01892549383).

South West Arts, Bradninch Place, Gandy Street, Exeter, Devon EX4 3LS (tel: 01392 218188; fax: 01392 413554).

Southern Arts Board, 13 St Clement Street, Winchester, Hants SO23 9DQ (tel: 01962 855099; fax: 01962 861186).

West Midlands Arts Board, 82 Granville Street, Birmingham B1 2LH (tel: 0121 631 3121; fax: 0121 643 7239).

Yorkshire and Humberside Arts, 21 Bond Street, Dewsbury, West Yorkshire WF13 1AX (tel: 01924 455555; fax: 01924 466522).

For Scotland information can be obtained from the Scottish Arts Council, 12 Manor Place, Edinburgh EH3 7DD (tel: 0131 226 6051).

For Wales information can be obtained from the Arts Council of Wales, 9 Museum Place, Cardiff CF1 3NX (tel: 01222 394711; fax: 01222 221447).

For Northern Ireland information can be obtained from the Arts Council of Northern Ireland, 185 Stranmillis Road, Belfast BT9 5DU (tel: 01232 381591; tax: 01232 661715).

Other Organizations for Writers
Societies exist for both general and almost all specialized interests in the spectrum of writing. Both the *Writers' and Artists' Yearbook* and *The Writer's Handbook* carry comprehensive lists of such organizations.

Glossary

Advance The moneys paid to an author in advance and on account of the earnings of the book concerned. Normally non-returnable. Often referred to in the USA as a 'guarantee'.

ALCS The Authors' Licensing and Collecting Society (see p.222).

Backlist After a book is published it becomes, if it continues to sell, part of its publisher's backlist. A publisher cannot exist on the sale of new books alone, but is constantly looking for books which will sell over a period of years – i.e. potential backlist titles.

Bastard title Another term for 'half title', q.v.

Binding Hardcover books are usually bound by being sewn and cased, i.e. the signatures are sewn together and a stiff binding is then attached by means of the endpapers. Paperbacks are more often 'perfect bound', i.e. the back edges of the signatures are trimmed, so that each page is separate, and glued and the stiff paper cover is then drawn on.

Bleeding Illustrations which go off the edge of the page, so that there is no surround to the illustration, are said to 'bleed'.

Blues See *Ozalids*.

Blurb The advertising copy which the publisher uses on the jacket or cover of a book, in the catalogue, and in various other ways. A blurb is not to be confused with a synopsis, and should not attempt to cover in detail all the contents of a book. It usually consists of some indication of what the book is about, couched in terms which are designed to intrigue the reader, plus a number of statements, which cannot always be relied upon to be entirely truthful, intended to persuade potential customers that the book is one which they cannot afford to be without. The best blurbs are short and pithy, and have both a selling and a teasing quality, like a good trailer for a film.

Boards The stiff cardboard used in binding a hardcover book. As a descriptive term in a catalogue, 'boards' means that the book has a hardcover binding (the boards often being covered with a decorative paper bearing the title, author's name and an illustration), but no jacket.

Brasses The title of a book, the author's name, the publisher's name or colophon, and sometimes decorative designs are printed on to the binding of a hardcover book by means of brasses (which are nowadays more likely to be made of other material than brass and called 'chemacs').

Camera-ready copy Most printing processes nowadays involve photography, for which material has to be produced which is error-free, with everything correctly positioned as it is to appear on the page, and which can therefore be called, with a literal meaning, 'camera-ready copy'.

Cancel page A page inserted in a printed book in place of a page which contains an error or other material which it is essential to change, even at the cost of this expensive process.

Case The binding of a hardcover book. Alternatively, the tray in which moveable type is stored, the upper part containing capital letters and the lower part small letters; 'upper case' has hence become a synonym for capitals and 'lower case' for small letters. For most practical purposes, however, moveable type is not now used (except perhaps by a few small jobbing printers).

Cased A book with a hardcover binding is often referred to as 'cased'.

Cast off A word count usually prepared in a publisher's production department or by a printer. The object is to work out accurately the number of pages that the book in question will occupy, given a specified type size and type area, and allowing for any special requirements such as illustrations, tables, or material set in a different way from that of the main text.

Chemacs See *Brasses*

CLA Copyright Licensing Agency (see p.222)

Cloth Nearly all hardcover books used to be bound in real cloth. Nowadays 'cloth' is more often a special kind of hard-wearing paper, frequently embossed with a pattern to give the impression that it is a woven fabric. The term is rarely used by publishers nowadays (it would be an incorrect trade description), but some traditionalists in the bookselling business still like to preserve it.

Co-edition A book produced simultaneously for two or more

publishers and for different areas of the world, or languages, in order to reduce printing costs.

Colophon The term is usually used in the book trade to describe the device which publishers use as their sign or trademark. It is often to be found on the title page and in many cases on the spine of the binding and jacket, while paperback publishers also place it on the front covers of their books.

Composition The conversion of the author's copy, which has been produced on a typewriter or word processor, into the type from which the book will be printed. The composition is usually done on a computer, producing camera-ready copy or film or a disc. This process involves re-keying all the copy, but use of the author's PC discs can eliminate most, if not all, such labour.

Copyright page Another term for 'imprint page', q.v.

Cover See *Jacket*.

Double-page Spread When an illustration or a group of illustrations runs across and fills two facing pages, it is called a 'double-page spread' (sometimes shortened to 'double spread'). The same term may be applied to a publisher's advertisement on two facing pages of, for instance, *The Bookseller*, or to two facing pages devoted to a single book in a catalogue.

Dummy A book made of the paper to be used in the finished article, and bound in the style that will be used for the book, but without the pages being printed. The dummy is used, among other things, for the preparation of the jacket, since it shows the size of the book, including the width of the spine. Dummies are sometimes prepared with a few pages of printed material, especially in the case of highly illustrated books, to give foreign publishers and bookbuyers in the trade an impression of what the final book will look like.

Dust Jacket See *Jacket*.

Edition An edition of a book is not the same as an impression. Each impression of the book, that is to say the first and subsequent printings, contains the same material. Each edition, on the other hand, is altered in some substantial way from the previous edition.

Em A unit of measurement in printing. Since it is based on the width of the letter 'm', its size can obviously vary with the size of the type. However, the term is frequently taken to mean a standard 12pt 'm', equalling roughly one-sixth of an inch. See also Point size.

Endpapers The four pages at the beginning and end of a hardcover book by means of which the case is attached. Endpapers are sometimes printed with a decoration or perhaps a map.

Extent The length of a book in words, or in typescript or printed pages.

Flap The part of the jacket which is folded inside the cover of the book. 'Front flap' and 'back flap' are terms which are frequently used.

Folded and Collated After printing, the sheets of paper are folded into signatures, which are collated or gathered into groups, so that each group contains all the signatures which make up the book.

Folio Although this word has a number of definitions relating to sheets of paper (a single sheet, for instance, or the size of sheet obtained by folding a standard basic sheet once), in printing and publishing it is normally used to mean the page number.

Format The size and shape of a book. See also *Paper sizes*.

Gutter The 'join' where two facing pages of a book meet.

Half-title A page of a book on which is printed the title of the book, or the title of a Part (in which case it should really be called a 'Part-title'), but which does not normally carry the author's name or that of the publisher.

ISBN International Standard Book Number. A world-wide system of identifying books by means of a ten-digit number. The first digit identifies the book's country of origin, the next four the publisher, the next four the individual title, and the final number is a check digit.

Imposition The arrangement of the pages for printing so that when the sheet is folded the pages will appear in their correct sequence.

Impression A printing of a book. New impressions are reprints without changes having been made to the contents. See also *Edition*.

Imprint The publisher's name printed at the foot of the title-page is the publisher's imprint. The printer's imprint, giving the name and address of the firm, is usually printed at the foot of the imprint (or biblio) page.

Imprint page The page of the book which contains all or most of the following details: the copyright notice and assertion of the author's moral rights, the printing history of the book, the ISBN, the publisher's name and address, British Library Cataloguing in Publication Data, the printer's imprint, and any other similar necessary information. It is usually on the back, or verso, of the title-page.

In print Books which are 'in print' are available from the publisher, as opposed to those which are no longer in stock and will not be reprinted and are designated 'out of print'. The phrase 'in print' is also used to indicate the number of copies printed of a book to date – 'There are fifty thousand copies of this book in print, made up of nine impressions,' or 'We have published ten of this author's books, totalling over two million copies of his work in print in paperback editions.'

Jacket Sometimes still called 'dust jacket' or 'dust wrapper', this is the loose paper cover on a hardcover book, usually carrying the title and the author's name on the front, often with an illustration, and a blurb and the retail price on the front flap. Paperbacks do not normally have jackets, and their stiff paper bindings are known as 'covers'.

Leading Space between lines of type.

Letter spacing Space between the letters of a word, often used when the word is entirely in capitals, as in a title.

Limp Binding in which boards are not used. Paperbacks could technically be described as having a limp binding, but in practice the term is normally used only for books bound without boards in cloth or imitation cloth.

List The books which a publisher produces – 'We are glad to announce that X has joined our list,' or 'Our list contains general non-fiction and medical books, but not fiction.'

Literal The equivalent in composition of a typing error. In America the term 'typo' is used.

MTA Minimum Terms Agreement (see Chapter 6).

Net Book Agreement A trade agreement which prevented booksellers from selling books at less than the retail price fixed by the publisher, thus protecting them from competitive price-cutting. It no longer exists, and booksellers are now allowed to sell books at discounted prices. See p.45.

Orphan When the last line on a page happens to be the first line of a paragraph, it is called an 'orphan'. It is a companion term to that other great typographical sin, the 'widow', q.v. 'Club line' is a less picturesque synonym, in this context, for 'orphan'.

Ozalids Proofs of highly illustrated books often come in the form of 'ozalids'. Authors are often appalled by them, but should be reassured that they do not reflect the quality of the finished printing. Since ozalids are blue, they are often referred to as 'blues'.

PA The Publishers Association, to which some 300 publishers, including almost all the major houses, belong.

Paper Three main kinds of paper are used for books: antique, a comparatively rough-surfaced paper, used for most books without integrated tonal illustrations; calendered paper, which has been subjected to a smoothing process, used for illustrated books; art paper, coated with china clay or other material to give a glossy surface for the fine printing of illustrations.

Paper sizes The most popular sizes of paper for books are Metric Crown, Metric Large Crown, Metric Demy and Metric Royal, of which quad sheets (i.e. sheets four times the basic sizes) measure in millimetres 768 x 1008, 816 x 1056, 888 x 1128 and 960 x 1272 respectively. The terms 'quarto (4to)', 'octavo (8vo)', 'sixteenmo (16mo)' refer to the number of times the basic sheet of paper is folded to produce a signature; quarto is folded twice, producing an untrimmed Metric Crown page size, for instance, of 252 x 192 mm; octavo is folded three times, producing an untrimmed Metric Demy page size, for instance, of 222 x 141 mm; and so on. Trimming will remove a few millimetres on the fore-edge and the top and bottom. Paper is used not only in quad sheets, but in larger sizes, and also in reels. The use of terms like Metric Crown 8vo to indicate the size and shape of a book have gone out of fashion, and most publishers now use the measurements of the trimmed page instead.

Paste-up A paste-up is usually prepared for highly illustrated books, taking the proofs of the text and illustrations and pasting them into the blank pages of a dummy to show the printer the exact position required.

Perfect binding See *Binding*

Plant costs This term normally refers to all the costs of production prior to the actual printing of the book. It therefore includes composition, preparation of film, manufacture of binding brasses, etc.

PLR Public Lending Right (see p.220)

PLS Publishers' Licensing Society. Joint owner with the Authors' Licensing and Collecting Society of the Copyright Licensing Agency (see p.222)

Point size Type sizes are indicated in points, this showing the height of the block on which, in the case of moveable type, the individual letter stands. So one refers to '10pt type', for example, or '36pt type'. A point equals approximately 1/72 inch.

Prelims The first or preliminary pages of a book, including half-title and title pages, imprint page, contents, etc., before the text begins.

Printing processes Virtually all books nowadays are printed by offset lithography. Letterpress – printing direct from type – which used to be the standard method for all short-run production and was basically the same process as Caxton used, is now quite outdated.

Print run The number of copies of a book printed at any one time.

Proofs Proofs come in various forms. Galley proofs are long strips of paper on which long columns of print, not yet split up into pages, appear. Paged galleys are also long strips of paper, but the columns of type on them have been divided into pages, although these have not yet been imposed. Other proofs may look like computer print-outs. Page proofs normally look much like paperbacks, the type having been split into pages and the pages imposed.

Recto A right-hand page in a book is called the 'recto'. A left-hand page is the 'verso'.

Remainder When publishers find that a book appears to have stopped selling, they may try to sell off the stock at a very low price to certain traders who specialize in such purchases. Books sold in this way are called 'remainders' and the people who buy them are 'remainder merchants'. The word 'remainder' is also used as a verb – 'I shall have to remainder this title.'

Running head The headline at the top of a page. Sometimes the title of a book is repeated on all pages, but more often the book title appears on the verso and the chapter title or title of a sub-section on the recto.

Sheets This term is used mainly in the context of 'folded and collated sheets'. When a book is printed the sheets have to be folded and collated before the book can be bound. Sometimes, however, the publisher does not wish at the time to bind all the copies printed, and may keep part of the stock in the form of folded and collated sheets. Folded and collated sheets may also be sold unbound – to library suppliers, for instance – and in many co-editions the originating publisher will supply the other publishers concerned with sheets rather than bound stock.

Signature When a printed sheet has been folded into pages it is called a 'signature'. Signatures usually consist of sixteen or thirty-two pages (although it is possible to have signatures of four or eight pages). For this reason the extent of a book is usually a multiple of thirty-two or sixteen, although this may not always be apparent if the publisher has chosen to ignore the prelims and to start numbering the book so that page one is the first page of the main text.

Spine The back, or what you might call the closed end, of a book, and especially the central part of the binding case, frequently rounded.

Subscription When publishers sell their books to booksellers and other trade outlets prior to publication they 'subscribe' them. Such advance sales are 'subscription' sales. The word 'subscription' is also used to mean the total number of copies of a book sold before publication.

Subsidiary rights Strictly speaking, all rights in a book other than those of the original publishers to produce their own editions of the book. In many contracts, however, the clause concerning subsidiary rights does not include paperback, bookclub, United States or translation rights, which are dealt with under separate headings.

Synopsis A summary of the complete contents of a book, usually prepared by an author in the hope of persuading a publisher to commission the book, or at least to agree to read it. A synopsis usually confines itself to factual details of what the book is about, rather than including comments designed to 'sell' the product, which are the province of the blurb, q.v. Synopses range in length from a mere list of chapter titles to several thousand words detailing, for instance, the characters and the twists and turns of plot of a long, complex novel.

Title Apart from the obvious meaning of the name of a book, publishers use this word as a synonym for 'book' – 'I am publishing twenty titles this Spring.'

Title page The page which carries the title of the book, usually in large type, the author's name, and, in most cases at the foot of the page, the publisher's name.

Title verso Another term for 'imprint page', q.v.

Trade paperback This term is usually applied to a paperback edition produced by a hardcover publisher rather than a mass market paperback house. It uses the same format, paper and size of type as would be used for a hardcover edition, differing only in having a stiff paper cover rather than a binding of cloth-covered boards and a jacket. The edition is usually comparatively small and the price therefore falls somewhere between that of a hardcover book and that of a mass market paperback.

Verso See *Recto.*

Volume rights A somewhat vague term, subject to varying interpretations, but usually taken basically to mean the rights offered or granted to a publisher to produce the work in book form, plus the right to issue bookclub, paperback and other reprint editions (or to license others to do so).

Widow   A short line appearing as the first line of a new page. Typographers dislike 'widows'. They also dislike 'orphans', q.v. In bygone days, when it was often quite costly to rejig the type, printers would do so in order to avoid widows and orphans. Nowadays, despite the fact that computer setting makes it comparatively easy to carry out any such adjustments, typesetters appear to be quite casual about these typographical infelicities, and they appear all over the place in considerable profusion.

Wrapper   see *Jacket*.

Appendix I
Proof Reader's Marks

The symbols for correcting proofs are taken from a British Standard BS 5261: PART 2 1976 *Copy preparation and proof correction - Specification of typographic requirements, marks for copy preparation and proof correction, proofing procedure.* Extracts from the new Standard are reproduced below with the permission of BSI. Complete copies can be obtained from them at Linford Wood, Milton Keynes, Bucks, MK14 6LE. All authors, printers and publishers are recommended to adopt the new correction symbols.

Instruction	Textual Mark	Marginal Mark
Delete and close up	through character or through character e.g. chara͡cter chara͡cter	
Substitute character or substitute part of one or more word(s)	through character or through word(s)	New character or new word(s)
Wrong fount. Replace by character(s) of correct fount	Encircle character(s) to be changed	
Change damaged character(s)	Encircle character(s) to be changed	
Set in or change to italic	under character(s) to be set or changed	
Set in or change to capital letters	under character(s) to be set or changed	
Set in or change to small capital letters	under character(s) to be set or changed	
Set in or change to capital letters for initial letters and small capital letters for the rest of the words	under initial letters and under rest of word(s)	
Set in or change to bold type	under character(s) to be set or changed	
Change capital letters to lower case letters	Encircle character(s) to be changed	
Change italic to upright type	Encircle character(s) to be changed	

Appendix I

Instruction	Textual Mark	Marginal Mark
Invert type	Encircle character to be inverted	
Substitute or insert full stop or decimal point	/ through character or ⅄ where required	
Substitute or insert semi-colon	/ through character or ⅄ where required	;
Substitute or insert comma	/ through character or ⅄ where required	,
Start new paragraph		
Run on (no new paragraph)		
Centre	[enclosing matter to be centred]	[ ]
Indent		
Cancel Indent		
Move matter specified distance to the right	enclosing matter to be moved to the right	

Instruction	Textual Mark	Marginal Mark
Take over character(s), word(s) or line to next line, column or page		
Take back character(s), word(s) or line to previous line, column or page		
Raise matter	over matter to be raised / under matter to be raised	
Lower matter	over matter to be lowered / under matter to be lowered	
Correct horizontal alignment	Single line above and below misaligned matter e.g. $mi_{sal}{}^{ig}n_ed$	
Close up. Delete space between characters or words	linking characters	
Insert space between characters	between characters affected	
Insert space between words	between words affected	
Reduce space between characters	between characters affected	
Reduce space between words	between words affected	
Make space appear equal between characters or words	between characters or words affected	

Appendix II
Model Royalty Statement

19(c)/79 Telephone: Littlewick Green 3104
Telegrams: Scholarly, Maidenhead
Registered Number 522538 England

EDWARD ARNOLD (PUBLISHERS) LTD.
Woodlands Park Avenue,
Maidenhead, Berkshire.

Our Ref: 123456

H.W. Smith,
Royalty Manager

31st March, 1979.

ROYALTY STATEMENT NO. 1.

Period Covered 1st July 1978 to 31st December 1978

To: C.O. Mittee Esq.,
    19 Bedford Square,
    London WC1B 3HJ

Author:	**GUILD & MITTEE**
Title:	**Royalty Statements for Authors**
SBN:	**0 7131 4142X**
Date Published:	**9th October 1978**

Printing Qty: **Previous Periods: —**
                           This period   : 50,000

SALES DETAIL		Published Price	Proceeds £	Royalty Rate	Royalty £	p
General Sales	10,000	£1.00	n.a.	10% of PP	1,000	00
General Sales†	2,000	£1.00		12½% of PP	250	00
Special Sales:						
Flat sheets to USA	5,000	n.a.	2,250	12½% of Rec	281	25
Subsidiary Rights						
as detailed		n.a.	n.a.	n.a.	25	00
Cumulative Sales	17,000					
†Change of rate after						
10,000 General Sales						
Note: n.a. = not applicable						
Total Royalties etc. Payable					1,556	25

	£	p		
Royalties Payable Your Share = 50%			778	12
Less: Advances Paid	*250.00			
Less: Unearned balance brought forward				
Less: Deductible Corrections and Contributions	* 18.85			
Less: Reserve for Returns				
Less: Authors' Goods Purchased	7.50			
			276	35
Sub-Total			501	77
Add: VAT © 8% on * items			40	74
Balance Payable/(Unearned)			£542	51

Appendix II

19(c)/79 Telephone: Littlewick Green 3104
Telegrams: Scholarly, Maidenhead
Registered Number 522538 England

EDWARD ARNOLD (PUBLISHERS) LTD.
Woodlands Park Avenue,
Maidenhead, Berkshire.

Our Ref: 123456

H.W. Smith,
Royalty Manager

31st March, 1979.

ROYALTY STATEMENT NO. 1 – DETAILS OF SUBSIDIARY RIGHTS

Author: Guild & Mittee   **Title: Royalty Statements for Authors**   **SBN: 07131 4142 X**

Date	Details	Total £ P	Author's Share %	Author's Share £ P
29 Oct 78	AMOUNT RECEIVED FOR EXTRACT REPRINTED IN THE BOOKSELLER	50.00	50	25.00
31 Dec 78	TOTAL Carried to Attached Statement			£25.00

247

ROYALTY STATEMENT NOTES

1. Publisher's imprint: i.e. if different from publisher's name.

2. Date: i.e. date on which the Statement is issued. Note, however, that if the Statement should be issued on or before 31st March in any year and the date of issue is in fact later than 31st March, tax problems may arise if the Statement is not pre-dated to the 31st March or before.

3. Royalty Statement No.: i.e. "No. 1", "No. 2." etc., adopting consecutive numbering for Statements issued in respect of each publication and, in the case of Statement No. 1, stating the publication date after "Title".

4. Sales details: i.e. cumulative sales, specifying each relevant category:

    > Home
    > Export
    > Special (with appropriate detail)
    > Remainder
    > Subsidiary Rights

    and, where relevant, stating the point at which the royalty rate changes.

    A separate detailed statement may be required for subsidiary rights.

5. Royalty rate: stating the basis of calculation, e.g. 10% x PP or 12½% x Rec.

6. If the publication has gone out of print since the previous Statement it would be helpful if the tabulation were to state, above the lower horizon line, "Put out of print on................(date)".

7. Printing numbers: if sheet or other stock has been transferred from one edition to another, confusion about the printing number may arise. It would therefore be helpful if

relevant details were set out, as briefly as possible, above the lower horizontal line.

8. Royalties: Only some of these items will be relevant. It may be easier not to pre-print this part of the Statement but to insert to typewriter or by computer printer the required items, sub-totalled and totalled.

9. VAT: i.e. VAT payable on relevant items, identified by an asterisk under "sales details".

    N.B. It is unnecessary to insert stock details.

Index